# CLASSIC
# Literary Walks

## by Jeremy Evans

The Oxford Illustrated Press

Thanks to those who accompanied me on these walks, most notably Lesley, Bryony, Ivory and Jasper. Others who came along and helped were Julian Holland, John Hackett, Penny and Dee, Keith Young, Paul and Jennifer, Alex Simmonds, and Will and Hal Sutherland. Your company was much appreciated.

© 1990, Jeremy Evans

ISBN 1 85509 204 2

**Published by:**
The Oxford Illustrated Press, Haynes Publishing Group, Sparkford, Nr Yeovil, Somerset BA22 7JJ, England.

**Printed in England by:**
J.H. Haynes & Co Limited, Sparkford, Nr Yeovil, Somerset.

**British Library Cataloguing in Publication Data:**
Evans, Jeremy
 Classic literary walks. — (Classic walks, no. 13).
 1. England. Literary associations - Visitors' guides
 I. Title II. Series
 914.204859

 ISBN 1-85509-204-2

**Library of Congress Catalog Card Number:**
90-83289

# CONTENTS

For Joan Hackett—who would surely have enjoyed these walks as much as we did.

# INTRODUCTION

*The 30 walks in this collection follow in the footsteps of some of the 'classic' writers who have made a profound impression on our literature over the last 300 years. With the exception of Dylan Thomas's Wales, all the walks are scattered throughout England, providing circular routes of about 5–10 miles.*

The link between the literary figure and the walk is made clear in the biographical details—sometimes the writer has lived in the area for a long time; in other instances the association may have been sparked off by no more than a brief visit. There are many features of interest along each route and every walk is accompanied by a fact panel to help you plan your outing.

## Fact Panel Information

**Map:** The number of the relevant Ordnance Survey map. If possible buy the 1:25000 Pathfinder or Outdoor Leisure size which will make it easier to find your way, particularly when the footpaths are poorly marked as is often the case. A compass is also useful, just to make sure you're pointing in the right direction.
**Start:** All the starting points are accompanied by suitable car parking places.
**Nearest BR Station:** In most cases this is quite a long way away from the start— such is our reliance on the car today.
**Distance:** An approximate mileage.
**Time:** I usually allow for a speed of just over 2 mph. Extra time should be allowed to look at the various houses and features on the route, and to stop for refreshments.
**Facilities:** A good walk should have a pub, a tea house, or at least somewhere to buy some victuals en route!
**Summary:** A brief guide to the route.

## Finding the Way

All these walks follow footpaths, bridleways, and other rights of way as shown on current OS maps. Some have excellent, well signposted paths; on others I found that signposting was poor or non-existent. In a few instances paths were virtually blocked off and even built over, and many of those crossing fields were ploughed up or covered by crops.

The fight to keep footpaths open has almost taken on the proportions of a crusade amongst walkers and certainly the more paths are used the more likely they are to survive, while those that are untrodden are in danger of being lost altogether. The Ramblers' Association is leading the cause, and if you want to complain about a blocked path, a lack of signposts or a difficult landowner, it may be most effective to contact them first and ask their advice about how to take positive action. The Association is located at 1-2 Wandsworth Road, London SW8 2XX. Tel: 071 582 6878.

The rights of the walker are too complex to explore in detail here, but are concisely covered in *The Rambler's Annual Yearbook* which is sent free to members. A good rule of thumb for the walks in this book is to stick to the paths as shown on the maps. However good your map, it can be difficult to find the way if there's no signposting, and reason dictates that the walker who strays off course in such circumstances cannot be held to blame. If there is an obstruction, you will have to walk around it; if the path has been sewn over I believe you are justified in following the path through the crop if practical—otherwise walk round the side. Remember that it is an offence for a farmer to plough paths round field edges, and paths across fields should be made good within two weeks of ploughing.

None of the walks in this book can be regarded as difficult or dangerous, but for most of them I would recommend wearing proper walking boots, taking sufficient clothing if the weather should turn wet or cold, and carrying a few supplies to eat and drink.

Finally, I hope you enjoy these walks as much as my family and I did; after you have completed them you can work your way through the many splendid books associated with each writer.

Jeremy Evans

# Walk 1: WITH JOHN MILTON IN CHALFONT ST GILES

*John Milton (1608–74) came to Chalfont St Giles to escape the plague in 1665.* Paradise Lost *had just been completed and Milton stayed in the village for a year until it was safe to return to London, little knowing that 'Milton's Cottage' would become his memorial and museum, with none of his London homes still standing.*

Most of us have heard of *Paradise Lost* but perhaps fewer of us have actually read it. By today's standards it is heavy going, but it was a best seller in its day. John Dryden hailed it as, 'One of the greatest, most noble and sublime poems which either this age or nation have produced', and it still appears regularly on the school curriculum.

So what is it about? Essentially it's a very long, blank verse poem recounting man's fall due to the machinations of the archangel Satan. Lying on the burning lake of hell Satan summons a council and advocates a battle for the recovery of Heaven. His second-in-command, Beelzebub, comments on the creation 'Of some new Race call'd Man' on which they could take out their revenge. With a certain amount of difficulty, Satan makes his way to Earth and having resolved 'Evil be thou my Good', he sets about ensnaring Adam and Eve through the forbidden tree of knowledge. After little success he has the idea of appearing as a serpent, and in this guise Eve falls subject to his evil ways. Adam decides to join her in death, if not in life:

'If Death consort with thee, Death is to mee
as life:
So forcible within my heart I feel
The Bond of Nature draw me to my owne.'

Satan returns to Hell to announce victory, and Adam and Eve are left to suffer God's judgement and leave the Garden. Milton does not allow matters to rest there, however, and in the much shorter sequel, *Paradise Regain'd*, Satan loses the battle when tempting Christ in the wilderness, falling in awe of Jesus' words,

**John Milton in middle age.** *Photo courtesy of the Milton Trust.*

'Tempt not the Lord thy God'. God is the victor and paradise is regained:

'Haile, Son of the Most High, heir of both
Worlds,
Queller of Satan, on thy glorious work
Now enter; and begin to save mankind.'

Milton was born at a house in Bread Street, Cheapside, in the City of London. His father was a well-to-do scrivener—a money lender and contract maker—and the young Milton showed early signs of precocious brilliance. By the age of 15 he was a scholar at Cambridge, staying there a full nine years before retiring to his father's estate in Buckinghamshire where he continued to study the classics and European literature with the vague notion of becoming a poet or a priest.

His early work from this period includes the masque (masked play) *Comus* which was first presented at Ludlow Castle on Christmas Eve 1634; his twin poems *L'Allegro* and *Il Penseroso*; and the elegy *Lycidas* written in 1637 which dwelt on his fears of premature death. He was to live for another 40 years but for the next 20 years or so he turned his back on poetry, preferring first travel and then politics.

In 1638 he set out on a 15 month European tour, travelling as far south as Nice. He was a free thinker who believed strongly in self-expression, and tells us that while in Florence he 'found and visited the famous Galileo, grown old as a prisoner of the Inquisition, for thinking in astronomy otherwise than the Franciscan and Dominican licensers thought'. Milton himself was by no means free from danger on his travels, being an ardent Protestant and critic of 'the Romans', and when he opted to return home his equally outspoken pro-republican pamphleteering hardly endeared him to King Charles I and the Royalists.

He led an active political life in London, surviving his monarch who lost his head in 1649 and becoming a pillar of the new Protectorate, acting as Latin Secretary to Cromwell's Council of State. This was an important position which provided him with the means to live in 'a pretty Garden-house in Petty France, Westminster', close to St James' Park. He was effectively the Protectorate's Public Relations/Advertising supremo, writing and publishing pamphlets to discredit the

*Chalfont St Giles today. Peaceful except for the motor car.*

monarchy. His most famous work in this line was *Pro Populo Anglicano Defensio*—the *Defence of the People of England*—a riposte to *Eikon Basilike* which purported to be the meditations of Charles I and had been dangerously successful. Milton's reply for the Protectorate made him a celebrity in London, and a heretic in Paris and Toulouse where his work was publicly burned.

The Restoration of the monarchy in 1660 did nothing to help Milton's cause and having published his last ditch, *Ready and Easy Way to Establish a Free Commonwealth*, he went into hiding. While the triumphant Royalists went on a bloodthirsty rampage, Milton's friends staged a mock funeral to put them off the scent. When the new king, Charles II, heard of this ploy he was apparently much amused that Milton should have escaped death 'by a seasonable show of dying'.

The last of his republican pamphlets were publicly burned by the common hangman, and after four months in hiding Milton ventured forth. He was arrested, and then released on payment of a heavy fine since several Royalists were willing to put in a good word for him. From then on he retired from public life and politics, although never wavering in his republican beliefs.

In much reduced circumstances he moved to a small house near Bunhill Fields in London where, apart from the brief stay in Chalfont St Giles, he spent the rest of his life. Perhaps sensing that the times were changing he had started work on *Paradise Lost* a couple of years before the Restoration, and when he decided to leave London due to the plague it was virtually complete. Chalfont was then deep in the heart of the country, and the cottage must have seemed extremely solitary after years

of noisy London life. It was found for him by Thomas Ellwood, a former pupil and helper of Milton's who was working as a tutor at Chalfont Grange. Milton and his wife moved there in July 1665.

At first Ellwood was prevented from visiting his mentor due to his imprisonment for attending a Quaker funeral—the sort of injustice Milton had for so long campaigned against. After his release he soon visited the cottage and was shown *Paradise Lost*, as he recounted in his memoirs:

'After some common discourse had passed between us, he called for a manuscript of his; which being brought he delivered to me, bidding me take it home with me, and read it at my leisure.' On his next visit Milton asked Ellwood how he liked it, to which he replied, 'Thou hast said much here of Paradise Lost, but what hast thou to say of Paradise Found?'. Milton made no answer at the time, but later, in London, he was able to show Ellwood *Paradise Regain'd*—'This is owing to you for you put it into my head by the question you put to me at Chalfont, which before I had not thought of.'

The extraordinary thing is that Milton composed this and many other works when he was blind. He suffered from steadily diminishing eyesight throughout his adult life, and doctors warned him of the consequences if he continued to spend long hours reading and writing. In 1651, at the time of writing *Pro Populo Anglicano Defensio*, his sight went altogether causing him to declare: 'Greater good was purchased with an inferior evil; so that by incurring blindness alone, I might fulfil the

most honourable of all duties.' He remained equally pragmatic about his affliction. When the future James II chose to call on him and mocked his blindness as God's vengeance for his republicanism, Milton replied that while he had only lost his eyes, Charles I had lost his whole head, implying much greater wrath from above.

Milton did not have the money to employ a secretary to work on *Paradise Lost*, so he depended on the services of anyone who could help pen his immortal thoughts. Having been unlucky in marriage—both his wives had died, the first inspiring Milton to write *The Doctrine and Discipline of Divorce*—he was blessed with a third wife who also proved to be an able secretary. She recounted how her husband composed principally in the winter—'his vein never happily flowed but from the autumnal equinox to the vernal'—and on waking in the morning would get her to write down anything from 20 to 30 verses which he had composed with the aid of a formidable memory. His work completed he lived to hear of its success and died a famous man, buried at the Church of St Giles in Cripplegate in a grave next to his father's.

## Bibliography

*Paradise Lost* was first published in 1667 and *Paradise Regain'd* in 1671. Other late works include a *History of Britain* (1670), *Logic* (1672), and the second edition of his *Poems* (1673). Milton has had many biographers and there are many critical studies of *Paradise Lost*. For those interested in buying a copy of *Paradise Lost* it's worth seeking out a Victorian edition which may include illustrations by Fuseli, Blake, John Martin or Turner.

# A Walk with John Milton

**Map:** OS Landranger 176.
**Start:** Milton's Cottage, Chalfont St Giles—OS Grid Ref. 988932. Car park down the west end of the High Street. Milton's Cottage is open March to October, weekdays except Mondays 10–1 pm, 2–6 pm; Sundays 2–6 pm.
**Nearest BR Station:** Seer Green.
**Distance:** 7 miles.
**Time:** Allow 3½ hours.
**Facilities:** Pubs and shops in Chalfont St Giles.
**Summary:** A circular walk from Milton's Cottage through pleasant countryside within easy reach of Central London.

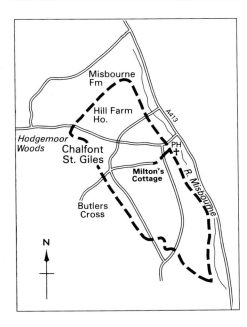

Chalfont St Giles is only 25 miles from the heart of London, and can be reached by car from the city in about 45 minutes. It lies in the countryside just beyond the suburbs, and provides Londoners with this pleasant, easy walk that's also good for dogs! Whether Milton's contemporaries would have recognised today's surroundings is, however, open to question.

If you come by car, park in the large free car park at the west end of Chalfont St Giles down by the green. From here head up the hill, passing road turnings to right and left. Milton's Cottage is about five minutes' walk, almost the last house on the left, opposite Milton's Restaurant as you head out of the village.

After numerous owners the cottage was 'saved' in 1887, following a rumour that an American was about to buy it and ship it piece by piece to his own country! It was put in the hands of trustees dedicated to maintaining both the cottage and its garden which is small, but delightful. The Custodian—a retired Colonel—proved most helpful on my last visit, and freely encouraged visitors to help themselves to the fruit from the mulberry tree which dominates the front garden. The best time for this pleasure is late August when it is well laden.

Experts believe that the cottage has changed little since Milton's day, and inside one can see two rooms which he lived in. The left hand room mainly features memories of old Chalfont St Giles; while the right is Milton's study-cum-thinking room containing all kinds of memorabilia—a lock of his hair, the magnificent gnarled root of his original mulberry, first editions of *Paradise Lost* and *Paradise Regain'd*, and many other early works and translations.

Having visited the house turn right down the hill. If you are ready for lunch—and remember that the house closes from 1–2 pm—the Feathers, which is the first pub on the left, has a pleasant garden and on my visit served excellent value-for-money food. Just opposite, on the other side of the road, go through a tunnel by a footpath sign pointing to the church which is an interesting building with a fine wooden porch. Follow the tarmac path which skirts the right hand side of the churchyard, turning left and right until you come to a somewhat basic concrete bridge crossing the River Misbourne, which on our visit was no more than a dried up ditch.

From here, and indeed on other parts of this walk, the way is not clearly signposted. Do not cross the bridge, but turn right at its side along a fence fronting some modern flats. Follow this fence round to the right, and then pick up the path through the grass ahead which grows long in summer, with trees on either side. The path continues more or less straight ahead all the way to the outskirts of Chalfont St Peter, keeping to the west side of the river as it passes over a stile and runs along the foot of a hill going up to houses on the right. Keep on for just over a mile, passing a few more stiles and kissing gates on the way.

Eventually you see buildings ahead, and the path comes to some tennis courts. Bear round the right side of them, walking on past a sports and cricket ground on the left. At this point a narrow path goes up between the modern houses to the right. Turn up it, and then turn right at the top following the footpath sign up the drive ahead. Go on over a stile where a footpath sign directs you diagonally across a field to the next stile. Here you head diagonally uphill across the next field, keeping to the right of a modern house on the hilltop.

Bear right at the top, following the footpath sign through a kissing gate along a narrow, overgrown, fenced track, with a field full of horse jumps on your left and a large, modern equestrian centre on the right which is Windmill Farm. The track leads out to a quiet lane by the entrance to Windmill Farm where you turn left and walk along for 100 yards or so, passing an extraordinary, oversize, 'Hollywood-comes-to-Chalfont-St-Giles', single-storey house which appears to have more accommodation for horses than humans. Just past this, and beyond the driveway to a somewhat splendid wooden barn on the right, a footpath sign points right through a kissing gate.

Walk along the narrow track here, and when it reaches the road bear right on another narrow track. This brings you to an orchard where you turn left along a wide crossing track, soon coming out to the road some way above Chalfont Grove.

Cross straight over here and follow the footpath sign ahead. After 75 yards or so take the right hand fork which brings you into the open with a belt of trees stretching ahead on your right. There's a crossing track, but no obvious indication of the footpath which should follow the trees running parallel to the road. However if you turn left and then look for a path going right, you will soon find it running alongside the hedge in the correct direction.

Follow this path on through an opening in the hedge, and at the side of a field turn right along a crossing track, heading into the trees ahead where you turn left along a well defined path beside a corrugated iron fence—this is the continuation of the footpath which became lost further back. Keep on ahead, following the path into the open and crossing a large field with two rather splendid clumps of broad leaved English trees. Go over the stile ahead, and then follow the narrow fenced path which follows a belt of trees on your right with an open field to the left.

This soon leads you to the road at Three Households. If at this stage you want to cut short the walk, turn right and it's about half a mile down the hill to Milton's Cottage. To continue, cross the road, following the footpath sign ahead over two stiles. Follow the footpath along a fenced track, and then along the side of a field towards a stile ahead. Go over this stile into the next field (you can see Hodgemoor Woods in the distance ahead), bearing right and left round its perimeter towards the

*Top:* **Milton's Cottage in Chalfont St Giles as seen from the garden.**

*Above:* **Milton's study, preserved today much as it was in his own day.** *Photo courtesy of the Milton Trust.*

next stile where you turn right along the side of a field, and then left just by the stile in the bottom right hand corner. This takes you round the perimeter of the field towards the right hand side of Hodgemoor Woods.

When you come to the woods, bear left round their edge for a short way until you see a stile leading into the woods. Turn right onto the narrow path here—it can be very muddy in wet weather, and has some spectacular reeds growing alongside it in summer. A short way on you come to a crossing track in the woods; turn right, and after about 75 yards the track forks right and left. Both ways lead to the road—going right is the unofficial way but quicker, bringing you to a left hand bend on the road.

Walk along the road and where it bends right after about 50 yards go straight ahead through a kissing gate next to a track which turns off to the left. When I passed this way, the two footpath signs that mattered had been turned in the wrong direction! Keep straight on, with trees on your left, and after a short while pass through a gate leading to a track running by the side of a tennis club (yes, another) on the right. Follow this down to an old sign pointing to Amersham left and London Road straight ahead, taking the London Road direction downhill past Hall Farm House, a nice old building which compares more than favourably with some of the 'conspicuous consumption' houses one passes on this walk.

Walk on down through the fields ahead, following a line of trees on your right. About halfway down the hill cross a stile on the right, and bearing a little to the right head on downhill to the next stile. Continue on in much the same direction until you come to a stile on the edge of a long belt of trees at the bottom of the hill. Enter the woods at this point, and turn right on the crossing track which follows a pleasant woodland trail leading towards Chalfont St Giles. Walk past Misbourne Farm with its shire horses over to the left, passing a stile in the fence a short way beyond.

Keeping straight on, you eventually join a lane. Where the lane bends left continue on along a track ahead, passing on your right a couple of bungalows with excessively grand gates. From there the track leads along past more of the plush houses of Chalfont St Giles, most of which seem to be guarded by dogs of the large and apparently ferocious variety. It brings you back to the village opposite the church, and if you left soon after lunch you'll be in plenty of time for an early evening drink—the village has five competing pubs, and they all have outside seating to tempt you on a summer evening.

# Walk 2: With John Bunyan at Elstow and 'House Beautiful'

*John Bunyan (1628-88) is best known for* The Pilgrim's Progress, *an allegorical tale first published in 1678 which became an immediate best seller and has remained popular ever since. The walks which follow visit his home near Elstow, and his 'House Beautiful'.*

*Above:* **Bunyan—handsome in this portrait despite many years in gaol.**

*The Pilgrim's Progress* is the story of a dream. It starts:

'As I walked through the wilderness of this world, I lighted on a certain place, where was a den [the gaol where Bunyan was imprisoned]; And I laid me down in that place to sleep: And as I slept I dreamed a Dream. I dreamed, and behold I saw a Man clothed with Raggs, standing in a certain place, with his face from his own house, a book in his hand, and a great burden upon his Back.'

Bunyan's aim was to write a tale that every man could understand, and the result is a combination of beautiful language and fast narrative. Christian, the central character, makes his difficult journey from the City of Destruction via such wonderfully named places as the Slough of Despond, House Beautiful, the Valley of Humiliation, the Valley of the Shadow of Death, Vanity Fair, Doubting Castle and the Delectable Mountains until he at last reaches the Celestial City. He meets some extraordinary characters on the way who expound about their opinions and problems— Mr Worldy Wiseman, the foul fiend Appolyon, Lord Time-server, Mr Facing-both-ways (prototype for our current politicians), Mr No-good, Mr Love-lust, Mr Heady, Mr High Mind, Mr Lyar, Mr Implacable, and Mr Two-tongues the parson!

*The Pilgrim's Progress* makes entertaining reading, and many sayings in current usage such as 'Hanging is too good for him' or 'Come wind, come weather', can be attributed to Mr Bunyan, as well as the hymn *To be a Pilgrim* which is the mainstay of many Sunday services. Bunyan's contemporaries loved the

*Right:* **The church at Houghton Conquest—the start point for this walk.**

book, and the only bone of contention arose from the fact that Christian's wife, Christiana, and their four children had been left behind in the City of Destruction, causing a lady called Charity to reprimand Christian while he is at House Beautiful. Encouraged by his success Bunyan made up for this oversight in the less well known *The Pilgrim's Progress II* which was published in 1684 and takes Christiana and the children on a similar but less taxing journey.

Bunyan came from a comparatively poor, uneducated family. He was born in a cottage on the outskirts of Harrowden—all signs of it have long since disappeared, and the surroundings would be unrecognisable to him. Thankfully, nearby Elstow is much better preserved. Knowledge of his early life is sketchy, but we know that his grandfather was a chapman (travelling salesman), his father a brazier (travelling metalworker), and as an adult John described himself as a tinker and later as a brazier, doing similar work to his father.

Bunyan was baptised on 30th November 1628 and would have worshipped at the fine Abbey Church of St Helena in Elstow which today has a stained glass window commemorating *The Pilgrim's Progress*. He would also have been a regular visitor of the Moot Hall on the Green which was the centre for the fairs held frequently at Elstow. By his own admission he was an irreligious young man, and remained that way during the Civil War. He was 'impressed' to join the parliamentary army in 1644 at the age of 16, and was billeted at Newport Pagnell for a couple of years where it seems likely that he found the time and resources to practise reading and writing which later led him to produce over 50 books, pamphlets and essays.

When the Civil War was more or less over, John was discharged and returned to Harrowden where he married his first wife and moved to a cottage in Elstow High Street before finding his final home at St Cuthbert Street in Bedford (both long since demolished). It seems the army had also given him time to ponder religious matters, and after much self-questioning he joined the congregation of an 'independent' church in Bedford where he was baptised in the River Ouse. This was one of the brief periods in seventeenth-century history when non-conformist religion was permissible, and by 1656 Bunyan had become a travelling preacher and religious pamphleteer with wide popular appeal.

The death of Oliver Cromwell and the restoration of Charles II in 1660 signalled a change. Independent church meetings or 'conventicles' were under suspicion for producing anti-state propaganda, and the repression of free religion began anew. Bunyan continued to preach even though he knew he was in danger, and was arrested on 12th November 1660 at a public meeting. He refused to undertake not to preach any more, and went off to Bedford Gaol with the words: 'I did meet my God sweetly in the prison again, comforting of me, and satisfying of me that it was His will and mind that I should be there.'

Despite spirited attempts by his second wife Elizabeth (his first wife died leaving four children) to secure justice for him, he was imprisoned for most of the next 12 years. For some of that time there was a real danger that he would be transported to the 'plantations', in which case all of his family possessions would have been sold to pay for the fare and there would have been no *Pilgrim's Progress*. At other times the gaol appears to have been fairly liberal, and Bunyan was allowed home for quite long periods; when the political heat was off he even resumed preaching round the villages for a short while. Despite Bunyan's imprisonment, he succeeded in writing nine books, one of which, his spiritual autobiography *Grace Abounding*, was published in 1666, and the episodes which made up *The Pilgrim's Progress* were begun during the latter years of his first prison sentence.

Bunyan was officially pardoned on 13th September 1672, as a result of Charles II's Declaration of Indulgence. Bunyan, who had become the leader of his church in Bedford, was again free to preach as he pleased, gaining the nickname 'Bishop Bunyan' before his right to preach was once again withdrawn in 1675. He nevertheless continued to preach, keeping one step ahead of the law for some 18 months before he was again imprisoned in Bedford Gaol for a short period during which time it is thought he finished *The Pilgrim's Progress*. When it was published on 18th February 1678, Bunyan added an introductory 'Apology' in case it was a flop—he need not have worried for it became an instant success, selling at one shilling and six pence and being reprinted in the first few months. It was reprinted 10 more times before Bunyan's death by which time there were at least 100,000 copies in circulation, as well as translations into French, Dutch and Welsh which paved the way for further editions in over 200 different languages and dialects. It was the missionaries' second favourite book!

Bunyan continued to write, though none of his other books had the immediate appeal of *The Pilgrim's Progress*. He also continued to work as a brazier and to preach when the political climate allowed, and by the age of 60 he was still travelling to meetings that would take him far afield. It was while riding from Reading to preach in London that he was caught in a rainstorm which soaked him through and led to illness and eventual death on 21st August 1688. He was buried in the Dissenter's Cemetery at Bunhill Fields in Finsbury.

## Bibliography

None of Bunyan's other works are as accessible as *The Pilgrim's Progress*, and they tend to be the reserve of Bunyan scholars. The better known examples include *Grace Abounding* (1666), *The Life and Death of Mr Badman* (1680), and *The Holy War* (1682).

*The Moot Hall at Elstow with the old Abbey Church in the background.*

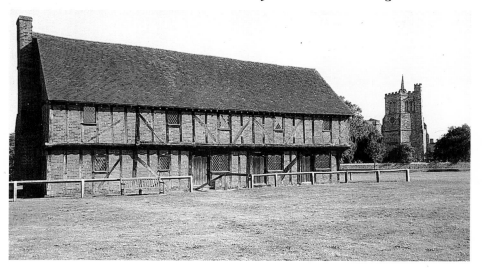

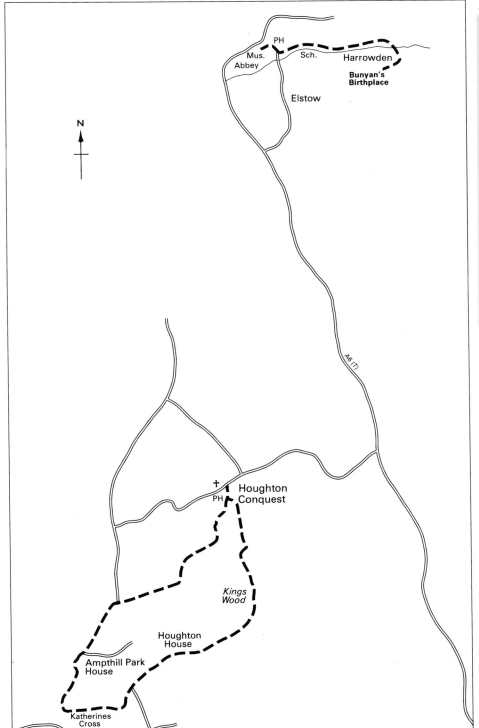

## A Walk with John Bunyan

**Map:** OS Landranger 153.
**Start:** Houghton Conquest, south of Bedford off the A6—OS Grid Ref. 045414 for walk via 'House Beautiful'. Parking on the roadside by the church. Moot Hall—OS Grid Ref. 048474 for walk from Elstow. Small car park nearby. The Moot Hall is open April to October, weekdays except Mondays 2–5 pm; Sundays 2–5.30 pm.
**Nearest BR Station:** Stewartby.
**Distance:** 'House Beautiful' walk approx 6½ miles; Bunyan's birthplace walk 2½ miles.
**Time:** For 'House Beautiful' walk allow a good 3 hours; for Bunyan's birthplace walk allow at least 1 hour.
**Facilities:** Pubs in Houghton Conquest and Elstow.
**Summary:** A fine walk via the ruins of Houghton House taking you along the only high country in the surrounding area; the additional walk to see Bunyan's birthplace is only recommended to committed pilgrims.

This is a full day out which can be divided into two parts—a circular walk south from the village of Houghton Conquest, where there was a 'Clerke School' during Bunyan's childhood, to visit Bunyan's 'House Beautiful' (Houghton House) and Ampthill Park; and then a visit to the Abbey Church and Moot Hall at Elstow with all their Bunyan memorabilia, possibly including a walk to the site of his birthplace in nearby Harrowden. If time allows, you could also visit the Bunyan Museum on the site of Bunyan's original church in Mill Street, Bedford, which is open from Tuesday to Friday, mornings and afternoons.

Start from the rather splendid church in Houghton Conquest—you can park just opposite in a lay-by. The restaurant/pub opposite, the Knife and Cleaver, proved excellent. It is a superior kind of pub with good snacks, and the owner was not at all thrown by our rough walking gear and was happy for us to leave our cars in his car park for the afternoon. Inside there is a pleasant conservatory where full lunches are served, while outside we found the apple tree orchard much to our liking. Predictably it is more expensive than the usual ploughman's!

From the Knife and Cleaver turn right along the road through Houghton Conquest, and then after about 75 yards turn first right down a dead-end side road. Follow this past the Methodist chapel on the right, and a little further on turn left at the footpath sign to Haynes West End, just past some old Nissen

*'House Beautiful' remains a wonderful ruin today.*

huts. After a couple of hundred yards you come into a field and turn right, following a sign for Houghton House. Walk along towards the woods of King's Wood on the hillside, turning right and then left through a signposted gate where there is an information panel on the wildlife preservation area you are passing through.

Head on up the left hand side of the field ahead, and at the top go through a gate into trees. The way here is not too clear, but you bear to the right, keeping along the bottom of the woods until you come to a stile going into the next field. Here you turn left uphill before the stile, heading up on a very indistinct and overgrown track that meanders its way up the left side of the main body of King's Wood. If in doubt keep straight on up along the side of the woods.

Near the top the low lying trees to the left begin to thin out and disappear, and the track improves until you go through a gate ahead. From there on you continue straight-ahead along a field by the side of the woods, with Bury Farm in open country over to the left. Continue keeping to the side of the woods

following them round to the right and then, where they end, go over a signposted stile by a gate and walk ahead, joining a track passing to the left of a small house on the hillside. From here there are fine views to the north, with the brick-making chimneys of Stewartby dominating the landscape.

Keep on down this track passing a reservoir pumping station with Houghton House coming into view on the right. Go past a large barn, and then turn back onto the track which leads to the house—a splendid ruin in a fine setting and also an excellent place for a picnic if the weather is suitable. There's an information board telling you about the house which was built in 1615 for the Countess of Pembroke, sister of Sir Philip Sidney, in the Jacobean and Classical style. James I visited the house in 1621 and 1624, and then in the late seventeenth century it became the home of Robert Bruce, Earl of Aylesbury, a key figure in the restoration of Charles II. The family were forced to sell the house in 1738 to the Duke of Bedford on account of their debts, and in 1764 he restored it for his son, the Marquis of Tavistock. Unfortunately the Marquis

died in an accident some three years later and his widow not long after, and from then on the house deteriorated rapidly.

Its contents were removed to furnish nearby Ampthill Park House, and in 1794 large parts of it were dismantled for other uses—it's thought that the fine panelling went first to Haynes Grange and then to the Victoria & Albert Museum, while the staircase ended up in the Swan Inn at Bedford. Despite these removals it remains a fine ruin today—what is more it's open all the year round, and it's free!

The connection with the 'House Beautiful' of *The Pilgrim's Progress* where Christian met a beautiful damsel named Discretion is only made clear by the fact that the house is on a hill:

'This Hill, though high, I covet to ascend,
The difficulty will not me offend . . .'

From Houghton House rejoin the track, passing a terrace of houses on the left and going over a cattle grid where the track, which is part of the Greensand Ridgeway, becomes concrete, with fine views of rolling farmland to the left. You soon come to the B530 road on a dangerous bend; cross carefully here, and walk down the pavement to where after about 75 yards another Greensand Ridgeway sign points through a gate on the right. Go ahead into the woods, ignoring the first turning to the left and a fork to the right. You soon come to an obvious crossing track where you turn left along an avenue of trees, which brings you out into the open at the top of Ampthill's very pleasant and fairly wild park.

Follow the Greensand Ridgeway sign to the right, and keep following the track in this direction, passing the two crosses at Katherine's Cross on your left and the very pretty pond at the base of the hill to the right, with glimpses across to Ampthill Park House. Follow the next Greensand Ridgeway sign, and where the track starts to go down and then comes to a distinctive crossing track, turn right off it to head downhill in the direction of Ampthill Park House. This brings you down past the pond on your right, coming to a stile where you follow a well worn path towards the house.

Keep straight on, passing a stile on the left and emerging at the bottom of the south driveway to the house. Turn right onto the lane that passes the front of this imposing building which is now turned into flats, and prepare yourself for the next section of the footpath which though clearly marked on the OS map is not at all clear on the land. Where the lane starts to bend right go straight ahead across the field beside it, even though there is no footpath sign. Head for a small footbridge, which when we passed by was marked by a post with a piece of blue plastic fluttering from the top that may or may not have been an indication of the path. Keep straight on across the next field, heading for the left hand side of the woods ahead. The way is not too obvious, but you bear to the left through a gap in the hedge and into the next field, walking along its right hand side until you come once more to the B530 road. Here you can walk left up the side of the field until you come to a footpath sign, or much easier cross straight over the road, heading for the footpath sign on the other side.

The footpath sign shows the way up the side of a field here, but the actual path runs along just inside the woods. It brings you out to a games field where you follow the hedge along the left hand side, squeezing round the end of a fence ahead and keeping alongside the hedge with King's Wood once more ahead of you and the ruins of Houghton House up on the hillside to the right.

At a footpath sign pointing right and left

*A view of the surrounding countryside from St Katharine's Cross.*

turn left through the hedge, and then follow the footpath right along the side of the field in the same direction. This is a redirected footpath which does not follow the route shown on the 1988 OS map—basically it follows round the edge of the field rather than going straight across. It proved to be extremely hard going on our last visit as the side of the field was badly churned up by ploughing, and it would no doubt be appalling to walk on in wet weather—having redirected it, the farmer concerned should do something to put it in proper order.

Keeping along the side of the field with King's Wood on your right, look for a stile set a few yards into the woods. All the way you have clear views of the church at Houghton Conquest encouraging you that it is not far to go, and once you find and cross this stile you continue to follow the edge of the woods to a gate by another information panel. Here you turn left along a track towards Houghton Conquest, and then right along the edge of a field as indicated by a yellow footpath sign, bringing you back to the lane leading to the road that runs through Houghton Conquest, with tantalising glimpses back to the fine old manor, shown surrounded by a moat on the OS map.

## With John Bunyan in Elstow

No doubt Bunyan could and would have walked from Houghton to Elstow—it's only a matter of some six miles and even today there is a footpath all the way. However, the countryside becomes less and less appealing, as it is completely flat and soon overrun by Bedford's suburban sprawl. I would advise driving along the A6, and then following the signs to the Moot Hall once in Elstow. This interest-

ing building is sited on the fine green opposite the old Abbey Church (locked on a Sunday afternoon), and has various Bunyan memorabilia as well as some splendid old oak furniture in the long room upstairs; the overhead fluorescent lights do not, unfortunately, help to recreate the atmosphere!

From Elstow you can walk to Bunyan's birthplace at Harrowden, but this is only recommended to the committed Bunyan pilgrim. The countryside is at best uninteresting, and at worst completely overrun by a depressing series of housing estates that will surely engulf poor Bunyan's birthplace before long.

From the Moot Hall turn right down the road running through the old part of Elstow, passing houses with such names as 'Bunyan Meade' on your way! Just before the bridge turn left onto a riverside path that appears to promise better things, but in the end proves disappointing. Follow this stream which is a tributary of the River Great Ouse for about a mile along a path which is clear and easy to follow, eventually coming to a bridge that crosses it. Go over here and head along a long, dusty track towards the suburban blight of Harrowden. When you come to another stream, a half hidden sign in the bushes invites the pilgrim—and no one else—to walk up the side of the field following this brook. There is no path and it may well be a muddy 'Slough of Despond', so determination is required. In the distance a solitary tree stands to the right, with Elstow Abbey in the background way, way beyond. When you reach this tree the stone marking Bunyan's birthplace is to the left, almost hidden in the undergrowth, at a point which divides the two fields. From here the way back is the way you came . . .

# Walk 3: With Laurence Sterne at Shandy Hall

*Laurence Sterne (1713-68) is hailed by his admirers as the inventor of the modern 'stream of consciousness' novel which he introduced with his fictional autobiography* The Life and Opinions of Tristram Shandy Gentleman. *It brought him fame and fortune in the last eight years of his life, a time when his home was the aptly named Shandy Hall in Coxwold, North Yorkshire.*

By today's standards *Tristram Shandy* is by no means easy reading, but in its time it was considered witty, sly, salacious, absurd, and very amusing. In brief, it is a novel about writing a novel; an endlessly complex work in which Sterne takes the reader on so many red herrings that the hero fails to reach birth before the third volume and is still waiting to become a man by the end of the ninth.

Sterne declared 'I write to be fed, not to be famous.' After the initial publication of the first two volumes in 1760 he continued to write two further volumes a year which were rapturously, and in some cases nervously, awaited. At the start of Volume VII he boasted that he could keep up this winning formula forever if his tubercular lungs allowed him that privilege:

'No—I think I said I would write two volumes every year, provided the vile cough which then tormented me and which to this hour I dread worse than the devil, would give me leave—and in another place—(but where, I can't recollect now) speaking of my book as a *machine*, and laying my pen and ruler down cross-wise upon the table, in order to gain the greatest credit to it—I swore it should be kept a-going at that rate forty years, if it pleased but the fountain of life to bless me so long with health and good spirits.'

The fountain of life did not bless him so well, for within three years he was dead. The following extract gives some idea of the convoluted literary style of *Tristram Shandy*:

'I wish I could write a chapter upon sleep.
A fitter occasion could never have Presented itself, than what this moment

*Laurence Sterne in pensive mood as painted by Sir Joshua Reynolds in 1760. Photo by NPG.*

*Here his body lies, transported to its resting place beside the church at Coxwold.*

offers, when all the curtains of the family are drawn —the candles put out—and no creature's eyes are open but a single one, for the other has been shut these twenty years, of my mother's nurse.

It is a fine subject!

And yet as fine as it is, I would undertake to write a dozen chapters upon button-holes, both quicker and with more fame, than a single chapter upon this.

Button holes!—there is something very lively in the idea of 'em . . .'

And so the subject rapidly moves from sleep to button holes and then back again to sleep with the help of Sancho Panza and Montaigne. By the next short chapter, however, the hero is waxing lyrical on the vexed subject of his nose:

'When the misfortune of my NOSE fell so heavily upon my father's head;—the

reader remembers that he walked instantly upstairs, and cast himself down upon his bed; and from hence, unless he has a great insight into human nature, he will be apt to expect a rotation of the same ascending and descending movements from him, upon this misfortune of my NAME; no.'

Sterne wrote whatever came into his fertile mind, and despite reports of piles of discarded paper in his study one would guess his writing came quite easily. Most of the Shandy characters were larger than life caricatures of people in and around York where Sterne earned his living as a cleric. One wonders what Doctor Slop—modelled on the local obstetrician Dr John Burton—would have made of his description? 'Imagine to yourself a little squat, uncourtly figure of a Doctor Slop, of about four feet and a half perpendicular height, with a breadth of back, and a sesquipedality of belly, which would have done honour to a serjeant of the horse-guards.'

And so on! Thankfully Sterne was not prey to the laws of libel which blight writers today, and *Tristram Shandy* was considered screamingly funny in the *It's A Crazy World* vein; 'shandy' being Yorkshire dialect for 'crazy'.

Laurence Sterne was born in the south of Ireland, where his father, the Ensign Roger Sterne, was stationed in the army. His ancestry was that of a gentleman but he had few expectations, and those he did have became severely reduced when his father died in true Shandean fashion, run through in a duel on account of an argument over a goose. Laurence had some rich relations and was fortunate enough to attend Jesus College, Cambridge with a little help from his uncle, Richard Sterne. On graduating he opted for the church, a career that many who were well educated but not well heeled chose to pursue. As such it was a job rather than a spiritual calling. Sterne himself could be a hell-raiser with his gang of cronies nick-named 'The Demoniacs', and later he pursued at least two extra marital liaisons. His Uncle Jacques, who acted as his first patron, was a political in-fighter who also happened to be Canon and Precentor of York Minster.

Uncle Jacques set him up as Prebendary of York, but the job had little to do with church matters. He was principally employed to churn out political invective on behalf of his uncle's Whig newspaper, and this he did through a particularly vicious by-election campaign of 1741. By the end he'd had enough, and finished himself forever, in his uncle's eyes, by publicly apologising for his part in the Whig campaign. With little hope of further advancement in the church he retired to Sutton-on-the-Forest as a rural vicar, and in 1744 was given a second living at Stillington nearby.

His sermons pulled in the crowds; indeed he was so good that he earned a handy additional income by occasionally standing in to preach at York Minster. He only discovered his true vocation as a comic writer in 1759 when he wrote *A Political Romance*, his satirical view of a dirty linen feud that was being waged by two top churchmen. The church was not pleased to have their less than spiritual affairs exposed to the public, and rather than lose his career altogether Sterne agreed to have the book burned and forsake publication. However he had got the bug, and soon turned out another satire— *The Life and Opinions of Tristram Shandy, Gentleman*.

He sent it to the London printer and publisher Dodsley, but the first version of what was to become Volumes I and II was rejected as too scandalous. Sterne rewrote it and toned it down—at about this time his wife was in the hands of 'a lunatic doctor', and even though he didn't greatly like the situation it made him more sober than he might otherwise have been. Then with money borrowed to pay for the printing, he published it himself in York in January 1760. He sent copies on to Dodsley, carefully suppressing the fact that the book had emanated from provincial York. Two months later he hitched a lift to London with a wealthy crony to find out how the book was selling, deserting his sick wife with a modicum of guilt. On enquiring in various bookshops he found it unobtainable, every copy having sold out, and from obscurity he was welcomed to the heights of the London social whirl with his reputation assured and his image immortalised by a first portrait by Reynolds.

More of *Tristram Shandy* was called for, and in the same year Sterne was also presented with the living of Coxwold by Lord Fauconberg, an old acquaintance from Newburgh Priory. He immediately moved there believing it to be a much healthier place to live, and rented an old house close by the church which was soon named Shandy Castle and then Shandy Hall in true Shandean style.

Sterne lived on and off at Shandy Hall for his last eight years, spending on average six months either side of the summer there. In between times he stayed in London or travelled through France as far as Naples which gave him the background for the two volumes of his unfinished travelogue *A Sentimental Journey*, as well as *The Flight From Death* in Volume VII of *Tristram Shandy*. He preached in the church at Coxwold until his voice gave out due to ill health, and used his earnings to refurbish and extend Shandy Hall. Most of his literary output emanated from there—seven volumes of *Tristram Shandy*, two of *A Sentimental Journey*, and *The Sermons of Mr Yorick* which proved equally successful.

Having avoided death for many years, Sterne finally died from pneumonia and pleurisy on 18th March 1768, in London. Following his funeral at St Georges in Hanover Square he was laid to rest in the burial ground near Bayswater Road. A final twist of the tale then took place in true Shandean fashion. His body was exhumed by grave robbers, and sold to a Cambridge surgeon for an anatomy lecture—such behaviour by the medical profession was not exceptional in those times. When he was on the dissecting table a horrified member of the audience recognised the great man. They stuck him back together and bundled him back into his grave, until 200 years later when he was to be disturbed again. The burial ground had been sold for development, and the Laurence Sterne Trust decided to exhume his remains and rebury them with due celebration at the churchyard of Coxwold. Finding his tombstone was of course easy, but with all the coffins long decayed the job of deciphering the right bones was not so simple. Various skulls were matched to the famous marble bust executed by Nolleken in 1766—one matched perfectly and had the top sawn off, the mark of the over keen surgeon.

## Shandy Hall Today

Shandy Hall, which originally dates from the mid fifteenth century, was in a state of severe neglect when it was rescued in 1967 by the Laurence Sterne Trust. This was the inspiration of Kenneth Monkman, a lifelong Sterne enthusiast—'I was bowled over by Tristram Shandy—it was incredible'—who visited the Hall on a Sterne pilgrimage. The old lady who lived there at the time was at first too ashamed to let him and his wife inside, but a little later she relented and the house eventually passed into the hands of the trust with the Monkmans acting as resident curators.

Shandy Hall has been open to the public since 1976 with its principal ground floor rooms restored as Sterne would have known them. The house is packed with Kenneth Monkman's extraordinary collection of Sterne memorabilia including the Nolleken bust; early Shandean paintings; and Shandean prints by Hogarth, Bunbury, Newton, Rowlandson, Cruikshank and other famous admirers. There are also complete runs of popular magazines and newspapers published throughout Sterne's lifetime, and important source books for Sterne including the original King James' Bible.

Shandy Hall is now a fine and very interesting house to visit, set in beautiful surroundings. The Laurence Sterne Trust has established an appeal with a target of £400,000 to safeguard its future— a visit by you will help Shandy Hall to survive, and you may even develop a taste for *Tristram Shandy*!

## Bibliography

The finest collection of Sterne books is owned by Kenneth Monkman, filling 600 feet of shelving at Shandy Hall and including more first and Sterne-lifetime editions than exist together anywhere else in the world. He has a comprehensive run of later editions from 1769 to the present day, as well as many old editions of *Shandy* translations into 15 languages.

*Tritstram Shandy* and *A Sentimental Journey* are widely available in modern editions. The first standard Sterne biography was by W.D. Cross (1904).

## A Walk with Laurence Sterne

**Map:** OS Landranger 100/Pathfinder SE47/57.
**Start:** From Shandy Hall at Coxwold, off the A19 north of York—OS Grid Ref. 531773. Easy roadside parking in Coxwold. Shandy Hall is open June to September, Wednesdays 2–4.30 pm and Sundays 2.30–4.30 pm.
**Nearest BR Station:** Thirsk.
**Distance:** Approximately 6 miles.
**Time:** Allow 3 hours.
**Facilities:** Pubs in Coxwold and Husthwaite.
**Summary:** A walk round the countryside south of Coxwold, with high level views over to Abbey Bank in the north.

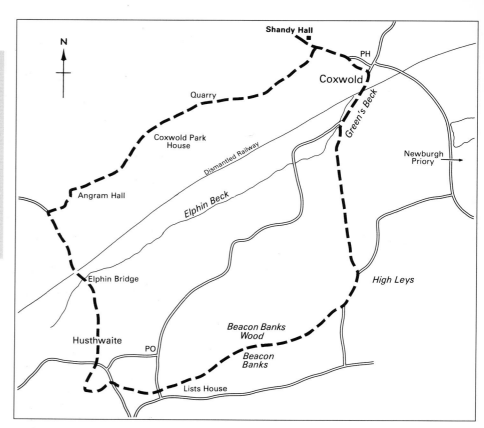

Park in the main street of Coxwold, a seemingly prosperous one street village. Opposite the church there's a splendid house whose owner has an even more splendid collection of Rolls-Royce cars, ancient and modern. At the top of the hill stands Shandy Hall, about halfway down is the church, and further down still is the rather smart pub.

There are many potential walks in the area. Sterne is known to have frequently visited Newburgh Priory which is about 1 mile along the road (open mid-May to late August, Wednesday and Sunday 2–6 pm) but poorly served by footpaths if you want a circular walk. To get there head straight down the hill, and bear right following a track on the right side of the road, passing a large lake on the left before you come to the Priory some 250 yards further on. Sterne also visited Byland Abbey which could be part of an alternative circular walk, following footpaths north from Shandy Hall, east towards Byland Abbey, and from there south-east via Wass Grange to return to Coxwold along the Coley Broach Road—a distance of around 11 miles, and thus best suited to those in an energetic mood.

This walk explores the country south of Coxwold, giving good views of the surrounding countryside and returning via Husthwaite. To start turn right down a track that runs between the houses opposite the pub. This track bears left past pretty gardens, and then runs down to the road where you turn right. Walk along for about 100 yards, passing the old railway line with the signal box still intact.

A little further on you come to a gate with a footpath arrow on the left, just before the road bends right. Go through this gate and cross the stream which is called Green's Beck, and then go through another gate immediately ahead. From here you bear round the right

*Shandy Hall as seen from the side garden—an eminently pleasant home for the great man.*

*Walking up the hillside towards Beacon Banks with the spectacular white horse above Abbey Bank in the background.*

side of the field, walking along past trees until you come to a plank bridge in the top right hand corner of the same field. Cross Mill Beck here, and bear left up the left hand side of the next field heading straight up the hill towards High Leys Farm which you can clearly see on the hilltop.

Keep on steadily uphill, passing Low Parks Farm over to the right. At the next gate bear right along the hedge until you come to another gate with a footpath sign. Go through this gate and straight up the hill, heading for a gate set slightly to the left of the farmhouse. At the top by the farm turn right along a track, and then keep to the right along the edge of Beacon Banks Wood on the hillside. Keep on in this direction with fine glimpses of the countryside to the north, including a spectacular white horse which is cut in the hillside above Abbey Bank.

The bridleway track carries on past a Trig Point, after which it starts to head down towards Husthwaite. Go through a gate and pass Lists House, a substantial building on the left, heading on down its drive until you come to the road. Turn left here, and after about 10 yards turn right through an unsignposted kissing gate which takes you down a path on the right side of a field which was inhabited by some amiable rare breed sheep when we passed by. Keep to the right and go over a stile by the trees in the bottom right corner; then keep to the left downhill in the next field, walking across ground that was very overgrown in summer and could be muddy in winter.

At the bottom go over a stile, and then walk by some cottages leading to the road. Turn right, and almost immediately turn left down a track. This leads to a farmyard where you bear round to the left, before turning right up the side of a field by a footpath sign just past the barn. Keep along this path for a short distance until you see a gate with a footpath sign in the hedge to the right. Go through here and then head up the narrow field ahead, passing by a spectacularly well ordered vegetable garden before passing through a gate and coming back to the road that runs through Husthwaite. If you want some refreshment at this stage, make for the pub by turning left down the hill.

To continue, head straight over the road and follow the track by the left of the church. This bears left, and then goes straight ahead over a stile and down and over another stile. From here head straight across the large field ahead, aiming for the farmer's dump of hay and turnips on the far side—walking across here could be muddy in winter. Bear round the right side of this dump—which may have been removed by the time you walk this route—and then turn left onto the road and walk over the Elphin Beck Bridge and over the disused railway line.

Head along this quiet road towards Angram Hall which you can see behind trees ahead to the right. The footpath shown on the OS map leaves the road about 100 yards after the bridges and heads directly across a field to Angram Hall. However we found no stile and the hedge looked pretty impassable, so we walked on and turned right down the drive-

way to Angram Hall, bearing left and right between the farm buildings before heading on past a solitary cottage on the left.

Keep on this track towards Coxwold Park House. About 200 yards before you reach this house, which is distinctive, there's a footpath sign pointing straight ahead over a stile and up the left hand side of a field, while the main track bears right towards the house. Walk along this footpath, and then go straight ahead at the next footpath sign which is ambiguous since it seems to want you to bear left through a mass of nettles—the 'gate' which effectively barred our way straight ahead had to be climbed over.

Walk on in the same direction along the right of the next field, with trees by your side and a farmhouse behind them. You come to an even more rickety gate with a footpath sign—go over this and continue down the right hand side of the next two fields. We found all these footpaths very badly overgrown. Eventually you come to a five bar gate and see Coxwold's farmstead and church ahead of you. The track bears to the left of the church past some trees. Head for the middle gate among the farm buildings with a substantial house to the right and barns to the left, bringing you back to the road a short way down the hill from Shandy Hall, and a short way up the hill from the church. Be sure to visit the latter. Laurence Sterne's tombstone lies against the south wall, marking the place where he was reburied with due ceremony in 1969.

# Walk 4: With Gilbert White in Selborne

*The Reverend Gilbert White (1720–93) and the Hampshire village of Selborne are today as closely linked as they were in the eighteenth century. It was there that the Reverend White wrote* The Natural History and Antiquities of Selborne, *published in 1788 as an edited series of letters which became a literary classic around the world. Surprisingly much of Selborne remains the same today as it was in those days, enabling us to faithfully retrace the footsteps of this unusual and enigmatic man.*

Although we know his book so well, we know little about the Reverend White's personal life. All that we do know has been gathered from those who corresponded with him, most notably his lifelong friend John Mulso. He never married, and in the later years of his life spent less and less time away from Selborne.

He was born on 18th July 1720 in his grandfather's vicarage, which stood where the Victorian vicarage stands today. His family then moved away for some time, before returning to occupy The Wakes, the house which now acts as Selborne's Gilbert White museum.

White left Selborne to attend Oxford University (less revered then than it is today), and on 30th March 1744 became a Fellow of Oriel College. During that period of his life he spent much time away from his home travelling in the south of England, but always returning to Selborne when circumstances permitted.

He wasn't rich, but by today's standards his life as a curate with responsibilities for various parishes appeared to involve little work and a lot of free time. This allowed him to indulge his lifelong passions—gardening, botany and other aspects of natural history—and to record much of his day-to-day life as it related to these subjects, but with very little reference to his personal life.

The Reverend White began to garden seriously at the Wakes in 1749. He planted trees, raised seedlings, and experimented with growing all manner of vegetables—artichokes, endives, broccoli, maize, wild rice, potatoes, and sea kale were but a few of the ones he tried. Thankfully for us the results of his efforts are recorded in *The Garden Kalendar* which he started to write day-by-day in 1751. The original manuscript can be seen in the British

*A pen and ink sketch of Gilbert White, one of only two known likenesses discovered in his personal copy of Pope's translation of Homer's* **Iliad.** *Photo courtesy of the British Library.*

Museum.

He was particularly enthusiastic about growing melons, a difficult crop at the best of times but one which was extremely fashionable in eighteenth century England. His melon 'hot bed' was more than 45 feet long, and his entries in the *Kalendar* concerning it are equally lengthy and protracted:

April 13: Worked-up a nine-light melon-bed with 18 good dung-carts of fresh, hot dung, & 80 bushels of fresh tan. I had made this

bed just a week before . . .'

And so it continued until the satisfactory end to the melon season on September 12th:

'Held a Cantaleupe-feast at the Hermitage: cut up a brace & an half of fruit among 14 people . . .'

White didn't of course do all this work himself, but employed village people and his faithful handyman Thomas Hoar who also helped to keep up the *Kalendar* whenever White was absent. Nor did Gilbert build the famous zigzag path up the Hanger as is widely assumed; this was the work of his brother, John White, a man who led a more turbulent life due to his frequent financial mismanagement.

## The Natural History of Selborne

White's interest in botany also grew apace, and in 1767 he was introduced to Thomas Pennant, a member of the Royal Society and a successful writer and journalist. Pennant specialised in natural history which was very popular at the time, and was very organised, employing a number of correspondents who could feed him with views and information from around England.

White was delighted to join their number, and began to keep the *Naturalist's Journal* to record his findings just as he had with the *Garden Kalendar*. Having assimilated enough information he would then write newsletters to Pennant, who would use the material in his editions of *British Zoology*.

White's *Natural History* was born out of these newsletters. In 1769 he met the

Honourable Daines Barrington, an enthusiast in the subject and another frequent correspondent who suggested that White was more than qualified to publish his own work. The Reverend White's own views on this matter were summed up thus:

'Out of all my journals I think I might collect matter enough, and such a series of incidents as might pretty well comprehend the Natural History of this district . . . I have moreover half a century of letters on this subject, most of them very long; all of which together might make up a moderate volume.'

Editing *The Natural History* took White another 14 years, for he was in no great hurry and had none of the business-like drive of Pennant. The first parts of the work were delivered to the printers in 1787, and it was finally published some two years later.

It was widely complimented. *The Topographer* of 1789 wrote of *The Natural History* thus:

'A more delightful or more original work has seldom been published . . . The book is not a compilation from former publications, but the result of many years' attentive observations to nature itself, which are told not only with the precision of a philosopher, but with that happy selection of circumstances which mark a poet.'

White lived out his last years peacefully. In 1793 he fell seriously ill, and his bed was moved into the old parlour at the back of The Wakes so he could look out on The Hanger. He died there on 26th June 1793. His extraordinary *Natural History* has lived on to become one of the world's great best sellers, a natural history and literary classic which has appeared in over 150 editions, and been translated into German, French, Danish, Swedish and Japanese.

## Selborne Today

Selborne would probably be recognisable to the Reverend White today, but he would certainly disapprove of the summer traffic, and raise a clerical eyebrow at the number of summer visitors to his house, for they now come from all corners of the globe to pay their respect.

No doubt he would be pleased to find his zigzag in such fine fettle, and the topography of Selborne Hanger and the Lythes virtually unchanged though with the wealth of wildlife sadly diminished by the more intense nature of modern life. He would also find the village

**The Wakes, the Gilbert White Museum in Selborne, and also the Oates Memorial Library and Museum.**

much more affluent than it was.

The opening letter of *The Natural History* describes the topography of Selborne in detail and begins:

'The parish of Selborne lies in the extreme eastern corner of the county of Hampshire, bordering on the county of Sussex, and not far from the county of Surrey. The high part to the south-west consists of a vast hill of chalk, rising three hundred feet above the village . . .'

That vast hill continues to brood over the village, and the road which passes through Selborne still divides it into two, though not quite as White described it—'one single straggling street in a sheltered vale'. The cliffs of the Hanger remain covered in White's favourite beech trees, some of which are over 300 years old, and Selborne Common (NT) beyond, is thankfully preserved in its original state.

To the north-east the flatter meadow land past Dorton and the Lythes is also well preserved. Here sandstone merges with the Surrey heathlands, and the two main footpaths through the deeply wooded valley (NT) on either side of the Oakhanger Stream are the same ones that White knew. This can be a magical landscape to walk through, and is at its best in spring or autumn.

## The Wakes

In the centre of Selborne, The Wakes is a must for all visitors. This is the house where White spent most of his very long life, gardening with innovatory enthusiasm, and making numerous forays into the surrounding countryside in order to research and write his *Natural History*. At that time the house was considerably smaller, though it frequently had 11 or more family members packed into its confined space. In the intervening years it has had numerous additions, and is now rather grand and about the size of a small country house with seven-acre gardens to match.

The Wakes opened as a museum in 1955. Most of it is dedicated to White memorabilia, but upstairs there are two separate exhibitions dedicated to the memories of Lawrence and Francis Oates. Lawrence was the well known Polar explorer who perished with Scott, having said the immortal words 'I am just going outside—I may be some time'; Francis was his lesser known uncle, an explorer of central Africa who made it his lifelong ambition to reach the Victoria Falls. He finally succeeded in 1874, but died of fever on the return journey.

The Wakes' gardens are as impressive as the house. The setting is magnificent with the Hanger rising behind, and its cultivation is in line with White's *Garden Kalendar* though his famous vegetable bed is no more. A short length of his fruit wall remains with a plaque reading 'GW 1761'; the herb garden not only grows his herbs but also sells them; and a descendant of Timothy, the Reverend White's pet tortoise, is in evidence together with various uncles, aunts and children.

Selborne boasts a most interesting privately owned bookshop a few yards up the road from The Wakes specialising in historical countryside and rural craft books, with a large collection of various editions of *The Natural History* and White biographies. The shop also has a separate section with an exhibition of rustic furniture and other oddments, most of which are for sale.

The Romany Folklore Museum at Limes End Yard at the southern end of the village is also well worth a visit (open 'Most days Easter to September'). This is a working museum with an indoor exhibition charting the life of gypsies in the Britain and abroad, a shop selling gypsy crafts, and an outside workshop with a collection of gypsy caravans in various stages of restoration.

## Bibliography

*Gilbert White's Journals*, edited by Dr John Aikin (1747-1822); Routledge & Kegan Paul 1970.
*The Garden Kalendar*, edited by John Clegg, The Scolar Press 1976.
*The Natural History of Selborne*. Since the first edition was published in December 1788, there have been scores of edited versions of *The Natural History* and a number are in print. A facsimile of the original first edition is published by the Scolar Press, 1976; a more recent version is published in paperback by Penguin, 1977.
The most recent biography of White is *Gilbert White* by Richard Mabey, Century Hutchinson, 1986.

## *A Walk with Gilbert White*

**Map:** OS Landranger 186.
**Start:** Grid Ref. 740338; public car park next to the Selborne Arms
**Nearest BR Station:** Alton.
**Distance:** 5 miles.
**Time:** Allow 2–3 hours.
**Facilities:** Two pubs and tea room in Selborne.
**Summary:** See Selborne Hanger, the zigzag, The Wakes, and the Short and Long Lythe, much as the Reverend White saw them in his time.

*The picturesque view of Dorton Cottage as one enters the Short Lythe on the east side of Selborne.*

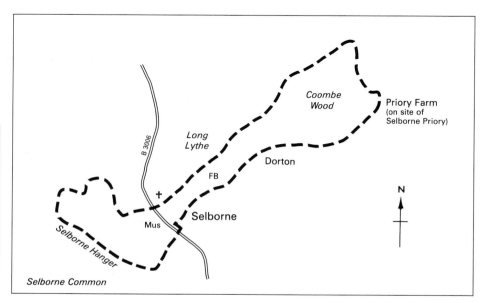

*The view of Selborne from the top of the Hanger, a short way from the famous zig-zag.*

There are any number of walks around Selborne, with the area criss-crossed by public footpaths and bridleways. However any walk must include the famous zigzag and Hanger to the south-west of Selborne, and Short and Long Lythe to the north-east—the frequent walking ground of the Reverend White where his observations formed the basis of *The Natural History*.

Approach Selborne on the B3006 Alton to Petersfield road, and leave your car at the public car park (on the right side if coming from Alton; on the left from Petersfield) which is clearly signposted and conveniently placed next to the Selborne Arms pub. This serves reasonable food, has a pleasant garden and play area for children, and also boasts a small collection of exotic caged birds.

Selborne Hanger becomes muddy in heavy rain, and at those times walking boots

or wellingtons should be worn. Otherwise the walk is undemanding and requires no special preparation or any great level of fitness, making it suitable for children. From the car park follow the signposts for the zigzag which ascends the Hanger ahead of you, and quite literally zigzags up the hill. This was built by brother John with some help and advice from the industrious Reverend White, and is today kept in order by National Trust volunteers.

Ten minutes is ample time to take you from the car park to the top of Selborne Hanger, from where you can see Selborne and its surrounding countryside spread out before you. The view has been greatly improved by the number of trees which were blown down in the gale of 1988, many of which would have been non-existent or mere saplings in White's time, and apart from the occasional modern blot on the horizon it must accord with White's

view during his frequent visits to the Hanger.

With the aid of a map the walk can easily be extended across Selborne Common towards Newton Valence, or south to Noar Hill and High Wood Hanger. However our prescribed route first pauses to view the Obelisk or 'Wishing Stone', which was placed at the top of the zig-zag by White and his brothers having been brought from the village of Farringdon, and then turns right along the top of the Hanger.

The path meanders downwards through woods. When you come to a National Trust sign turn right along a sunken lane, one of the few that remain from the Reverend White's time when many if not all of the lanes were hollow or 'sunken', as indeed was the very poor track which connected Selborne to the outside world at Alton. These lanes were pressed deep into the soft sandstone ground by years of erosion and horse-drawn traffic, as described by

*The surrounding countryside looking east from Selborne—another view from the Hanger.*

the Reverend White:

'In many places they are reduced sixteen or eighteen feet beneath the level of the fields; and after floods and in frosts exhibit very grotesque and wild appearances. These rugged, gloomy scenes affright the ladies when they peep down into them from the paths above, and make timid horsemen shudder when they ride along them . . .'

You then turn right down a crossing track, emerging on a metalled lane by a corner house which is now named Fisher's Buildings. This was the village poorhouse, wrecked by a mob protesting against church taxes in 1830. Justified though they no doubt were, most of the rioters suffered the penalty of being deported.

From here turn into Gracious Street which has a number of aptly gracious houses, and onto the main road where the entrance to The Wakes—the Reverend White's home and now his museum—is a few yards to the right. If overtaken by thirst, the second pub in the village is conveniently opposite, a short way up the hill.

The walk continues by crossing directly over the road and onto the Plestow ('Play Place')—Selborne's village green. A pathway leads into the churchyard where you can't fail

to see the remains of the magnificent yew tree which is estimated to be at least 800 years old, and measured 23 feet around its base during the Reverend White's period as curate. Walking round the left side of the church you will find the Reverend's grave to the north of the chancel, the fifth headstone out from the wall. A simple inscription is marked with the initials 'GW', but inside the church a stained glass window commemorates Selborne's most famous resident.

Beyond the churchyard the path goes downhill over grass, and across a small footbridge fording Oakhanger Stream . The well-defined path passes to the left of the thatched Dorton Cottage—very picturesque and no doubt equally so in the time of the Reverend White. One now enters the Short Lythe, leaving the woods by a stile and crossing into more woods at the start of the Long Lythe—his walks along here inspired his poem 'Summer Evening Walk'.

From here go over a stile, keeping left along the edge of a field before bearing right downhill towards another bridge. Then head left up the hill, turning right through a gate on the edge of the wood and crossing another field diagonally. Fork right following the path through woods towards Priory Farm which stands on the former site of Selborne Priory, founded in 1232 and suppressed in 1484. This

suppression was due to the scandalous lifestyle of the monks, about which White commented:

'They used to attend junketings and feastings . . . had pawned their plate . . . also got into a method of laying naked in bed without their breeches, for which they are much reprimanded.'(!)

From Priory Farm the footpath continues straight on towards Oakhanger Farm and the mesolithic site at The Warren, but we turn right over a stile, cutting across a field on the west side of the farm buildings and joining a bridleway track signposted to Selborne. This retraces and runs parallel to the outward route, but is on the other side of the Oakhanger Stream.

Just before the village you reach the old Via Canorum, the 'Monks Way', which originally linked it to the priory. By bearing left you eventually emerge on the main road, a little way down from the car park where you started. With the aid of the local Pathfinder OS map (SU63/73) this walk could easily be extended in a number of directions; indeed those who are particularly energetic can follow footpaths all the way to Chawton and combine this Gilbert White walk with the Jane Austen one featured elsewhere in the book.

# Walk 5: With William Wordsworth in Grasmere

*William Wordsworth (1770–1850) must be the best known British poet. Most of his life was spent in the Lake District, and today three of the houses he lived in can be visited by the public. The walk which follows visits his first Grasmere home at Dove Cottage, and his last home at Rydal Mount where he lived in a splendid setting for 37 years.*

One almost suspects that Wordsworth changed his name by deed poll, for when a man's life, fame and immortal reputation are based on the use of words, the fact that he is called 'words worth' seems almost too good to be true. He produced a vast amount of verse, earned the title of Poet Laureate and left us with perhaps his most famous lines:

'I wandered lonely as a Cloud
That floats on high o'er vales and hills,
When all at once I saw a crowd,
A host of golden Daffodils;
Beside the Lake, beneath the trees,
Fluttering and dancing in the breeze.

. . . Ten thousand saw I at a glance,
Tossing their heads in a sprightly dance . . .'

William Wordsworth was born in Cockermouth at the northern end of the Lake District on April 7th 1770. His famous sister, Dorothy, who became his constant companion, was born there on Christmas Day a year later—the large Georgian house they were brought up in is in Main Street, and is now owned by the National Trust and open to the public.

Wordsworth attended St John's College, Cambridge, which he didn't much care for, and then set off on his first walking tour of the Continent which took him to Germany, Switzerland and most notably, France, where he became an enthusiastic supporter of the Revolution, and also found time to father a daughter as a result of an affair with Mademoiselle Annette Vallon. His radical enthusiasm for the new style of French liberty

**Wordsworth as painted by B. R. Haydon in 1842.** *Photo by NPG.*

was later tempered by the mass guillotinings of the 'Terror', and having abandoned plans to marry his French girlfriend he later became a more conservative figure, a fate which befalls many who start out with idealistic aspirations.

In 1795 he received a legacy of £900 which enabled him to exist as a full time poet. From then on his sister Dorothy lived with him, a useful arrangement for posterity since she chose to record the minutiae of their life together in her famous *Journals* and other writings—she has been described as 'probably the most distinguished of English writers who

never wrote a line for the general public'. They moved into a house in Dorset, and then to Alfoxden House in Somerset, featured in the Samuel Taylor Coleridge walk in this book.

A comparatively brief stay there ended a decade of wandering before Wordsworth returned to the Lake District for the last 50 years of his life, although he remained an enthusiastic traveller elsewhere. From that time on he produced a vast quantity of poetry inspired by the Lakes and established himself as their literary godfather with references in his verse that can be traced to Keswick, Helvellyn, Grasmere, Easedale, Rydal, Patterdale, Borrowdale and many other well known locations. He walked all over the Lakes, and apart from verse wrote a *Guide To The Lakes* published in 1810, which became a best seller with five editions sold out by 1835. However, as is often the case with travel writers, he was in two minds about the tourists he was encouraging exclaiming: 'These Tourists, heaven preserve us!' Despite his misgivings, he ended his guide by describing the Lakes as 'a sort of national property, in which every man has a right and interest who has an eye to perceive and a heart to enjoy'.

He was an energetic walker who always championed rights of way, which were as open to dispute then as they can be today. One of Coleridge's nephews remembers walking with him across 'private' land:

'I remember asking him if we were not trespassing . . . He said, no; the walks had, indeed, been inclosed, but he remembered them open to the public, and he always went through them when he chose . . . He had evidently a pleasure in vindicating these rights, and deemed to think it a duty.'

*The view over Rydal Water—classic Lakeland scenery.*

Wordsworth never owned a home in the Lake District—he rented them all. He found the house which is now known as Dove Cottage on a walking tour of the Lakes with Coleridge in November 1799, took it at a modest £5 per year, and returned immediately to settle in with Dorothy the following month. From the start they both loved Dove Cottage, and indeed Grasmere which Wordsworth described as 'blissful Eden' in one of his many poems on the immediate area.

Two years later Wordsworth married Mary Huthchinson, a decision which required him to leave Dove Cottage briefly before returning in triumph with his bride. This short separation from the cottage was enough to inspire an eight verse outburst entitled *A Farewell*, ending with a eulogy on the wonderful garden and orchard which he and Dorothy so enjoyed:

'O happy Garden! whose seclusion deep
Hath been so friendly to industrious hours;
to soft slumbers, that did gently steep
Our spirits, carrying with them dreams of flowers,
And wild notes warbled among leafy bowers;
Two burning months let summer overleap,
And, coming back with Her who will be ours,
Into thy bosom we again shall creep.'

The years Wordsworth spent at Dove Cottage were his most productive and by all accounts exceptionally happy, but by 1808 the tiny house was full to overflowing with William and Mary, Dorothy, three young children (two more followed), and visitors who included Thomas De Quincey and Coleridge. The Wordsworths moved reluctantly, passing

on Dove Cottage to De Quincey who then appalled them by tearing down some of the trees in the garden to make more light!

It is surprising that the Wordsworth clan ever considered moving to Allan Bank. This was a newly built house on the outskirts of Grasmere, and in a letter William had already described its owner as 'A wretched Creature, wretched in name and Nature, of the name of Crump, goaded on by his still more wretched Wife,' and the house itself as 'a temple of abomination in which are to be enshrined Mr and Mrs Crump'. Despite these feelings it was the Wordsworths who were enshrined there, and while he revised his opinion of the Crumps he was right to have been suspicious of the house which proved to have smoking chimneys which couldn't heat the rooms and was too expensive to maintain.

After two years the Wordsworths moved

on in 1811 to the Rectory opposite Grasmere's church, and this proved to be an even less happy choice with the same smoking chimneys and an unhealthily damp atmosphere. Two of Wordsworth's children died there the following year within six months of one another, and after burying them in the adjacent churchyard—the place of rest for William and Mary in later years—the family decided to find a new home as soon as possible.

By this time Wordsworth's finances had been improved by his appointment as Distributor of Stamps for the area, and in 1813 they took the lease on Rydal Mount from Lady Fleming of Rydal Hall, some two miles distant. This was a far finer place and Wordsworth delighted in the views from the old ninth-century mound (or 'mount') which stands in front of the house, looking over towards Lanty Scar which he knew as 'Aerial Rock':

'Aerial Rock—whose solitary brow
From this low threshold daily meets my sight;
When I step forth to hail the morning light;
Or quit the stars with a lingering farewell . . .'

He also created the garden and its walks which remains magnificent today, preferring when possible to compose in the open air:

'This Lawn, a carpet all alive
With shadows flung from leaves—to strive
In dance, amid a press
Of sunshine, an apt emblem yields
Of Worldlings revelling in the fields
Of strenuous idleness'

In 1825 disaster seemed imminent. Lady Fleming announced that she wished to let Rydal Mount to a relative, and the Wordsworths would have to go. William immediately bought the land below 'at an extravagant fancy price' with the vague idea of building a house. When Lady Fleming apparently remained adamant in her intention Wordsworth bewailed the prospect of losing his home:

'The doubt to which a wavering hope had clung
Is fled; we must depart, willing or not;
Sky piercing hills! Must bid farewell to you . . .'

Thankfully she changed her mind, and William passed on the land to his daughter Dora—she died in 1847 from tuberculosis and it became known as 'Dora's Field'. The Wordsworth's lived on at Rydal Mount where William died at the fine age of 80 on April 23rd 1850, followed by his sister in 1855 and

*Above:* **No question as to why Wordsworth chose the Lakes as his home—their beauty is unsurpassed and this view, which he must have known, can have changed little if at all.**

*Below:* **Dove Cottage, the home which Wordsworth discovered while on a walking tour in 1799.**

his wife in 1859. The house reverted to the Fleming family, until in 1969 they appropriately sold it to a great great granddaughter of the poet who opened it to the public in 1970.

Dove Cottage is today a place of pilgrimage for many thousands of visitors and is run by the Wordsworth Trust. You are given a guided tour lasting about 30 minutes, and since it's so small you need to time your visit to avoid the worst of the crowds in the holiday season. The adjacent museum is very extensive, and beautifully laid out with the bonus of a large section on Byron—it's worth allowing plenty of time if the idea interests you. The shop is rather small for the number of people it has to accommodate but they do stock a good range of relevant books.

Rydal Mount is very different—large, light, spacious, and displaying a taste for home comforts which had not concerned the ascetic poet in earlier life. The main rooms are all on view and make for an extremely interesting tour, and there is a very good Wordsworth bookshop which is a much better place to browse than the shop at Dove Cottage. The aforementioned garden remains very fine.

## Bibliography

Wordsworth's poetry is available in numerous editions, as are his letters and those of Dorothy and Mary. Wordsworth's *Guide To The Lakes* (1810) is available from the Oxford University Press, who also publish David McCracken's *Wordsworth & The Lake District*, an interesting guide to his poems and their places. There are innumerable biographies and critiques of Wordsworth and his work.

## A Walk with William Wordsworth

**Map**: OS Outdoor Leisure 7—The English Lakes SE area.
**Start**: From Dove Cottage at Town End near Grasmere, on the A591 in Cumbria—OS Grid Ref 342070. Park by the Dove Cottage restaurant. Dove Cottage and the Wordsworth Museum are open 9.30–5.30 pm daily, last admissions at 5.00 pm. Rydal Mount is open 9.30–5.00 pm daily in summer; 10–4 pm daily excluding Tuesdays in winter.
**Nearest BR Station**: Windermere.
**Distance**: Approximately 4 miles.
**Time**: Allow 2–3 hours.
**Facilities**: Cafe/restaurant by Dove Cottage; pub at Rydal.
**Summary**: An easy walk round Rydal Water from Dove Cottage to Rydal Mount, Wordsworth's first and last Grasmere homes. The route packs some splendid scenery into its short distance.

The car park by the Dove Cottage restaurant is small; if it's full, you can park a short way into Grasmere where there is also an Information Centre. Dove Cottage itself is set a short way back from the road, and all the buildings that block its view of Grasmere have been built since Wordsworth's time there. Before the new road was built in 1831 it was a very quiet and remote place.

Facing Dove Cottage, turn right up the hill, and where the road bends right by a farm carry straight on up a tarmac track following

the sign to Rydal. Keep on along what was known as the 'Coffin Track', ignoring a footpath sign off to the left which shows the way to Alcock Tarn. The track continues past a few houses before dropping downhill and bearing round to the right on an unmade surface. Here Nab Scar towers above you, while to the right there is a fine view over Rydal Water down the hillside.

The track runs more or less straight all the way to Rydal. The only point where it becomes less obvious is when it forks left and right—up towards a parapet wall, or down to follow the side of the woods. Take the right fork here, and then the next left fork continuing for a few yards uphill until you come to a gate set in a stone wall. Go through the gate and continue to follow the same easterly direction, staying well above Rydal Water as the woods are left behind and the track takes you into more open country. After 30-45 minutes' walking the track starts to drop down into Rydal. It passes the back wall of Rydal Mount on the right, and then takes you through a gate and on to a crossing lane. Turn right here, and the entrance to Rydal Mount is a few yards down the hill.

To continue walk on down the hill, passing Lady Fleming's Rydal Hall on the left—on one occasion Wordsworth and Coleridge were told off for exercising their 'right of way' in the grounds. A short way on turn right through a wrought iron gate into the Rydal Chapel churchyard. The chapel was built by Lady Fleming in 1824; Wordsworth was a warden, and his family occupied the front pew on the left. Walk along the path by the side of the chapel, and at the end a gate leads to 'Dorothy's Field' which is now owned by the National Trust. Although well covered by trees, the hillside displays plenty of Wordsworth's daffodils in the early spring.

From the church turn right along the main road which thankfully has a pavement. About 100 yards further on, a footpath sign points off to the left, just opposite the large hotel/pub where you may care to stop for lunch—alternatively there are many excellent places for a picnic along this walk. Follow the footpath sign away from the road and over a footbridge, and where the path forks right and left take the right fork which heads through Steps End to follow the side of Rydal Water. Once again the way is easy to follow, with the path going through woods and then coming out into the open by a gate past Jobson Close.

From here you have the choice of continuing along the side of Rydal Water on the low lakeside path which is unmarked on the OS map but well used by the public, or

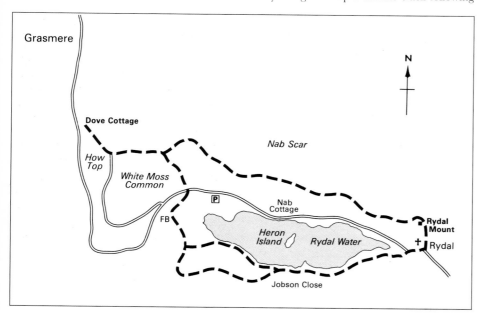

*Rydal Chapel, the church where Wordsworth prayed, just below his last home at Rydal Mount.*

forking left onto the OS map bridleway which follows the hillside. On the far side of the water you get a clear view of Heron Island which inspired *Inscription Written with a Slate Pencil*; beyond it is Nab Cottage, a solitary white building, the farmhouse home of Thomas De Quincey's wife and now a guest house. Hartley Coleridge—the son of the great poet—also lived and died there, and both he and the 'opium eater' would no doubt have been horrified by the amount of traffic which roars past the front door today.

The lakeside path eventually bears left away from the lake, heading uphill by the side of a wall. As it climbs higher past an old, black barn you come to woods on the right in the lee of Ewe Crag towering above. Just before a sign pointing on to Grasmere there's a stone gateway through the wall, near to where the upper bridleway comes down to join the lower path. Turn through this gateway into the

Woods, following the track downhill and round to the left, and ignoring a less obvious fork right that leads down to a wildlife nature reserve—unless you wish to explore it.

A little further on the main track bears right to a substantial wooden footbridge which crosses the River Rothay that connects Rydal Water to Grasmere. On the other side you bear right with the track, taking the next right hand fork which soon bears left up to the road where you should see a red postbox by a footpath sign on the opposite side. It's easy to get confused here; if you've turned up to the road too early, turn right and walk along it for a short distance until you find the right place.

Follow the footpath sign into the woods, and then take the narrow path that forks left up past a waterfall. You continue to follow the side of the stream which feeds it, heading uphill on its right side. Just past a small yellow footpath blob on a ground level rock (easily

missed), cross to the other side of the stream to continue up its left side—take care as the stones are likely to be slippery. The path becomes more indistinct and overgrown, but persevere on up and you soon come out of the trees onto a grass plateau which is up to the left. This is White Moss Common, a spot well known to Wordsworth, which gives a most magnificent view over to Ewe Crag and beyond. Behind is the track that connects Dove Cottage to Rydal Mount, and it's a short walk back to your starting point.

You may like to wander into Grasmere to see Allan Bank and the Rectory, though neither are open to the public. From Dove Cottage cross the main road and follow the B5287. Grasmere Church is on the right with the Rectory opposite. From there bear left past the Wordsworth Hotel. Allan Bank is on the left up a private road, a few hundred yards past the Red Lion.

# Walk 6: With Sir Walter Scott at Rokeby

*Sir Walter Scott (1771–1832) was the most successful, most affluent and most prolific writer of his day. He made a fortune and then lost it, spending his last few years paying off creditors and suffering ill health. His poem* Rokeby *occupied three months of an extraordinarily productive life.*

Rokeby is a beautiful eighteenth century house in the far north of England near Barnard Castle. Scott was a close friend of John Morritts who inherited the house at the age of 20, and was a guest on his journeys south from Abbotsford. These visits led to his long, narrative poem *Rokeby*, published in 1813 when his standing as a poet was declining, not helped by Byron's publication of *Childe Harold*.

The narrative of the poem is complex. The scene is set at Rokeby after the Battle of Marston Moor (1644) which is described at length. Oswald Wycliffe, Lord of Barnard Castle, and Bertram Rissingham shoot Philip of Mortham, leaving him for dead in order to get his land and treasure which necessitates an attack on Rokeby. The attack is repulsed, but having held Lord Rokeby a prisoner since Marston Moor, Oswald threatens to execute him unless his daughter marries Oswald's son who, it transpires, is far too gentle and poetic to take advantage of her consent and withers away and dies. As Oswald is about to do the dreadful deed, Bertram, smitten with remorse, rides in and kills him, and is slain himself. Redmond O'Neale, the page who had heroically defended Rokeby, is found to be the lost son of Mortham, marries Mathilda, and all live happily ever after.

There are plenty of references to the surroundings in the poem:

'Stern Bertram shunned the nearer way,
Through Rokeby's park and chase that lay,
And, skirting high the valley's ridge,
They crossed by Greta's ancient bridge.'

*Rokeby* also contains two songs which have outlasted the poem itself—*A Weary Lot is Thine*,

***Sir Walter Scott, as painted in 1832 by W. Allan.*** Photo by NPG.

*Fair Maid* and *On Brignal Banks*:

Yet Brignal Banks are fresh and fair
And Greta woods are green,
And you may gather garlands there
Would grace a summer queen.

Scott was a quite exceptional man. Hardly writing anything until he was 30, he died when he was 61 having produced vast quantities of work which included four volumes of collected ballads, his own editions of Dryden and Swift, as much poetry as Shelley, 27 novels, a nine volume life of Napoleon, 12 volumes of correspondence, a 700 page *Journal*, and endless essays and reviews. He was not even a full time writer, working also as a judge, businessman

and landowner, and during the last 15 years of his life he was more often than not extremely ill. The majority of his work was hugely popular, and was avidly read and imitated throughout the 19th century.

Scott was born in Edinburgh, the ninth child of a hard working Writer to the Signet (lawyer). He also entered the legal profession—polio, which had left him lame, precluded him from the military life he would have preferred, and the nearest he got in this direction was helping with the Royal Edinburgh Volunteer Light Dragoons. He was successful in law, becoming Sheriff Deputy of Selkirk and Principal Clerk to the Court of Sessions in Edinburgh which enabled him to combine life in the city and country.

In 1786 he saw the Highlands for the first time, developing the romantic appreciation of Scottish landscape and history which proved to be the backbone of his writing. Inspired by Percy's *Reliques*—a fashionable book of ancient songs and poems—he made his own collection in *The Minstrelsy of the Scottish Border*, which he followed by his first highly successful narrative poem, *The Lay of the Last Minstrel*, published in 1805 with 44,000 copies sold by 1830. Amongst many other works, the poem *Marmion* followed in 1807 and *The Lady of the Lake* two years later—both hugely popular.

Scott recognised that Byron was a superior poet, and after Rokeby turned to the first of his historical Waverley novels which today are sold by the yard in secondhand bookshops. *Waverley* (1814), based on the story of the Young Pretender and the unsuccessful Scottish Jacobite rising of 1745, was the most successful novel ever published in English, paving the way for the series that followed.

*Above:* **The splendid ruins of Egglestone Abbey, as seen from the road to Barnard Castle.**

*Below:* **The way along the north bank of the River Tees—overgrown in summer, but easy walking so long as it's dry.**

These ranged historically from the eighteenth century tales of *Rob Roy* and *Guy Mannering* to the medieval shenanigans of *Ivanhoe* of which 10,000 copies were sold in a fortnight!

When Scott was too ill to write he dictated his novels and other works to trusty retainers who acted as his secretaries—*Ivanhoe* was written in this fashion, as was *The Bride of Lammermoor* (which became Donizetti's *Lucia de Lammermoor*), conceived at a time when Scott was delirious with pain from gallstones. When he was not writing or dictating, Scott was obsessed by his home at Abbotsford, the Gothic creation which is rather well described in an early edition of his poems edited by W.M Rossetti (brother of the Pre-Raphaelite D.G.):

'Famous, fully occupied, happy in domestic life, surrounded by numerous friends and acquaintances, wealthy and yet loving society, Scott seemed one of the most fortunate of men. He had a rather weak minded ambition—that of living like a feudal lord; and for a while he realised it with considerable éclat. In 1811 he bought a hundred acres of moorland on the Tweed, near Melrose—moorland bleak and bare. "Cartley Hole" did not sound so well as "Abbotsford"; he called it by the latter name, and about 1814 left for the house at Abbotsford, which he rebuilt. He filled it with costly and curious odds and ends of all sorts; exercised a large hospitality; and endeavoured to revive the aspect of olden times. Many other purchases of land followed, at heavy prices.'

Abbotsford is open to the public from Easter until late October.

Scott was secretly a major shareholder with James Ballantyne who printed his books, and with Constable, his publisher. Despite his incredible success both those companies managed to go bankrupt in 1826, saddling Scott with a debt of around £114,000.

He vowed to pay off his creditors in full, saying 'My own hand shall do it'; he succeeded, but the effort broke him physically, and the publications of his last years which included the vast *History of Napoleon* were written to make quick money, and would never become lasting classics.

With the end of his debts in sight, Scott went to Italy for the winter of 1831 in an effort to recover his health—he had suffered two strokes in the previous months, brought on by drinking champagne against medical advice. He returned to Abbotsford on 11th July the following year in a pitiable physical and mental state, and finally died on 21st September to be buried at Dryburgh Abbey.

## Bibliography

The Waverley novels are generally considered Scott's masterpieces, notably *The Antiquary* (1816), *Old Mortality* (1816), *Heart of the Midlothian* (1818) and *Redgauntlet* (1824). All these novels were published anonymously, and he only admitted to being their author in 1827, the year after his ruin.

*Scott's Life* by his son-in-law J.G. Lockhart (1837) is 'considered one of the great biographies of English literature' by *The Oxford Companion to English Literature*, and of course he has had many more biographers in the intervening years.

## A Walk with Sir Walter Scott

**Map:** OS Landranger 92.
**Start:** Egglestone Abbey, south of Barnard Castle in Durham—OS Grid Ref. 061151. Large free car park; the Abbey is open all year round. Rokeby Park is open 2–5 pm on Mondays from June to mid-September; Tuesdays from mid-July to mid-September; Thursdays during August.
**Nearest BR Station:** Darlington.
**Distance:** Approximately 8 miles.
**Time:** Allow 2–3 hours to the Morritt Arms, 1 hour to return to Egglestone Abbey, and at least 1 hour to see Rokeby Park.
**Facilities:** Hotel/pub by Greta Bridge.
**Summary:** A fine walk along the north and south banks of the River Tees, diverting to the River Greta. Beautiful views of the river valley and lots of variety throughout.

You can park next to the ruins of Egglestone Abbey, an interesting old ruin in a fine setting with an information panel by the entrance. Walk down from the Abbey to the road, bearing right then left over the bridge that crosses the River Tees, with views up and down the rapids. Bear left up the road towards Barnard Castle, ignoring a pathway to the right which goes down to the riverside but soon peters out.

Continue uphill for about 75 yards towards some farm buildings; before reaching the driveway there's a step over the wall on the right side of the road which is the unmarked start of the footpath. Before crossing, however, it's worth walking up the road for another 75 yards or so for the splendid view of the Abbey. From here Scott's characters might also have seen the lofty towers of Barnard's Castle, but nowadays you have to go all the way into town if you want to see its ruins. The most one can see is the white spire of the Barnard Castle School, a short distance from the Bowes Museum which is well worth a visit later in the day.

Climb over the step to cross the wall and walk across a grassy field, bearing diagonally right towards the trees in its far right hand corner where you go over a stile. From here onwards you generally follow a straight line east, with the trees that line the heights of the northern river bank of the Tees immediately to your right and fields rising gently to your left in a tranquil, rural setting. I last did this

*Rokeby, a wonderful home which played host to Scott and inspired his poem dubbed 'Rokeby' in a rather different setting.*

walk in June when the paths here were well overgrown but accessible apart from occasional nettle patches. In wet weather the combination of high grass on one side and high corn on the other could make this a very wet walk; in winter it could also be muddy.

A short way on ignore a yellow footpath sign which appears to direct you onto a track going right into the trees—this soon peters out. Keep on along the edge of the field with the trees immediately on your right, picking up the occasional footpath sign as you pass stiles and go through gates. After a time a footpath sign indicates that you should bear left across the grassy field ahead, moving away from a bend in the river where the trees disappear for a short time. Follow the sign over to the far side of the field, bearing left towards steps in the stone wall with a copse of trees on a hillock up to the left.

Go over the wall and continue in much the same direction, heading for the top left hand corner of the next field. A short way to

the left of the gate ahead you will see more steps over the stone wall. Cross over and then follow a stone wall along on the left until you come to a ladder going over a wall straight ahead, with a gate on the left by a small shed and a gate on the right leading into trees. Go over this ladder and continue to follow the trees on your right with fields on your left. As you pass East Shaws Farm away to the left, the path goes into a belt of trees, down into a gully which is very overgrown with a stream at the bottom, and up the other side, bearing right and left to resume its course along the edge of the trees opposite the farm buildings at Sledwich Hall.

A little further on you come to another break in the trees where a footpath arrow indicates that you bear left on a narrow sheep track, following a line of trees on the hillside above the river. (There is a ladder over a wall some way down in the valley by the river which you should ignore.) After passing through more fields the track takes you towards

houses on the outskirts of Whorlton. Keep to the right following alongside the trees, and when you come to a red brick house bear right through a gate and along a narrow track on its right hand side. After passing a large house on the left, you emerge on the road just below Whorlton.

Turn right here, and take the steps which go down to the right at the side of the road. This leads you to the tollgate building by the splendid wood and steel suspension bridge just upriver from Whorlton Lido which is a popular bathing spot during fine summer weather. Cross the bridge and head along the road, and after about 75 yards go over a step in the wall on the right. Head diagonally left across the grassy field, making for the right side of a clump of trees by the roof of a house which is obscured by the slight hill you are climbing.

When the house which is on the corner of the road by Thorpe Hall comes into view, bear over to a gate in the wall on the right to join an overgrown, disused track, running along the edge of a field towards the ruined farmhouse at West Thorpe. You pass these ruins well above the river, following the track left round the edge of a belt of woodland until you come to a stile at the end of the trees. Go over the stile, following the footpath sign along the edge of a hedge with fields stretching down to the river on your right.

Continuing in this direction you soon come to a gate with the large and romantic building of Mortham Tower beyond. The footpath sign tells you to bear right here, crossing a field for about 30 yards before joining the driveway that runs up to the front entrance of the house. Here you have a choice—either turning left along the drive bound for Greta Bridge, or turning right down towards the bridge at 'The Meeting Of The Rivers' where the River Greta floods down to join the Tees, and then walking along the riverside on the south side of Rokeby Park. This is a much more direct route, but it's worth the detour to see Greta Bridge which figures so largely in Scott's *Rokeby*, particularly if your timing is right so that you can stop for lunch at the excellent Morritt Arms nearby.

Turn left up the driveway towards Mortham Tower, bearing left round the side of its outbuildings which include a delightful, run-down stable block. The footpath follows the boundary wall round to the right on the edge of a field, heading uphill and then bearing left and right to follow a wall down the side of another field. Eventually you will see the infernal A66 ahead of you, with its hideous new road bridge over to the right. The footpath track heads down towards this bridge, passing under its left hand side on a very muddy track which is well used by the local cattle.

This track then bears up to the left, but you keep straight ahead along the bank of the River Greta, heading towards the romantic Greta Bridge which is a world away from its modern rival. From here you join the old road via a hole in the wall about 50 yards to the left of the bridge. Turn right along this minor road over the bridge, making for the Morritt Arms (opposite the south entrance to Rokeby Park) which has a fine garden and serves good pub food.

This entrance to Rokeby Park is not, however, open, for no other reason than that it's on the wrong side of the A66. To continue from the Morritt Arms turn left along the old road, bearing right uphill past a dead end sign. It is unusual and rather pleasant to walk along a disused road which is very slowly turning back to nature. You will come to some steps on the right which lead down to the busy A66, which is otherwise well hidden from this walk. Turn left along the walkway for about 100 yards, crossing where convenient to take the right hand turning signposted to Egglestone Abbey and Barnard Castle. On the north side of the road you will get your first glimpses of Rokeby through the trees, and it's a short and not unpleasant walk down the lane which leads to its main entrance.

Rokeby is a charming house, and by stately home standards it is light, homely and domestic—the Morritt family are still in residence. It is in a most enviable position with its tennis courts perched high above the River Greta, and there's a lovely walk along the side of this river which soon drops down to meet the Tees at 'The Meeting Of The Rivers'.

After visiting Rokeby Park, turn right out of the main entrance. Where the road bends round to the left, turn down the private lane on the right and almost immediately turn left onto a narrow track marked by a footpath sign. This follows the side of the River Tees with many glimpses of its fine rapids through the trees. After meandering along for some way it becomes a straighter tarmac track, eventually forking right and left. Here you take the right fork which leads you to the first bridge you crossed, and you then follow a zigzag uphill to rejoin the road. Turn right back to your starting point at Egglestone Abbey, after a most enjoyable walk along the rivers.

*The fine old bridge near 'the meeting of the rivers'.*

34

# Walk 7: With Jane Austen in Chawton

*With six novels and a small number of shorter stories to her name, Jane Austen (1775-1817) is regarded as the consummate master of the English language whose witty tales of domestic intrigues and romances amongst the well-to-do classes have a timeless appeal. The last eight years of her life were spent in Chawton; a period which saw her most important literary output.*

**Jane Austen as remembered by her sister Cassandra, around 1810.** *Photo by NPG.*

**Jane Austen's house at Chawton as it looks today.**

So many of the writers in this book led sad, unfortunate lives, often the result of great poverty and frustration. Jane Austen does not fit into this category. She came from a large, prosperous family with excellent connections, and from what we know she enjoyed her life and the company of those around, producing her immortal novels with relative ease.

She was born on 17th December 1775, the second youngest of eight children, living in a large and spacious rectory at Steventon, eight miles from Basingstoke in Hampshire.

Unlike the tragic Brontes the six sons and two daughters all survived their father, George Austen. Their mother, Cassandra, whose polished ancestors included a Lord Mayor of London, was outlived by all but Jane. They did well for themselves, too. Frank and Charles went into the navy and retired as Admirals; Edward, adopted by childless and extremely wealthy relatives, inherited both their Chawton and Godmersham (Kent) estates and their name, and fathered six sons and five daughters (his wife was Elizabeth Bridges whose

family later produced a Poet Laureate); Henry combined three careers as soldier, clergyman and banker in the City; and James, who was Jane's favourite and the eldest of the children, succeeded his father as Rector of Steventon and married a cousin who had lost her French husband's head to the guillotine. The sixth brother, George, was an invalid and little is known about him.

On the female side Jane's sister, Cassandra, who was two years older than her, never married after the man she was engaged to was lost on a clerical mission to the West Indies. She lived with Jane who likewise never married, and was enormously fond and protective towards her—too much so, for on Jane's death she destroyed all Jane's correspondence that might be considered too intimate or improper, which in those days covered any multitude of minor sins. Cassandra's character is reflected in Jane Bennet in *Pride and Prejudice*.

When George Austen retired in 1800, the two daughters moved with their parents to Bath, a popular town of the time which figured largely in Jane Austen's first novel to be accepted by a publisher, *Northanger Abbey*. Jane did not approve of this move however, preferring the country life of Steventon where the family had many friends and led a lively social life. When her father died four years later the two sisters and their mother moved to Southampton where brother Frank had a house, and then in 1809 on to the 'cottage' at Chawton with a friend, Martha Lloyd, who came to live with them. This was provided by brother Edward who was by then the principal landowner of the village; Chawton House was a short way down the lane. Jane was delighted with their new home, writing to Frank in a manner which characterises her light, witty style:

'Our Chawton Home, how much we find
Already in it to our mind;
And how convinced that when complete
It will all other houses beat
That ever have been made or mended,
With rooms concise or rooms distended.'

Jane Austen wrote with the full support and encouragement of her family. *Love and Freindship* (her spelling) and *A History of England by a partial, prejudiced and ignorant Historian* were produced at the age of 14; while one of her first attempts at a mature novel, *First Impressions*, was written around 1797 when she was 21. Her father sent it to a bookseller and offered to pay for its publication, but even on these terms they rejected it. Later her brother Henry took over her father's role, promoting and pushing his sister's work for all it was worth, and some 12 years later she rewrote and revised *First Impressions* at Chawton, turning it into *Pride and Prejudice* which is now generally considered her best loved book.

Other early works were *Elinor and Marianne*, written around 1795 which later evolved into *Sense and Sensibility*, and *Northanger Abbey* written around 1798-9. The latter was the first book to be successfully sold to a publisher in

1803; they paid £10 for it, but chose not to publish it until 1818 when it appeared with *Persuasion* after Jane's death.

Between completing *Northanger Abbey* and starting the final revisions of *Sense and Sensibility* and *Pride and Prejudice* there was a long eight or nine year period of apparent unproductivity. She wrote little in Bath except an abandoned novel called *The Watsons*, and nothing in Southampton—probably due to a combination of feeling unsettled after leaving Steventon, her father's death, and another move before they found Chawton. Once established in this quiet Hampshire village she produced most of her great work, completing the revisions of her earlier books in the first years and starting *Mansfield Park* in 1811, followed by *Emma* in 1814, and then *Persuasion* a year later. By that time her fatal illness, usually thought to have been Addison's disease (a tuberculosis of the kidneys) or leukaemia, had taken its grip, and Jane Austen scholars claim they can detect a lack of her typical vitality and perfection in what was to be her last completed book.

In the winter of 1816 she started work on a novel named *Sanditon*, but it was never finished. By the spring of 1817 her condition was so bad that she and Cassandra moved to rooms in Winchester where they could be near to her physician. The move was to no avail, and she died on 18th July and lies buried in Winchester Cathedral.

Thankfully, her novels were successful in her lifetime. The Prince Regent kept a set of them in each of his residences, and Sir Walter Scott spoke of 'that exquisite touch which renders ordinary commonplace things and characters interesting'. Later, in the nineteenth century, a Jane Austen fan club developed which remains in full swing today, with avid enthusiasts from all corners of the globe reading and rereading her six fine novels with glee and setting out on pilgrimages to her house at Chawton. The moral climate, social manners and relationship between the sexes may have changed, but for many the domestic wit and wisdom of Jane's marriage seekers remains as true today as it was in the opening lines of *Pride and Prejudice*:

'It is a truth universally acknowledged, that a single man in possession of a good fortune, must be in want of a wife.

However little known the feelings or views of such a man may be on his first entering a neighbourhood, this truth is so well fixed in the minds of the surrounding families, that he is considered as the right-

ful property of some one or other of their daughters.'

As one who was so good at writing about the ways and means of seeking a husband (or wife), it seems strange that neither Jane nor her sister, ever married. From what we know she was jolly and amusing to be with, and brother Henry describes her as 'very attractive . . . rather tall and slender . . . her whole appearance expressive of health and animation . . . her countenance had a peculiar charm of its own to the eyes of most beholders'. With Cassandra's extensive censorship of her correspondence there are few clues to her romantic inclinations. We know that at the age of 20 she was briefly attracted to Mr Tom Lefroy, who later became Chief Justice of Ireland; she also dallied with an Oxford don named Mr Blackall; and while in Bath she accepted a proposal of marriage from a rich widower who was much older, and then changed her mind the next morning and rejected him. Finally Henry Austen's *Memoir* tells of a tall, dark stranger:

'A gentleman, whose charm of person, mind and manners was such that Cassandra thought him worthy to possess and likely to win her sister's love . . . Cassandra felt no doubt of his motives. But they never met again. Within a short time they heard of his sudden death . . . if Jane ever loved, it was this un-named gentleman.'

After Jane's death the family lived on at Chawton. Her mother died ten years later, Martha Lloyd married Frank Austen, and Cassandra lived there alone until 1845 when she died at the ripe old age of 72. Both were buried in Chawton churchyard close by Chawton House. Jane's 'cottage' was then divided into three for use by farm labourers, and only rescued a hundred or so years later when T. Edward Carpenter purchased it and opened it as Jane Austen's museum in 1949. Considering its chequered history the curators of the Jane Austen Memorial Trust were remarkably successful in assembling their large collection of memorabilia, including the table on which Jane used to compose all her great works while sitting in the dining parlour.

## Bibliography

*Pride and Prejudice* (1813), *Emma* (1816) and *Mansfield Park* (1814) are generally regarded as Jane Austen's finest works. The other three novels are *Northanger Abbey* (1818), *Persuasion* (1818), and *Sense and Sensibility* (1811). All these works have been published in countless editions all over the world; there are also any number of literary and personal biographies.

## A Walk with Jane Austen

**Map:** OS Landranger 186.
**Start:** Jane Austen's house at Chawton, south of Alton off the A31 in Hampshire— OS Grid Ref. 708376. Free car park opposite Jane Austen's house. The house is open 114.30pm daily.
**Nearest BR Station:** Alton.
**Distance:** 7 miles.
**Time:** Allow 3 hours.
**Facilities:** Pub and café in Chawton; pub at Upper Farringdon; ice creams near Woodside Farm.
**Summary:** A walk which retraces the steps of Jane Austen to places she would have known. Footpath signposting is good and it's easy walking, although may be muddy in parts.

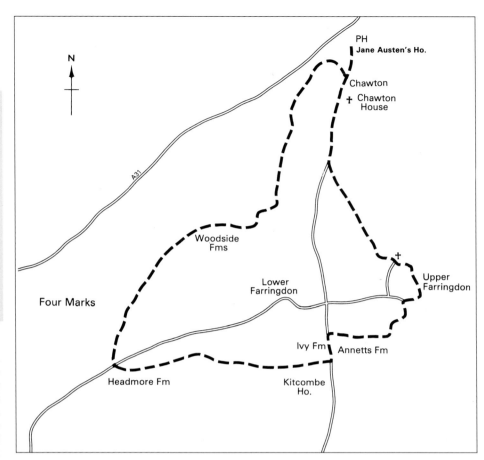

Jane Austen's house has a rather spartan interior, but is made more interesting by the various writings and scripts illustrating her life and work on its walls. It has a pleasant, small garden with several benches outside where you can rest if the weather is pleasant, and opposite on the other side of the road there's a good café serving snacks and excellent cakes, with a pub next door.

From the front entrance of the house cross the road to the corner café, and turn right onto the old, narrow road which goes straight ahead past the recreation ground and fields on the left, passing the substantial buildings of Manor House Farm before coming to the driveway leading up to Chawton House where Edward Knight (née Austen) lived and Jane was a frequent visitor. From here you can walk down and inspect the pretty church, although the imposing house is not open to the public.

Go back up to the road, turn left and continue for a couple of hundred yards until it comes to a dead end. Here you have to go up some steps on the right to join the A32, walking along the grass verge for some 500 yards until you reach a footpath. Pass the entrance to Southfield Farm on the right, and then when you come to a belt of trees on the right turn left over a stile by a footpath sign in the corner of a field. Bear right across this field, heading for a track to the left of a gate on the far side. When we walked here last, the path had been completely sewn over, so just follow the direction of the sign.

*Chawton House, where Jane's brother lived. At the time of writing, it seemed destined to be turned into a hotel, having been sold by its Austen descendant.*

The footpath on the far side leaves the field through trees, continuing along a wide track between fields and heading up into more woods, before dropping down towards Upper Farringdon. Walk on past swings and a children's whirlygig with some modern houses on the right; then turn left and follow the footpath sign towards a strange, red brick building which turns out to be a most elaborate Victorian village hall.

From here you can walk round the splendid church of Upper Farringdon where Gilbert White was assistant curate for some 24 years, going out of the far gate of the churchyard and turning left along a lane past some of the very bijoux residences of this affluent hamlet. Take the first turning on the right which takes you to the Rose & Crown pub, a pleasant enough place to stop with a large garden, although on our visit it disappointed us greatly by failing to serve food at an unreasonably early lunchtime hour!

At the pub turn right, and walk along the left hand side of the road ahead for about 100 yards. Just opposite a house with some rather splendid topiary in its front garden you'll see a track to the left with a bridleway sign. Follow this through trees, bearing right and ignoring the footpath stile that goes straight ahead. The track bears left again before coming into the open at a crossing track which runs along the top of a field with fine views out over the valley. Turn right here, heading downhill and then turning right again, following the bridleway sign and leaving the main track which curves round to the left above Annetts Farm. This bridleway appears to have been rerouted to the detriment of its users, since it brings you down to the A32 about 100 yards further north than is shown on the OS map.

Turn left along the side of this busy road and after about 300 yards take the right turning signposted to Kitcombe Kennels by a dead-end road sign. Follow this quiet tarmac lane up past a large house on the right with a notice for the kennels; here you bear left onto a rough track, following the side of the woods. Continue uphill for a short way, and where the track bends round to the left follow a footpath sign up to the right—the near right, not the extreme right which is another path. Watch out for this sign, for it's easily missed in the trees.

Follow the path up through the trees, eventually coming to a stile on the edge of the woods which is again well hidden. Go over and cross the field ahead, bearing diagonally right towards a gate by a clump of woods. You will find the next stile to the right of the gate just on the edge of these woods; cross over and

*The green lane which leads down to the thatched cottage above Woodside Farm where they sell the most excellent ice creams.*

*. . . and the cottage itself, a most welcome place to stop in summer!*

follow the side of the woods, heading on across the field beyond to a stile. Climb the stile and cross over a track and another stile, following the footpath between two bungalows—the right hand one is painted a distinctive yellow—until it joins the road at the crossroads north of Headmore Farm.

Cross over to the right, following the footpath sign which is easily spotted, and going over the stile into the field beyond. Walk on past the electricity sub-station and over another stile, heading across the next field towards the bright yellow footpath blob on the far side. Here, keep round the edge of the field, and then bear right following the footpath sign. Walk on until you come to a crossing track going left and right. Turn left and then almost immediately turn right onto a green lane which heads along the edge of the woods. At first the lane appears to be badly chewed up, but the surface soon improves and becomes a pleasant

woodland trail, bringing you down to the thatched cottage above Woodside Farm where they sell the most excellent home-made ice creams!

The track here becomes a tarmac lane, going downhill past the big farmhouse on the right and then on down past another farmhouse on the left. The OS map shows a footpath bearing left across the fields here, but this route appears to have been eradicated. Carry on along the lane for a few hundred yards, going uphill and then turning left at a footpath sign where the lane bends right. Follow the footpath along the edge of the field and round to the right until you come to a signposted footpath crossroads by an old building. Turn left along an old railway line, and follow this wide and quite rutted track along and under a bridge until you eventually come to a gate.

Go through the gate and into the next

field, following the footpath signs along the left hand side and then bearing right to walk through the clump of trees ahead, with the busy A32 over to your right. From here in summer you can often see the steam locomotives of the Watercress Line chugging along the old railway that connects Alresford to Alton, sending up clouds of steam as a reminder of the past. On the far side of the trees go over a stile and turn right down the side of the next field which brings you to the road a short way from the big roundabout. There is a stile opposite, but unfortunately no very obvious path back to your starting point and no footpath shown on the map. In the circumstances, it is easiest to walk up to the roundabout, and then take the right hand turning which leads you back to Jane Austen's house.

# Walk 8: With John Keats in Hampstead

*John Keats (1795-1821) was born in Moorfields (now Moorgate) on the edge of the City of London and lived in Hampstead for most of the last four years of his short life. Illness, financial worries, and lack of public appreciation for his work did not make his stay there easy, but his love for Fanny Brawne and the friendship of Charles Brown, who recorded much of Keat's work for posterity, provided some comfort and inspiration.*

Keats' melancholy lines linger in the memory:

'Ah, what can ail thee, wretched wight,
Alone and palely loitering;
The sedge is wither'd from the lake,
And no birds sing.

I see a lily on thy brow,
With anguish moist and fever dew,
And on thy cheek a fading rose
Fast withereth too.

I saw pale kings and princes too,
Pale warriors, death-pale were they all;
They cried — 'La Belle Dame sans merci
Hath thee in thrall!'

These three stanzas taken from *La Belle Dame Sans Merci* were written in April 1819, Keats gloomily foretelling his own death. On a walking tour with Charles Brown through the north of England and Scotland in the summer of 1818 Keats covered 642 miles before developing a sore throat which never left him. He abandoned the expedition and returned to Hampstead to find his 19-year-old brother Tom severely ill with consumption. John Keats had been a medical student, and he nursed Tom through the final stages of his illness until he died on 1st December that year. John's sore throat and general malaise did not leave him, and was finally brought to a crisis point. On 3rd February 1820 he travelled to London without a coat, and opted to ride back to Hampstead on the outside of a carriage because it was cheaper. Developing a fever he

**John Keats as painted by his friend Joseph Severn in 1819, two years before he died.** *Photo by NPG.*

took to his bed and then coughed violently into his pillow. His friend Charles Brown was with him:

'I heard him say "That is blood from my mouth". I went towards him; he was examining a single drop upon the sheet. "Bring me a candle, Brown, and let me see this blood." After regarding it steadfastly, he looked up in my face with a calmness of countenance I can never forget and said, "I know the colour of that blood—it is arterial blood—I cannot be deceived by that colour—that drop of blood—it is my death warrant—I must die."'

He was to die a year later at the age of 25.

On 13th September 1820 Keats left Wentworth Place and Hampstead for the last time, bound for Italy where it was thought the dry winter climate might cure him. With him went the artist Joseph Severn who was a couple of years older, and after the long and difficult journey they lodged in Rome at 26 Piazza di Spagna—now the Memorial House of both Keats and Shelley. His condition worsened, and Severn completed his last pen and ink drawing of the poet on 28th January 1821. With Severn beside him Keats died at about 4am on 23rd February:

'Severn—Severn—lift me up—I am dying—I shall die easy, don't be frightened—be firm and thank God it has come.'

Severn stayed in Rome and lived to the old age of 86. His memorable portrait of Keats reading in his sitting room at Wentworth Place (National Portrait Gallery) was painted shortly after the poet's death; his idealised portrait of Keats listening to the nightingale on Hampstead Heath was completed over 20 years later.

Keats' father and mother died when he was 15 leaving four children—John the eldest, George, Tom, and Francis Mary or 'Fanny'. With a sizeable trust fund John left school in 1810 and was apprenticed to a surgeon, later entering the medical schools of Guy's and St Thomas's. His first introduction to Hampstead was in 1816 when a friend showed some of his early verses to the radical journalist Leigh Hunt who lived in the delightfully named Vale of Health. In those days Hampstead was a much admired village on the outskirts of London—even today it retains much of its character, despite the unspeakable volume of cars that grind through it.

*Keats' House in Hampstead is open and closed at unpredictable times!*

Keats was much attracted to Hampstead, and became a frequent visitor of Hunt's who encouraged his poetry by publishing *In Solitude*. In April 1817 Keats and his brothers took lodgings at No 1 Well Walk—the cottage they stayed in has since disappeared, but it stood next to the Wells Hotel which was then The Green Man. By this time Keats had abandoned medicine and become a full time poet. His first volume of *Poems* was published in 1817 with a dedication to Leigh Hunt: 'And I shall ever bless my destiny . . . seeing I could please With these poor offerings a man like thee.'

This sizable volume included *To Hope* and *On First Looking Into Chapman's Homer*, but it was unsuccessful and the publisher would have nothing more to do with Keats' work. *Endymion*, described on the title page as 'A Poetic Romance Inscribed to the Memory of Thomas Chatterton 1818', was his next published work. This very long poem celebrated the romance that surrounded the death of Chatterton who had died at the age of 18 some 50 years earlier. It starts:

'A thing of beauty is a joy forever;
Its loveliness increases; it will never
Pass into nothingness; but still will keep
A bower quiet for us, and a sleep
Full of sweet dreams, and health, and quiet
breathing.'

Unfortunately, the immortal first line has now become a well worn cliché and Keats' critics at the time branded the poem to the 'Cockney school of poetry'. Fortunately for posterity the young poet persevered. During 1819 he wrote five of his six great odes while in Hampstead: *To Psyche, On Indolence, On Melancholy, To a Nightingale, On a Grecian Urn*. His second volume of poems—*Lamia, Isabella, The Eve of St Agnes, and Other Poems*—was published in 1820 by his new and very supportive publisher who insisted on including the unfinished *Hyperion* which was 'to have been of equal length with *Endymion*, but the reception given to that work discouraged the author from proceeding'. This volume was better received by the critics, but nevertheless only sold in small numbers. Apart from a dedicated circle of admirers, Keats' reputation was to be posthumous, with many of his remaining poems saved by Charles Brown and published after his death when his fame as a Romantic poet became such that Tennyson declared him the greatest poet of the nineteenth century.

Keats' monument in England is Wentworth Place, which is now open to the public in the guise of 'Keats' House'. It was built during the winter of 1815 by Charles Dilke and Charles Brown, and in those days was divided into two homes with separate entrances. Keats knew both owners, and was accompanied by Charles on that ill-fated walking tour which precipitated his decline. While Charles was away he let his half to a Mrs Brawne and her three daughters, and when Keats returned early, he caught sight of the only love of his life, Fanny Brawne, the eldest daughter.

When Charles returned he re-occupied his half of the house, and the Brawnes went to live elsewhere. Tom Keats died, George Keats departed for a prosperous life in America, and Charles invited the solitary John to come and share his home. In 1819 Dilke moved to far-off Westminster where his son was at day-school, and the Brawnes came back to occupy the other half of Wentworth Place. Keats soon became engaged to 19-year-old Fanny Brawne, who lost him forever less than two years later. She went into mourning for seven years, eventually marrying after an interval of 12 years.

In 1820 Charles Brown took off on another holiday in Scotland, and let his half of the house. The plan was for Keats to go with him, but he was too ill to travel. He moved into lodgings in Kentish Town, stayed for a time with Leigh Hunt, and then on 12th August moved back to Wentworth Place for the last time to be nursed by the Brawnes before his final departure for Italy.

Charles Brown left Wentworth Place a year after the poet's death. Years later it was bought by the actress Eliza Chester who converted it into one house and extended it. By 1920 it had fallen into disrepair, and was only saved by public subscriptions, largely raised in the United States. It was opened to the public in 1925, and in the garden a new plum tree has replaced the one under which Keats completed *Ode To a Nightingale*. The final verse is a fitting epitaph to one of England's greatest poets:

'Forlorn! The very word is like a bell
To toll me back from thee to my sole self!
Adieu! the fancy cannot cheat so well
As she is fam'd to do, deceiving elf.
Adieu! adieu! thy plaintive anthem fades
Past the near meadows, over the still
stream,
Up the hill-side; and now 'tis buried deep
In the next valley glades:
Was it a vision, or a waking dream?
Fled is that music—Do I wake or sleep?'

## Bibliography

Keats' poems are available in numerous editions, as are biographies and literary criticisms. His letters, written between 1814 and 1821, were first published in 1848 and 1878—they were later described by T.S. Eliot as 'the most notable and most important ever written by an English poet'.

41

## A Walk with John Keats

**Map:** London A–Z.
**Start:** Hampstead underground station. Parking is terrible—use public transport! Keats' House is open Monday to Saturday 10–1 pm and 2–6 pm; Sunday 2–5 pm.
**Distance:** About 6 miles.
**Time:** Allow at least 4 hours, preferably considerably longer to allow time for visiting the various houses that are open to the public.
**Facilities:** Endless pubs, cafés and restaurants in Hampstead; pubs en route; buttery at Burgh House and café/restaurant at Kenwood.
**Summary:** An action packed London walk. Hampstead is one of the most village-like areas close to the city—although incredibly busy—and its heath is the closest that Central London comes to wild countryside. If you care to explore further, it has many more literary associations.

*Kenwood on Hampstead—a magnificent and imposing mansion.*

If you don't mind asking the way it's easy enough to find your way on this walk. Otherwise you will be wise to go armed with a copy of the *London A-Z* for the street walking, and a map of Hampstead Heath to give you some idea of its main features. Both are available from bookshops in Hampstead.

From Hampstead underground station cross Hampstead High Street towards the bank on the corner, and walk straight on down St Fitzjohn's Avenue. After about 75 yards cross at the Belisha beacons, and go straight up Church Row towards the Parish Church of St John-at-Hampstead. After the hurly-burly of Hampstead you will find an air of tranquillity in the restful garden cemetery, and the church itself is a fine building. Keats' memorial bust was placed on the right side of the lectern in 1894.

From the church go up Holly Walk. You can walk up through the old and somewhat overgrown graveyard, leaving through a gate in the top left hand corner. From here carry on up the hill, passing a memorial to the composer Sir William Walton in Hollyberry Lane, and then bearing right along Mount Vernon past the plaque for the physiologist Sir Henry Dale—a large number of eminent people have lived in this very pretty corner of London, and still continue to do so.

Bear round to the left with the first of many pubs encountered on this walk situated opposite. Cross at the green, and go up Holly Grove to the main entrance of the late seventeenth-century Fenton House (NT) on Windmill Hill which is well worth a visit. It

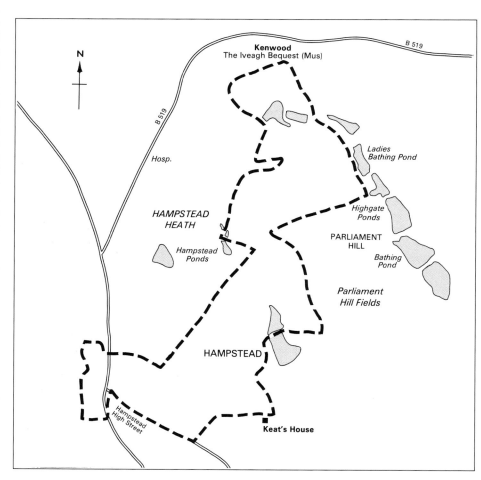

*A glade on the Heath—it's almost more perfect than the country, despite being in the heart of London.*

has a pleasant walled garden and a collection of porcelain and early keyboard instruments inside. It's open from early March until the end of October, Saturdays to Wednesdays 11-6 pm.

From the entrance to Fenton House cross the road, turn right, and a short way on turn left down a narrow lane that takes you steeply down to Heath Street which is the main and very overcrowded road through Hampstead. Cross straight over at the Belisha crossing, going straight ahead down New End past the Duke of Hamilton pub which has a pleasant terrace if it's 'sitting outside weather'. Go on down past Ye Olde White Bear—which doesn't look at all 'olde'—passing through New End Square which brings you to Burgh House.

Burgh House is open Wednesday to Saturday, 2-5 pm, and admission is free. Israel Lewis moved here in 1776 and stayed for 46 years—it was then called 'Lewis House'—and the three Keats brothers lived nearby when they lodged at No 1 Well Walk. John Keats

recorded in one of his letters the kindness of Lewis who brought fruit from his garden for the dying Tom Keats. Another letter refers to 'Old Mr Lewis—very good natured, good looking', and there are other facsimile letters on display at Burgh House written to Fanny and George Keats which mention Lewis House.

Burgh House is a light, airy building, filled with information on many of the better known artists and writers who have lived in Hampstead, including Alfred Lord Tennyson and John Constable. It has old paintings and ancient maps of the area on display, and many interesting publications concerning past and present happenings in the area are on sale. To make your visit even more agreeable, a buttery serves food which can be eaten on the grand terrace—all in all it's worth a look!

From the entrance to Burgh House turn left and then left again along Well Walk. The house where Keats lived was on a site next to the Wells Hotel on the corner, but has long

since been demolished. The painter John Constable also lived along here at number 40. Carry on along Well Walk, and go straight over Heath Road and onto Hampstead Heath, taking care to avoid fast traffic coming down the hill from the left.

The heath can claim to be London's finest and wildest area of parkland, with plenty of delightful diversions for those who are new to it. For dog owners the heath is a welcome exercise ground and for those with children there is kite flying on Parliament Hill Fields, a play area near Gospel Oak in the south-east corner, a wealth of waterfowl to keep youngsters happy. It has a maze of tracks, paths, woods and ponds, and despite being in the middle of London it's surprisingly easy to lose your bearings and get lost. The route which follows is a guide to seeing some of the heath's many landmarks, though you can vary it as you wish—just ask someone if you are uncertain of the way.

43

*The fine bridge that leads you through to the fenced 'woodland area' of Hampstead Heath.*

Walk on down to the bottom of the hill, and there bear left on a track which brings you to one of the heath's many ponds with a fine bridge crossing behind it. Walk to the right, round the side of the pond, before bearing left over the bridge and continuing on a track over another bridge which takes you through tranquil woods towards the fenced-off 'Woodland Area' of Kenwood which is closed at sunset. Go through the gate on the right and walk down through the woodland area; then turn left downhill when you come to a covered seat. Keep on downhill with occasional glimpses of magnificent Kenwood through the trees over to the right, bearing round the pond at the bottom and going over the bridge.

From here head straight across the grass towards Kenwood, or if you prefer take the tarmac path which goes round to the right. The house which Robert Adam started to remodel in 1764 is in a magnificent setting and open free of charge from 10 am every day. Sadly, it is very under-furnished with the large echoing rooms filled with the paintings it is mainly noted for. It has an interesting bookshop, and round the front the café/restaurant is a pleasant enough place to stop with out-

side seating in an old, walled enclosure in summer.

From the café bear round to the right, heading down towards Kenwood Pond with the covered stage or 'bowl' beyond—the well known venue for alfresco evening concerts. Before you reach the fine old bridge, bear left through a gate out of the fenced area along another tarmac track, and then bear right downhill to cross a small fenced bridge in a valley which can be muddy—if you prefer to avoid the mud, make your own route via the tarmac walkways.

Go uphill and join a tarmac track with glimpses of the Post Office Tower in the distance bringing you back to the reality of London. Just before Highgate Ponds turn hard right on a gravel track going uphill with trees and a grassy hill to the left. Walk to the top, and bear left before heading down and joining the track which runs between Hampstead Ponds. From here bear left uphill past the main pond, keeping left along the track which leaves the heath and takes you down towards the junction of South End Road and South Hill Park.

About 75 yards before this junction turn

right and cross South End Road into Keats Grove—you can't miss it; there's a post office on the corner, with a large and rather inappropriate neon sign for Rothmans cigarettes! Keats' House is about a hundred yards on the left, next to the public library. The first time I called it was closed due to cuts in council spending, despite being advertised as open. It may be wise to check that it really is open by telephoning 071 435 2062 on the day. Next to it the Keats Memorial Library holds part of the collection of 6,000 volumes relating to the poet and his contemporaries.

From here it's a short way back to the centre of Hampstead—turn left into Downshire Hill and right when you reach Rosslyn Hill, which will take you up to the underground station via the bustling High Street. For this walk you should allow at least four hours. With the wealth of diversions on offer it could easily be extended into the evening—Hampstead has many restaurants, and the concerts at Burgh House or in the open at Kenwood could help to complete a memorable day.

# Walk 9: With Samuel Taylor Coleridge in Nether Stowey

*Samuel Taylor Coleridge (1772–1834) was born at Ottery St Mary in the West Country and came to live in the Somerset village of Nether Stowey in December 1796. In his short time there he wrote all his most memorable poems, including favourites such as* The Rime of the Ancient Mariner, Kubla Khan *and* Christabel *guaranteeing his place as one of the best loved of all English poets.*

'It is an ancient Mariner,
And he stoppeth one of three.
"By thy long grey beard and glittering eye,
Now wherefore stopp'st thou me?

The Bridegroom's doors are opened wide,
And I am next of kin;
The guests are met, the feast is set:
May'st hear the merry din."

He holds him with his skinny hand,
"There was a ship," quoth he.
"Hold off! unhand me, grey-beard loon!"
Eftsoons his hand dropt he.'

*The Rime of the Ancient Mariner*

After one of the most agreeable and productive periods of his life, Coleridge left Nether Stowey after a three year stay to lead a life of wandering until in 1816 he eventually settled in Highgate, North London, where he lived until his death. During these years he suffered from illness and opium addiction, and his marriage proved to be an unhappy failure. He lost many of his former friends including the Wordsworths, but his reputation as a great Romantic poet was already secure by the time *Christabel and Other Poems* was published in 1817 and remains as strong as ever today.

At the age of 24, Coleridge, his young wife Sara, and their baby son Hartley came to live in what is now known as 'Coleridge Cottage' in Nether Stowey. With them came Charles Lloyd, a short lived and unsuccessful paying guest, and a nanny to care for young Hartley. Coleridge had hoped to move his family into

**Samuel Taylor Coleridge, painted by Paul Vandyke in 1795.** *Photo by NPG.*

a house near Over Stowey but when that plan fell through, the cottage was provided for them by Thomas Poole, a good friend who had met Coleridge in his early days of religious enthusiasm when he served as a Unitarian preacher. Poole is buried at Nether Stowey, and his association with the poet is commemorated on a tablet inside the church.

In those days the surroundings were very different. Coleridge Cottage stood alone (there was no sign of Lime Street) and there was a large garden at the back where Coleridge would dig and plant with enthusiasm:

'Our house is better than we expected. There is a comfortable bedroom and sitting room for C. Lloyd and another room for us, a room for Nanny, a kitchen and outhouse. Before our door a clear brook runs full of very soft water. We have a very pretty garden, large enough to find us vegetables and employment; and I am already an expert gardener, both my hands can exhibit a callum as testimonials of their industry. We have likewise a sweet orchard . . .'

Poole lived at what is now 19 Castle Street, with a lane connecting the two back gardens. The cottage would now be unrecognisable to both him and the poet, having lost its thatched roof and most of its garden, and suffered piecemeal extensions in the nineteenth century when it became a pub. It was only 'saved' when an appeal was launched on the 200th anniversary of the poet's birth. A memorial plaque was placed on the wall in 1893 and the cottage was leased by a committee which included Coleridge's grandson. After years of fundraising and numerous difficulties it was eventually bought outright and handed over to the National Trust in 1909. The two front rooms that one sees now are a reconstruction of what the cottage may have been like, furnished with mementoes donated by members of the Coleridge family, among others. The original plans to demolish the extensions and

*The gleaming white cottages on the way to Holford Combe.*

recreate the garden were never achieved, but by adopting Coleridge's 'willing suspension of disbelief' the result is perfectly satisfying.

In a letter of 1797 Coleridge described a typical day at Nether Stowey:

'From seven till half past eight I work in my garden, from breakfast till 12 I read and compose, then read again, feed the pigs, poultry, etc. till two o'clock: after dinner work again till tea; from tea till supper, review. So jogs the day, and I am happy. I have society—my friend T. Poole, and as many acquaintances as I can dispense with . . . We are very happy.'

Coleridge paid his fellow poet William Wordsworth a visit at Racedown in Dorset, and this inspired William and his sister to move to Alfoxden House from July 1797 until September the following year. Alfoxden (now the Alfoxton Park Hotel) was a large, Queen Anne house built by the St Albyn family in 1710, and Wordsworth was able to afford to rent it by virtue of a £900 legacy left to him to enable him to work as a poet. The house is about two miles west of Stowey, and the two poets trudged over the hills between their homes on an almost daily basis, working on what was then very 'progressive' poetry. The result was their combined *Lyrical Ballads* (1798) which included *The Rime of the Ancient Mariner*, and initially met with a poor reception.

At this time Coleridge was still fit and healthy, and the poets walked further and further afield. It was on a walk to Dulverton (look at the map—it's a long way!) that the *Ancient Mariner* was conceived as Coleridge explained in his own footnote to the first verse of Part IV of the poem:

'For the last two lines of this stanza, I am indebted to Mr. Wordsworth. It was on a delightful walk from Nether Stowey to Dulverton, with him and his sister, in the autumn of 1797, that this poem was planned, and in part composed.'

"I fear thee, ancient Mariner!
I fear thy skinny hand!
And thou art long, and lank, and brown,
As is the ribbed sea-sand . . .

Another poem—*The Lime Tree Bower My Prison*—was based on an unfortunate incident closer to hand, as recorded by a letter of July 1797:

'The second day after Wordsworth came to me, dear Sara accidentally emptied a skillet of boiling milk on my foot, which confined me . . . and still prevents me from

*The fine open moorland which distinguishes the Quantocks above Nether Stowey.*

all walks longer than a furlong. While Wordsworth, his sister, and Charles Lamb were out one evening, sitting in the arbour of T. Poole's garden which communicates with mine I wrote these lines:

"Well, they are gone, and here must I remain,
This lime-tree bower my prison! I have lost
Beauties and feelings, such as would have been
Most sweet to my remembrance even when age
Had dimmed mine eyes to blindness! They, meanwhile,
Friends, whom I never more may meet again,
On springy heath, along the hill-top edge,
Wander in gladness...' "

The frustration of an invalid who can't go for a customary walk recorded for posterity!

A number of famous and infamous visitors came to the houses of Coleridge and Wordsworth. The poets were fairly radical thinkers who had both approved of the French Revolution, and apart from Thomas Poole and Charles Lamb their guests included the poets Thomas De Quincey and Robert Southey, and the political theorists William Hazlitt and John Thelwall, the latter an arch radical. At a time of mild hysteria brought on by the French wars, the locals became suspicious of the Wordsworths with their strange northern accents, and particularly of Dorothy who was dark and looked 'foreign'. Tales were told of them trudging the hills at night armed with stools and notebooks, and an investigator was sent down by the Home Office. Unlike D. H. Lawrence at Zennor (see Walk 26) he reported that they were harmless cranks, but not long

afterwards, the Coleridge clan left Nether Stowey for an enlightening tour of Germany where the works of Kant and Schiller awaited them. They never returned to the area.

**Bibliography**

The following poems were written by Coleridge at Nether Stowey: *Osorio, To The Rev George Coleridge, This Lime Tree Bower My Prison, The Rime of the Ancient Mariner, Fire, Famine and Slaughter, Kubla Khan* and *Christabel* in 1797; *Frost at Midnight, France: An Ode, Lewti, or the Circassian Love-Chaunt, Fears in Solitude, The Nightingale; A Conversation Poem, The Three Graves, The Wanderings of Cain* in 1798; *The Devil's Thoughts* (with Southey) in 1799.

Coleridge's daily *Notebooks*, collected *Letters*, and early and late poems are all available in modern editions, as are many biographies.

# A Walk with Samuel Taylor Coleridge

**Map:** OS Landranger 181.
**Start:** The free car park at Robin Upright's Hill, on the minor road to Crowcombe about 1½ miles south-west of Nether Stowey—OS Grid Ref. 162382. Coleridge Cottage (NT) in Nether Stowey, on the A39 in Somerset, is open from Easter until late September, Tuesday to Thursday and Sunday 2–5 pm.
**Nearest BR Station:** Bridgwater.
**Distance:** Approximately 7–8 miles.
**Time:** Allow 3 hours, plus time for stops.
**Facilities:** Pubs in Nether Stowey and at Holford on A39; hotel at the north end of Holford Combe serves non-residents.
**Summary:** A short stroll for Coleridge or Wordsworth, but quite an energetic walk by today's standards. The Quantocks are much as the poets would have known them, and the route passes close by Alfoxton Park.

The Quantocks lie to the west and south-west of Nether Stowey. They remain unspoilt, and offer such fine views that you should ideally reserve this walk for a bright clear day. Much of the route is exposed, and in wind and rain it could be hard going.

To visit Coleridge Cottage, the best place to leave a car is the library car park at the top of Castle Street where there is an Information Centre. From here you can walk down past Thomas Poole's house at Number 19, turning sharp left for Coleridge Cottage. Then retrace your steps to the library car park from where you can either walk up to the top of Robin Upright's Hill, or if you prefer drive up. Follow the minor road up the hill to Bincombe and on towards Over Stowey, forking right for Crowcombe. After a little over 1½ miles the car park is visible on the left side of the road at the top of the hill, just by a turning to Walford's Gibbet—they have fine place names in this area!

From the car park turn left onto the road, and then bear right onto a long, level track which runs ahead into the distance. There are fine views out over the hills from here, with Hinckley Point power station brooding in the background—Coleridge and Wordsworth would surely have been appalled by its appearance and significance. On a clear day you can see the coast of South Wales in the distance beyond Bridgwater Bay. Keep straight on, passing a track which joins from the left and then going over a crossing track.

After 20 minutes or so you will be ready to turn onto a clearly defined track which bears off along the ridge to the right, taking you along Black Hill. You turn right at a crossing track, leaving the main track which goes straight ahead past Hurley Beacon, and follow the ridge track along Black Hill, passing a rack of fire beaters. From here on the tracks on the Quantocks are mainly unsignposted and tend to be all over the place, so a little navigational skill and initiative are called for! After a time you will see a hillock ahead on the left, with a few stunted trees—it's marked as 'Cairns' at 311 metres on the OS map. Bear left on a wide, grassy track up to this hillock, leaving the main gravel track which continues on downhill.

At the top of the hillock walk on down the other side, with the deep, wooded valley of Hodder's Combe to your left. Keep left on the track which goes gradually downhill, ignoring any right forks or turnings. After a time another track joins from the left, and at this junction a narrow path goes straight down the hill towards the cleft in the combe known as Lady's Edge. The path may be well disguised by ferns, but if you miss it you can simply turn down into the combe at the next suitable turning. The path downhill soon bears right, joining another wider track coming down from the right—if you've overshot it's probably the one you'll come down on. It then bears left downhill into the trees, and zigzags to take you to the floor of the valley where you cross a minor

*Coleridge's Cottage in Nether Stowey. He would find it almost unrecognisable today—in his day a stream flowed past the front door.*

48

stream and then bear right along the side of the main stream that runs through Hodder's Combe. This is a very pretty track which will take you the length of the combe to the village green at the south-west end of Holford. If you feel energetic, however, it's worth taking the extra loop past the Alfoxton Park Hotel where Wordsworth lived, adding about a mile to the distance.

The turn-off point is marked by a track which goes left across the stream and then bears right uphill—it can't be missed as the main track bears a little to the right here, and after 50 yards or so passes a large clearing on the left. Head up the steep, narrow track which takes you up the side of the combe through trees, bringing you out into the open on the side of Longstone Hill where it bears left. Walk on ahead over a crossing track, with a big clump of trees a short way downhill to the right and open moorland on the left and ahead. The track goes down and up a little, and close by the end of the trees comes to a large wooden signpost at a complex bridleway intersection by Pardlestone Hill.

Take the middle track to Alfoxton going down through trees—not the ones to left or right. It brings you downhill to a tarmac lane at a hairpin bend, where you carry straight on downhill. Follow round to the right over an unusual cattle grid and on through a farmyard with a strange building to the left, joining a driveway and passing by the back of Alfoxton Park Hotel which is over to the right. There are no footpath or bridleway signs, but it is a right of way. Unfortunately, the hotel doesn't serve passing travellers, but for such a smart hotel the rates appear reasonable and you may care to stay there.

Follow the drive over the next cattle grid at the main entrance. Here a bridleway sign points down to the left, but the footpath you want is unsignposted, heading up a narrow, indistinct track through the trees on the right. Walk up here, keeping to the right as much as possible and looking for a gate by the fence in the corner of the field ahead; when I walked this way it was wired up and you had to climb it. Carry on straight ahead across the field which is used for grazing, with trees on all sides, keeping to the left of the fence that runs down its centre. You will find the next stile directly ahead, taking you downhill on a narrow path that bears left down towards the 'Dog Pound'.

This is a venerable building, erected by the family of Sir Lancelot Brereton who, we are told, was a descendant of the St Albyn family who had owned the estate of Alfoxden (now Alfoxton) since the fifteenth century. It's

*The Alfoxton Park Hotel where Wordsworth once stayed—the locals were convinced that he and Coleridge were up to no good with their odd behaviour on the moors.*

right next to a lane by a 'Pedestrians Beware' sign on the outskirts of Holford. Follow the lane ahead, and then bear round to the right by the side of the village green—ignore the left turning here unless you want to walk down to the nearby pub on the main road, which serves reasonable food with outside seating. Keep on ahead towards a row of dazzling white thatched cottages, and bear left and right round the back of them following the sign for Holford Combe.

Keep on up the lane ahead past a number of pretty cottages, passing a small triangular green on the left. After a time the lane bears round to the left by a large, thatched building on the right which is a hotel. This serves coffee, bar snacks and tea to non residents in fine surroundings close by a water wheel. Beyond here the tarmac track turns into an unmade lane, and a little further on you come to a clearing close by a stream on the right. From here you can walk on through Holford Combe and from there find your way up to Robin Upright's Hill, but personally I prefer the less direct route which takes you on the high ground up towards Dowsborough Fort.

Just by the start of the clearing a track

bears uphill to the left. Walk up here past a 'Private Land—Keep to the Bridleway' sign, and at the top bear right through a gate. Walk straight on across a clearing with trees all around, heading towards a gate on the far side. Go through and turn right on a track heading uphill, which soon brings you back up to open moorland by the side of Woodlands Hill. Ignore a track forking to the left and a less distinct track forking to the right, keeping straight ahead up to a cairn on a hillock. From there head for the top of the big hill ahead which is Dowsborough Fort.

From the commanding height of this old hill fort you get a fine view, and it's a surprise to find a small forest of low lying trees on the top. Turn right at these trees, following a track which bears left and then walk downhill through very pretty woodland. Ignore a grassy track forking off to the left, keeping on downhill until you eventually turn right at a T-junction, following the next track to the road. Turn right up the road, ignoring the track which goes on ahead to Great Bear, and after five minutes' brisk walking you are back at the Robin Upright's Hill car park.

# Walk 10: With Alfred, Lord Tennyson in Farringford

*Alfred, Lord Tennyson (1809–92) spent much of the last half of his life at Farringford, a large Georgian house on the outskirts of Freshwater on the Isle of Wight. As Poet Laureate he entertained many eminent Victorians there, composed much fine poetry, and took his daily constitutional on 'Tennyson Down'.*

Tennyson's best known poem is also one of his slightest:

'Half a league, half a league,
Half a league onward,
All in the valley of Death
Rode the six hundred.
"Forward the Light Brigade!
Charge the guns!" he said:
Into the valley of Death
Rode the six hundred.'

He wrote *The Charge of the Light Brigade* at Farringford in 1854, having read an account of the charge—one of the many disasters of the Crimean War—in *The Times* while at breakfast. He apparently completed the six stanzas in 10 minutes with tears streaming down his cheeks, and it was an instantly huge success, not least with the men in the Crimea. Two thousand copies were distributed in the army hospitals, and one chaplain reported, 'Half are singing it and all want to have it in black and white, so as to read what has so taken them . . . The poet can now make heroes, just as in days of yore.'

More typical of Tennyson's output was his own favourite poem *Maud*. Despite the well worn phrase 'Come into the garden, Maud', this is a complex work that underlines the poet's frequently depressed nature. Unlike his jingoistic verse, its tale of death, ruin, and unrequited love was greeted by many Victorians with incomprehension when it was published in 1855:

'Come into the garden, Maud,
For the black bat, night, has flown,

**The craggy features of Tennyson, as photographed by his near neighbour Julia Margaret Cameron on the Isle of Wight in 1869.** *Photo by NPG.*

Come into the garden, Maud,
I am here at the gate alone:
And the woodbine spices are wafted abroad,
And the musk of the roses blown.'

Alfred Tennyson was the most popular of all Victorian poets. He was born at Somersby Rectory in the Lincolnshire wolds, and experienced a childhood that was by no means easy, being one of eleven brothers and sisters crammed into a pleasant but comparatively small home. His father, the Reverend George Clayton Tennyson, was the main problem. Having been effectively passed over by his own father he was a deeply frustrated man, prone to mental instability, violence, and drunkenness. His death in 1831 was probably a happy release all round, but his life left its mark on at least some of his children—one brother spent his life in a lunatic asylum, another was an opium addict, and Alfred himself was subject to very black moods.

Alfred Tennyson's first book of verse, *Poems, Chiefly Lyrical*, was published in 1830 while he was still at Cambridge. A small circle there lionised him, but some critics chose to slate his work, a fate which also befell his *Poems* of 1833.

As a result Tennyson continued writing, but refused to publish any more work for the next decade. Much of his greatest work was produced in these silent years when he lived off money from his wealthy grandfather. Most notable of these was *In Memoriam*, a long series of connected poems written between 1833 and 1850 when it was at last published and hailed as the greatest poem of the Victorian age. It celebrated Tennyson's intense friendship with Arthur Hallam who had died at the age of 22 in 1833, and for the Victorians it represented a message of hope and faith.

Two other fine poems composed in this period were his *Morte d'Arthur*, and the semi-autobiographical *Ulysses*. Published in 1842 they established him as the foremost poet of a generation which had seen the premature deaths of Keats, Shelley and Byron not long before. From then on much of his poetry turned to celebrating Victorian values and life, and it found a ready popular market which

*Above:* **Looking west from the Tennyson Monument towards the Needles.**

*Right:* **Farringford Park, Tennyson's Isle of Wight home which is now a hotel.**

secured his reputation as an eminent figure of the age despite his moody behaviour and strange poetic appearance—a wide brimmed 'wideawake' hat, a long flowing cloak, a trailing black beard, gaunt features and piercing eyes.

In 1850 Tennyson succeeded William Wordsworth as Poet Laureate, commencing a long and enthusiastic relationship with Queen Victoria. His eulogies were to earn him a fair amount of ridicule:

'Revered Victoria, you that hold
A nobler office upon Earth
Than arms, or power or brain, or birth
Could give the warrior kings of old.'

In the same year he at last married Louisa Sellwood; having proposed to her in 1836, he had broken off the engagement in 1840 on account of his depression and lack of finances. They lived in a variety of homes, and then in November 1853 they were rowed across the Solent in an open boat for their first view of Farringford. Tennyson was most impressed, taking the lease and then buying it outright with his earnings from *Maud* two years later:

'The house . . . seemed like a charmed palace, with green walls without, and speaking walls within . . . friends' faces lined the passages, books filled the shelves, and the glow of crimson was everywhere; the oriel drawing-room window was full of green and golden leaves, of the sound of birds and distant sea.'

Farringford included the adjacent farm and a good deal of land, and was in those days very remote with clear views of the sea. There was no public transport, and the many visitors who came would usually walk the three miles from the ferry terminal at Yarmouth on the other side of the island. Tennyson loved the place—he had a platform built on the roof to study the stars, he tended the large garden, and would frequently take long walks over the downs by day or night.

Prince Albert called at Farringford in 1856, but Queen Victoria never came despite her intentions. Instead, Tennyson went to meet her at Osborne Castle near Cowes, where he and his family became occasional and welcome visitors. Victoria described her first meeting with him in her diary:

'Tennyson who is very peculiar looking, tall, dark, with a fine head, long black flowing hair and a beard—oddly dressed, but there is no affectation about him.'

Tennyson's many visitors at Farringford included Charles Kingsley, Edward Lear, Swinburne and Arthur Hugh Clough. Exotic interest was provided by a visit from the Italian freedom fighter, Garibaldi, and from Queen Emma of the Sandwich Islands who arrived at midnight (having lost all her luggage on the road) and entertained the poet with Hawaiian songs on the lawn. But Tennyson had gone to Farringford for solitude, and by 1861 he was worrying about building plans in the area:

'Imagine my disgust at having Freshwater so polluted and defiled with brick and mortar, as is threatened; they talk of laying out streets and crescents.'

He would turn in his grave if he could see the way it's been built over now!

Another problem was the day trippers who came to catch sight of him. This he resolved by building a magnificent, isolated house near Haslemere which he called Aldworth. With the aid of his large earnings it was completed in 1868, and from then on he only spent winters at Farringford when trippers and holidaymakers were less likely to bother him. In summer he stayed at Aldworth, with occasional spells in London—most notably when be began to write for the theatre in the 1870s—and annual European holidays or trips round the West Country.

Tennyson was known for endlessly chewing on his pipe and frequently drinking a bottle of port or more each day. Despite this regime he stayed extremely fit and healthy throughout most of his old age, a keen walker whose daily constitutional was to stride over the downs above Farringford between 11 pm and 1 am whatever the weather. In 1884 he at last accepted the offer of a baronetcy which he had refused for nearly 20 years. He continued to lead a busy life with Farringford and Aldworth frequently packed with visitors, but after a bad bout of rheumatic illness at the age of 79 he knew that his life was drawing in. A year later, crossing the Solent to Yarmouth he wrote his final great poem *Crossing the Bar*:

'Sunset and evening star,
And one clear call for me!
And may there be no moaning of the bar,
When I put out to sea.

But such a tide as moving seems asleep,
Too full for sound and foam.
When that which drew from out the boundless deep
Turns again home.

Twilight and evening bell,
And after that the dark!
And may there be no sadness of farewell,
When I embark;

For tho' from out our bourne of Time and Place
The flood may bear me far,
I hope to see my Pilot face to face
When I have crost the bar.'

He died peacefully at Aldington on 6th October 1892 after a short illness. From there he was taken to Westminster Abbey and buried with due ceremony. His wife survived him by four years, and lies buried at Freshwater Church.

## Bibliography

Tennyson's most famous poems include *In Memoriam*, *Morte d'Arthur*, *Locksley Hall*, *Ulysses*, *Maud*, *Idylls of the King*, and *Locksley Hall Sixty Years After*. His dramas—Henry Irving and Ellen Terry appeared in *The Cup* and *Becket*—have not stood the test of time so well. His son Hallam Tennyson was the first of his many biographers.

*The Tennyson Monument at the top of the Tennyson Trail—he was revered as a great Englishman.*

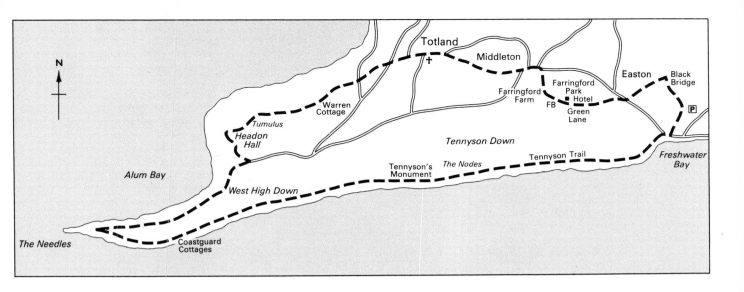

## A Walk with Alfred, Lord Tennyson

**Map:** Outdoor Leisure 29—the Isle of Wight.

**Start:** Pay & Display car park at Freshwater Bay—OS Grid Ref. 347858.

**Nearest BR Station:** Lymington on the mainland; ferry to Yarmouth.

**Distance:** Approximately 7½ miles (plus 3 miles each way if you need to return to the ferry point at Yarmouth).

**Time:** Allow 4 hours including visit to the Needles Battery.

**Facilities:** Pubs and cafés in Freshwater; cafés at Alum Bay; Farringford Hotel open to non-residents.

**Summary:** A bracing coastal walk up to the Tennyson Memorial, visiting the Old Battery above the Needles, and returning via Tennyson's home at Farringford.

This walk presumes you start from the car park at the bottom of the hill where the A3055 passes Freshwater Bay. In summer you would have plenty of time to make it part of a day excursion from the mainland, crossing on the Lymington-Yarmouth ferry (Tel: 0705 812001). There is no direct bus route to Freshwater, but there are taxis or better still, it's a very pleasant one hour walk—follow the dismantled railway called the Causeway along the east side of the River Yar to link with the signposted Freshwater Way leading to Freshwater Bay.

From the Freshwater Bay car park turn right and walk along the road past the hotel/pub on the left, heading up towards a sign for the 'Tennyson Tea Rooms'. Just before you reach this, there's a footpath sign to the left directing you onto the Tennyson Trail. Walk up the lane, and then bear right through a gate at the end, heading up the hill through another gate past a National Trust sign.

From here on it's a steady climb on hard, sea-water-soaked turf with fine views of the island opening out behind you as far as St Catherine's Point. Keep on up, heading for the Tennyson Monument which at first looks like a stick on the top of the hill. As you approach nearer it becomes a sizeable stone cross, with the word 'Tennyson' engraved on the west side.

From here there are fine views looking west towards the Needles, and south-west over Headon Warren which is the way this walk returns. Carry straight on downhill from the Monument, walking along the clear track with a belt of low lying trees to your right. You soon come down to a half-size replica of the old beacon which was replaced by the Tennyson Monument; carry straight on here, going over a stile by a gate where you follow the sign for the left hand coastal path that leads to the Needles.

This climbs gently uphill through a landscape of scattered gorse and the occasional thistle. Ahead to the right you will see a lonely row of old coastguard cottages in a commanding position on the cliffside which are now let out as National Trust holiday homes. Walk on past the back of them, following a wire fence round to the left until you come to a stile. Go over this and then bear left downhill on a track which appears to be about to throw you into an abyss. With a slight scramble it brings you down to the New Battery in surroundings reminiscent of *The Guns of Navarone*, with fine views of the nearby Needles and Scratchell's Bay which was Tennyson's own particular favourite.

Walk through the gun emplacements, bearing right on a track which starts to head uphill. Then follow the NT sign down to the Needles Old Battery (Open Easter to end October daily except Friday and Saturday) which is well worth a look round, although not expressly placed here for the protection of the Poet Laureate.

From the Old Battery walk out over the bridge and straight ahead along the tarmac track which follows the edge of White Cliffs, with fine views over any yachts that happen to be moored in Alum Bay Chine below. This brings you down to a small house on the corner where the road bends left downhill— look closer and you will see it is entirely populated by garden gnomes and their friends. Walk on down through the amusement park which among other things boasts the 'largest ice cream in the world'. This place is likely to be packed with holidaymakers in the summer, with chair lifts swinging down to the beach and music blaring. Tennyson would have shaken with rage at the sight of it and it does seem rather staggering that it should have been placed in what is otherwise a beautiful part of the island.

Walking past the amusement park you

*The Needles, on the westernmost tip of the island close by the Needles' Battery.*

come to the B3322 road which connects it to the outside world. Turn right here, and after about 75 yards follow the footpath sign up a track to the left, going through a gate on the right a short way on to by-pass the tea shop/café ahead. The path takes you up Headon Warren in a zigzag fashion, passing more old fortifications with good views of the south side of the Needles. Keep on following this path uphill through a well preserved landscape of peat and heather, skirting round the side of a fence cordoning off a tumulus and then continuing to follow the path in the same direction.

The large house over to the right on the opposite hillside is Weston Manor, and up on the hilltop the Tennyson Monument is always in sight. Eventually the path heads down towards a cottage, passing close by its left side and joining a hard track which takes you on past a small reservoir on the left before reaching the road. Cross straight over here, and head downhill on the lane ahead. After a short time this brings you back to the B3322 opposite a church. Cross straight over, and once more go down and then up the lane ahead, heading uphill past the Catholic church and school on your right.

A little further on you pass a footpath sign on the left, and then turn off at the next footpath sign on the right, heading across a field towards woods. Follow the path through the trees here, and then carry straight on past Stonewind Farm, heading up the farm track which has driveways to houses either side. You join the road on a bend, and follow it to the left for about a hundred yards. Just opposite the second left road turning, turn right up a track by a clump of trees as indicated by a footpath sign.

This leads you over a cattle grid through Farringford Farm. Turn left at the top of the track by the bridleway sign, and follow a sunken track ahead with trees on either side. Not far on you will see a bridge crossing overhead, and just past it there is a green wooden door on the left. This is the back entrance to what is now the Farringford Hotel (Tel: 0983 752500) where you may care to stop for lunch or tea. Ask to see the library where Tennyson did some of his writing, now preserved with a small amount of the poet's memorabilia including photos by his near neighbour, Julia Cameron. His cloak and hat hang in a glass cabinet, and the writing table and chair are said to be original. In the corner a small door

leads to a spiral staircase—Tennyson's escape route to the back garden when unwanted visitors came to call.

Otherwise Tennyson's home is sadly greatly changed, with an interior that has little in common with Hubert Parry's description of 1892:

'It is the most old fashioned house I ever knew, with dim candle lamps in the passages, four poster beds, hundreds of Mrs Cameron's photographs, ugly wall papers and early Victorian furniture.'

From the green door continue along the track down to the road. Turn right, and then take the turning first left opposite the unusual thatched church. Walk down this lane, passing a Freshwater Way footpath sign on the left—this leads north towards Yarmouth if that's the way you want to go. A little further on turn right down a track, as indicated by a footpath sign, and follow the path across a marshy area of field towards Freshwater. When you reach the road bear left at the footpath sign, and you are soon back at the car park.

# Walk 11: *With Emily Bronte to 'Wuthering Heights'*

*Emily Bronte's short, rather tragic life produced one brilliant masterpiece,* Wuthering Heights, *and a quantity of highly regarded poetry. Born in 1818, she suffered the same fate as her sisters and one brother, dying at a young age in 1848. In her lifetime,* Wuthering Heights *was greeted with incomprehension; only after her death was it recognised as a work of genius.*

The appeal of *Wuthering Heights* has survived the passage of time and it is still immensely popular today. It begins by introducing the reader to the surly, glowering Heathcliffe; his strange manners, his repressed household and his gloomy house on a hill above the moors:

'Wuthering Heights is the name of Mr Heathcliffe's dwelling, "Wuthering" being a significant provincial adjective, descriptive of the atmospheric tumult to which its station is exposed in stormy weather. Pure, bracing, ventilation they must have up there at all times, indeed: one may guess the power of the north wind blowing over the edge, by the excessive slant of a few stunted firs at the end of the house; and by a range of gaunt thorns all stretching their limbs one way, as if craving alms of the sun. Happily, the architect had the foresight to build it strong: the narrow windows are deeply set in the wall, and the corners defended with large jutting stones.'

Running to 300 pages or so, *Wuthering Heights* is a short book by Victorian standards, but there is no shortage of material within its covers. Heathcliffe, Hindley, Cathy and the other tragedians are all embroiled in a tale of passion where emotions rage. Indeed in its own day the novel was branded as depressing but today it is recognised as a wonderful outpouring of a vivid imagination.

The history of the Bronte family does, however, make depressing reading. Their illnesses and deaths were mainly caused by tuberculosis and other associated problems, and followed in relentless succession. Emily's father,

**The Bronte Sisters as painted by their brother Branwell in 1834. Controversy rages over which sister is which.** *Photo by NPG.*

Patrick Brunty (he later changed his name to Bronte while at university) was Irish, one of 10 children, and poor. He taught himself to read and write, worked as a teacher, entered the church, and from there found his way to St John's College, Cambridge in 1802. He married Maria Branwell from Penzance 10 years later, and after a number of clerical livings the Bronte parents and six very young children moved to the Parsonage at Haworth in 1820.

Eighteen months after arriving at Haworth, Emily's mother died of cancer

at the age of 38, leaving the children to the care of their father and an aunt. The two eldest Bronte children—Maria and Elizabeth—were both sent to a school for the daughters of poor clergy near Kirkby Lonsdale, and a rigorous regime and poor sanitation ensured that they did not live beyond their teens. Maria died in 1825 at the age of 11; her 10 year-old-sister followed her later the same year.

It is interesting to speculate whether Maria and Elizabeth may also have developed the extraordinary literary talents that their sisters later displayed; neither parent showed any sign of genius, although Patrick Bronte wrote a little. Their brother, Branwell, seemed destined to become a great painter. His legacy is the famous portrait of his three sisters which is now in the National Portrait Gallery of London. Unfortunately that was all he left for he couldn't cope with working as a portrait painter or in the more menial occupations which followed. With a depressive nature he became a heavy drinker and opium addict, and died at the age of 31 in September 1848. His black, distressing lifestyle possibly provided material for the character of Hindley Earnshaw, one-time master of Wuthering Heights, whose life was equally purposeless.

Emily caught a cold at Branwell's funeral which proved fatal and she died the following December aged 30. Less than six months later Anne died while on a rest cure in Scarborough at the age of 29. Charlotte survived to enjoy fame as the author of *Jane Eyre, Shirley* and *Villette*. She married her father's curate at Haworth in June 1854, but the tragedy was completed the following March when she died from complications in pregnancy, aged 38.

Extraordinarily, Patrick Bronte survived

to live on at the Haworth Parsonage until 1861 by which time he was 84, while Charlotte's husband soon remarried and lived to be almost 90! Much of the population of Haworth suffered the same fate as the Bronte children. Looking at this Pennine village, now prosperous with Bronte tourism, it is difficult to believe that the average age of death among its inhabitants, according to a report published in 1950, was 25.8 years, with 41.6 per cent failing to reach the age of six. The prime causes of death were terrible sanitation and polluted drinking water, resulting in endless illnesses that proved fatal to those of a less robust constitution. The village had expanded rapidly in the early eighteenth century due to growth of the weaving industry for which northern towns were famous, and while a few profited, the masses suffered in overcrowded conditions, contending with typhus, cholera, dysentery, smallpox and tuberculosis.

After the deaths of Maria and Elizabeth, the four children were educated at home by their father and an aunt, until they were of an age to educate themselves. All had tremendous imaginations, and as children they invented the mythical lands of Angria and Gondal. In 1838, at the age of 20, Emily took a job as a teacher at a school near Halifax, but only stuck it for six months before returning to Haworth. Both her sisters tried similar work as governesses and teachers, but none of them enjoyed it and the only benefit for Charlotte and Anne was that it provided background material for their novels. Emily's writing relied solely on her superb, brooding imaginination and the inspiration of the moors.

The three girls planned to run their own school at the Parsonage. To get the necessary qualifications Charlotte and Emily went to study at an academy in Brussels, but both returned to Haworth after less than successful experiences and the Bronte school never materialised. They then turned to their writing. Charlotte and Anne had been writing poetry openly and were surprised to discover the 'wild, melancholy and elevating', beauty of their sister Emily's poetry. Emily was not keen on the idea of publishing her work, but Charlotte and Anne persuaded her otherwise and at a cost of £30 they went into print with *Poems By Currer, Ellis and Acton Bell* in 1846. The elaborate, asexual pseudonyms of Currer (Charlotte), Ellis (Emily) and Acton (Anne) Bell, were used because they felt that as women, they stood less chance of success, and their secret was only revealed in 1848 when Charlotte and Anne visited the publisher of *Jane Eyre* in London.

Their collection of poems sold two copies!

*The Bronte Parsonage at Haworth—seemingly a fine home, but the whole village suffered appallingly from poor sanitation.*

Undeterred they sat down to write novels—it is extraordinary to think of these three sisters writing together at the same table, producing their selection of timeless masterpieces! Charlotte's first attempt was *The Professor*, based on her time in Brussels. It was rejected by every publisher she sent it to, but she swiftly followed with *Jane Eyre*. Published in October 1847, it was an immediate success, unlike her sisters' books which appeared together two months later. Neither Emily's wild, passionate *Wuthering Heights*, or Anne's carefully written account of the governess *Agnes Grey* were well received during their authors' lifetime.

Anne went on to write *The Tenant of Wildfell Hall*, while Charlotte added *Shirley* and *Villette*. Emily's *Wuthering Heights* ranks with *Jane Eyre* as the most popular of the Bronte sisters' works, and *The Oxford Companion To English Literature* also acclaims her as 'much the most considerable poet of the three sisters, and one of the most original poets of the century, remembered for her lyrics . . . her passionate invocations . . . and her apparently more personal visionary moments'. The first and last verses from *No Coward Soul Is Mine* seem a fitting epitaph for her life:

'No coward soul is mine,

No trembler in the world's storm-troubled sphere: I see Heaven's glories shine
And Faith shines equal arming me from Fear . . .
There is no room for Death
Nor atom that his might could render void,
Since Thou—Thou art Being and Breath,
And what Thou art may never be destroyed.'

## Bibliography

Charlotte (Currer Bell): *Jane Eyre* (Smith Elder, 1847), *Shirley* (Smith Elder, 1849), *Villette* (Smith Elder, 1853), *The Professor* (Smith Elder, 1857), *Emma* (unfinished).
Emily (Ellis Bell): *Wuthering Heights* (T.C. Newby, 1847).
Anne (Acton Bell): *Agnes Grey* (T.C. Newby, 1847), *The Tenant of Wildfell Hall* (T.C. Newby, 1848).

*Wuthering Heights* and the other Bronte novels have appeared in countless editions around the world. *The Complete Poems of Emily Bronte* are published by the Columbia University Press. There are innumerable biographies of the Brontes.

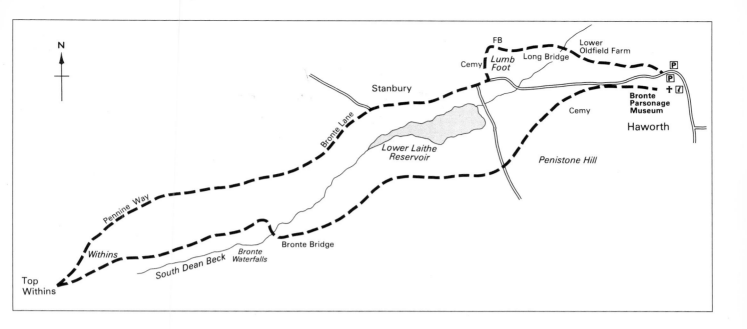

# A Walk with Emily Brontë

**Map:** OS Outdoor Leisure 21.
**Start:** From the Bronte Parsonage in Haworth, south of Keighley in West Yorkshire—OS Grid Ref. 029373. Car parking near to the Parsonage in Haworth. The Parsonage is open daily excluding 1st–24th February and 24–26th December; 11–5.30 pm April to September, 11–4.30 pm October to March.
**Nearest BR Station:** Keighley.
**Distance:** Approximately $7\frac{1}{2}$ miles.
**Time:** Allow 3-4 hours.
**Facilities:** Pubs, cafés, and tea houses in Haworth.
**Summary:** A walk across the moors to Top Withens which inspired *Wuthering Heights*, and then returning via some glorious Yorkshire countryside.

*Top Withins, reckoned to have been the inspiration for Wuthering Heights.*

The main Haworth car park is at the top of the hill, conveniently near the Information Centre and only a few minutes' walk from the Parsonage. Alternatively, if you carry on as the road bears left towards Stanbury there is another car park even closer to the Parsonage. Haworth itself was once a one-street village, and its cobbled Main Street is now a major south Pennine tourist attraction. It's well packed with shops, cafés and pubs, and if one can avoid the most crowded times in high season it remains a pleasant enough place to explore. The Parsonage also suffers from over-crowding so try to plan your visit on an out of season weekday.

The Parsonage is a fine looking building close by the church; all the Bronte family except Anne were buried here. In front of the Parsonage there is a small pleasant garden, and inside it's well laid out with a museum of Bronte history and a shop at the rear. This walk starts from the Parsonage — it is the local 'classic' route. It takes you onto the moor, past the Bronte Bridge and Falls to the ruined house at Top Withens which is claimed to be Emily's inspiration for Wuthering Heights. It's

57

*Crossing the stream by the Bronte Bridge and Bronte Waterfall. Locals swim and bathe here in summer.*

an easy walk despite being across open moorland, but is best tackled with walking boots and protective clothing in case the weather deteriorates.

Start by the side of the Parsonage and walk past the shop on your left, going ahead along a narrow path which passes houses on the right. Carry on into the next field and follow the stones which show the track of the footpath. This brings you down to the far right hand corner of the field, and onto the road just west of Haworth.

Turn left along the road here, and almost immediately bear left uphill following the sign for Penistone Hill. This is a quiet road, and there's a path which follows the right hand side past several benches, with good views out over the valley of the River Worth. Go past the viewpoint, having passed a walled cemetery on the left, and carry on along the road with views of Lower Laithe Reservoir to the right. Eventually you come to a T-junction; cross straight

over here, going onto a track and following the footpath signs for the Bronte Falls and Withens.

This track is tarmacced for a while and is still well surfaced as it begins to drop down the left side of a ravine towards Sladen Beck which is very picturesque and a popular spot with locals for picnicking and swimming in the summer. Down by the stream you come to a plaque set in a rock with the Bronte Falls to the left—they're usually at their best in winter. Here you can also see the Bronte Seat which is a stone-shaped chair, and the Bronte Bridge which is nothing more than a few slabs of rock across the stream.

Cross over here, and go straight up the steep hill on the other side, heading up through a narrow gate where you follow the sign to Withens. There's a small, old, farmhouse just above this gate named 'Virginia'. Follow the track off to the left, passing over several walls via ladders or squeezing through holes, with

Top Withens coming into sight on the hillside ahead. The well defined track heads downhill to cross a tributary of South Dean Beck, and then back uphill, soon coming to the remains of a building where it joins the Pennine Way. Turn left along the Pennine Way here, and walk a few hundred yards up to the ruins of Top Withens, a comparatively small and very basic building with a most wonderful, panoramic view. It has a plaque erected by the Bronte Society on one wall, stating that the situation—though not the building itself—resembles that of the house, Wuthering Heights, in Emily's novel.

Stop here for a picnic if you wish; it's a pleasant spot, but the local sheep are used to being fed titbits and tend to be over inquisitive. To continue, retrace your steps along the Pennine Way and continue along this well trodden route until the track becomes sandy peat underfoot, and then passes a couple of modern farmhouse conversions on the left.

*Crossing the River Worth below Lumb Foot on the final stage of the walk back to Haworth.*

A short way on, the Pennine Way turns 90 degrees left off this track. If you wish to extend this into a longer walk of around 10 miles, with the aid of an OS map you could make your way via the Pennine Way to the footpath that runs parallel to Oldfield Lane, and return to Haworth via Street Lane and Hey Lane on the other side of the valley. The Pennine Way takes you to the south-east corner of Ponden Reservoir, and then turns west and north to pass Ponden Hall which was Emily's model for Thrushcross Grange.

To continue without this extra loop, ignore the left turning onto the Pennine Way and carry straight on down the hill, keeping along the track which turns to tarmac at Back Lane and eventually comes to the road at Hob Hill by a bus stop. Here you turn right along the road for about one mile, walking through Stanbury. Approximately half the route is on pavement, and after a road turning on the right which runs down the east side of Lower Laithe Reservoir you turn left onto a footpath which is signposted about 200 yards further on.

Go steeply downhill on the narrow path between two walls, heading into more rural Yorkshire countryside with another walled cemetery over to the right. Keep on downhill until you reach a house at Lumb Foot; here you turn left onto a track, and then hard right downhill on the other side of the house, heading down towards two bridges which cross the River Worth. Cross the right hand bridge which gives a good view of the very pretty, cast iron, Victorian bridge on the left. Continue on a farm track, and after about 75 yards where this bears left uphill, keep straight ahead on a grassy track which follows the river with a clump of trees on the left. Keep the next bridge on your right, walking on ahead across a stile, then across another stile and straight on along the side of a field in very pretty countryside.

Eventually you come to a wider part of the river with the splendid old stone Long Bridge on the right. Cross over this bridge, and then bear left uphill away from the river on a deep track which could be very muddy in wet weather. This brings you up to Lower Oldfield Farm, a modernised building in a commanding hillside position. Climb up the ladder over the wall, and bear left round the front of the house and along a narrow track. Keep on ahead through fields, with the houses on the outskirts of Haworth on your right. Keep left past yet another cemetery—they are very frequent on this walk!—following the path which bears right and soon rejoins the road at Haworth. Cross over here, and it's a short walk back to the top of Main Street.

# Walk 12: With Charles Kingsley in Malham

*The eminent Victorian Charles Kingsley (1819–75) is today remembered mainly for his novels* Westward Ho! *and* The Water Babies. *The latter was inspired by a visit to Malham Tarn in the Yorkshire Dales, where the sooty streaks of black moss that triggered the creation of Tom the chimney sweep can still be seen today.*

Charles Kingsley dedicated *The Water Babies* to:

'My Youngest Son Grenville Arthur and All Other Good Little Boys.
Come read me a riddle, each good little man;
If you cannot read it, no grown-up folk can.'

He described it as 'A Fairy Tale for a Land-Baby', and it was an immediate success. Unlike most of his work, it has stood the test of time. It was a favourite with Queen Victoria who thought it fine reading for her children, and after its publication in 1863 was reprinted almost annually throughout the remainder of the nineteenth century.

Kingsley was a keen amateur naturalist and by all accounts unusually liberal and loving with his four children. He wrote it for the simplest of reasons, as his daughter Rose, explained:

'The writing of *The Water Babies* had for its reason a gentle reminder, one spring morning at breakfast, of an old promise, to the effect that as the three elder children had their book—*The Heroes*—the baby, my younger brother, then four years old, must have his. My father made no answer, but got up at once and went into his study, locking the door, and in an hour came back with the first chapter of *The Water Babies* in his hand, written exactly as it stands. At this pace, and with the same ease, the whole book was completed.'

It was serialised in *Macmillan's Magazine* between 1862–3 before being published as a book, with

**Charles Kingsley, painted by L. Dickinson in 1862.** *Photo by NPG.*

illustrations to the first edition by Sir Noel Paton. Many artists illustrated subsequent editions, with Kingsley's imaginative and descriptive powers launching wonderful images of Tom staring with shock into the mirror, gasping at his first sight of Ellie, swimming with the fishes, and meeting the many strange creatures that the author placed in his path.

Kingsley paid a short visit to Tarn House on the north side of Malham Tarn. He walked the moorland and saw all the magnificent sights of the area, and it is said that the white limestone cliffs streaked with black moss at Malham Cove gave him the idea of Tom, the chimney sweep. He had planned to use Yorkshire as the setting for two other novels which

he started and later abandoned, eventually using it as the background for the first two chapters of *The Water Babies*.

The story tells of Tom, the poor little chimney sweep, who 'lived in a great town in the North country, where there were plenty of chimneys to sweep, and plenty of money for Tom to earn and his master to spend'. This ogre, appropriately named Mr Grimes, sends him to clean the chimneys at Harthover Place—'really a grand place . . . so large the Duke of Wellington, with ten thousand soldiers and cannon to match, were easily housed therein'. Put to work, Tom gets lost in one of many chimneys and finds himself in a bedroom 'where lay the most beautiful little girl that Tom had ever seen'. Then, he sees, standing close to him, 'a little ugly, black, ragged figure, with bleared eyes and grinning white teeth. What did such a little black ape want in that sweet young lady's room? And behold, it was himself, reflected in a great mirror'.

Shocked by his appearance, Tom is discovered and chased out of the house as a common thief. He makes for the woods and heads 'out on the great grouse-moors, which the country folk called Harthover Fell—heather and bog and rock, stretching away and up, up to the very sky'. Kingsley's description of the imaginary Harthover Fell is excellent, as is Tom's eyesight!—'Behind him, far below was Harthover, and the dark woods, and the shining salmon river; and on his left, far below, was the town, and the smoking chimneys of the collieries; and far, far away the river widened to the shining sea; and little white specs, which were ships, lay on its bosom. Before him lay, spread out like a map, great plains, and farms, and villages, amid dark knots of trees . . . And to his right rose moor after

*The extraordinary limestone pavement above Malham Cove.*

moor, hill after hill, till they faded away, blue into blue sky.'

Having found his way over Harthover Fell, Tom risks climbing down Lewthwaite Crag (Malham Cove), much to the amazement of his pursuers, who by this stage have been informed of his innocence by noble Ellie.

'When they looked at that awful cliff, they could never believe he would have dared to face it. "Heaven forgive us!" said Sir John. "If we find him at all, we shall find him lying at the bottom."'

However, Tom is made of sterner stuff, and comes safely across the moors to Vendale which Kingsley based on Littondale, an area some five miles to the north-east of Malham around the village of Arncliffe. The chasing party almost catch him, but all they find are

his clothes by the side of the river (the River Skirfare). They assume he has drowned, but Tom has been transformed into something very different:

'Tom found himself swimming about in the stream, being about four inches, or—that I may be more accurate—3.87902 inches long, and having round the parotid region of his fauces a set of external gills (I hope you understand all the big words) which he mistook for a lace frill . . . In fact, the fairies had turned him into a water-baby.'

And that was the end of Yorkshire for the recreated amphibious Tom, who continues his adventures elsewhere, leading a busy underwater life and meeting many strange creatures including the morally improving Mrs Doasyouwouldbedoneby and Mrs Bedonebyasyoudid. Kingsley finishes the tale by reuniting Tom with Ellie ('Thank God that you have plenty of cold water to wash in; and wash in it too, like a true Englishman')—and cautioning his young readers:

'But remember always, as I told you at first, that this is all a fairy tale, and only fun and pretence; and, therefore, you are not to believe a word of it, even if it is true.'

Since its heyday, *The Water Babies* has been dissected and analysed as a moral fable that exposed Kingsley's various personal problems. It was never intended to prompt so much criticism, and the author would surely be amazed that he would be remembered for such a minor work, while his fame as a distinguished Victorian figure is almost totally forgotten.

In his day he was a prodigiously busy man

*Above:* **The splendid view of Malham Cove as you head back towards Malham village.**

*Facing Page:* **Janet's Foss—the waterfall near the start of the walk.**

*Left:* **Wild, open country above Gordale Scar.**

who almost certainly worked himself into an early grave. Devoutly religious, he was well known in his early post-Cambridge years for his leadership of the Christian Socialists, upholding the rights of downtrodden workers and publicising their plight in his early novels *Yeast* and *Alton Locke*. Despite being ridiculed and criticised by many members of the Victorian Establishment, his career as a cleric, academic and writer proved highly successful. His books invariably sold well, and with royal patronage he scaled the heights to become a Canon of Westminster and Chester cathedrals, and Professor of Modern History at Cambridge.

Kingsley was a man of contradictions. On the one hand he was a reforming radical fighting for better conditions for the less fortunate; on the other he firmly held the view that the workers should know their place. He believed the British were best and was by today's standards exceptionally racist, applauding any defence of the Empire, no matter how bloody it might be. Above all he hated Catholicism with extraordinary venom—this culminated in a literary duel with the turncoat Catholic Cardinal Newman, who on the strength of it wrote his *Apologia pro Vita Sua*, a spiritual autobiography which *The Oxford Companion to English Literature* labels 'a literary masterpiece'.

Kingsley's busy life came to an end after a long and exhausting lecture tour of the USA during 1874. He returned to the Rectory at Eversley in Hampshire—his home on and off for over 30 years—and cared for his wife who was severely ill. He nursed her until he developed pneumonia, and died believing that she was already dead. His wife however outlived him by many years, writing his first biography *Charles Kingsley; His Letters and Memories of His Life*, published in December 1876.

## Bibliography

Charles Kingsley's novels have a social, spiritual, or jingoistic content. His first were *Yeast* and *Alton Locke*, both published in 1850 after having been serialised in magazines. *Yeast* was inspired by the Irish famine of 1846—'I shall be very hard on the landlords because they deserve it'—and *Alton Locke* by the plight of those working for tailors. *Hypatia* (1851) was his first historical novel with heavy religious overtones, while *Westward Ho!* (1855) was overtly jingoistic and militaristic, prompted by the Crimean war. Among his other novels *Two Years Ago* (1857) was a veiled plea for sanitary reform, and *Heroes* (1856) was the simple history of Greek mythology dedicated to his three eldest children, later prompting *The Water Babies*.

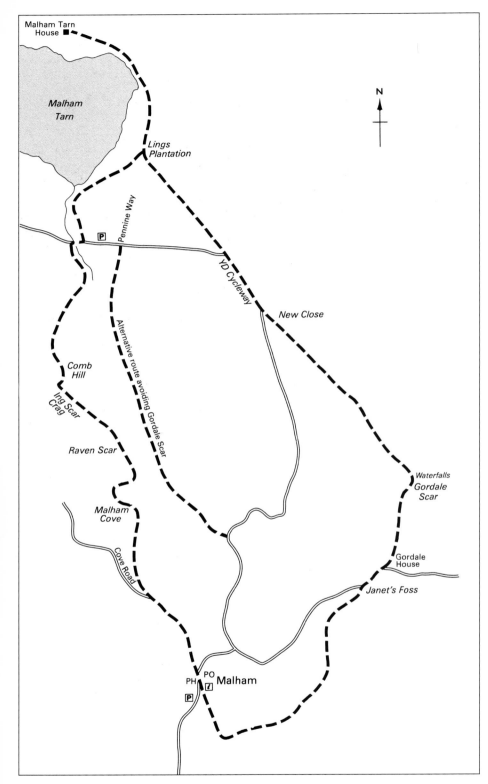

**Map:** OS Outdoor Leisure 10—Yorkshire Dales Southern area.
**Start:** Malham village Information Centre—OS Grid Ref. 901628. Large car park behind Information Centre with fixed charge for all-day parking.
**Nearest BR Station:** Gargrave.
**Distance:** Approximately 7½ miles.
**Time:** Allow 4 hours.
**Facilities:** Pubs, cafés, shops in Malham.
**Summary:** A fine walk with incredible scenery.

The large car park on the outskirts of the village of Malham is the best place to park, not least because the Information Centre next to it has interesting displays, books and maps of the area—on my visit the staff were also friendly and knowledgeable.

This is the 'classic' Malham walk, taking in some fine sights on its well trodden way. The signposting is excellent, and the only part demanding a degree of fitness is the climb up Gordale Scar (about 15 feet straight up). It's easy enough, but it is a climb and if you don't wish to try it, or have a dog, you may do better to take the alternative route from Janet's Foss to Malham Tarn via the Pennine Way.

From the Information Centre turn left, and walk towards the centre of the village passing a footpath turning to the right. After about 150 yards, just before you come to the first hotel, cross the road and go over the little bridge, turning right along the left bank of the River Aire. Turn left into a field as indicated, and walk on along the well defined path to the next wall. Here you take the footpath to the left, walking towards Janet's Foss along the side of another field, and crossing the next wall using the ladders which are so carefully provided.

The path follows the left side of a stream, bearing left into Wedber Woods on National Trust land. An information panel tells you what to expect, but when we last walked here the most unusual sight was that of three goats, grazing free and unfettered in the woods. They are pretty nimble footed, but you should take care as the going here can be slippery in wet weather. You soon come to Janet's Foss at the end of the woods—the 'Foss' is a splendid waterfall dropping into a still pool where sheep were washed prior to shearing.

From here the track takes you a few yards up to the road at Gordale Bridge where you turn right—it's a quiet, dead-end road, though

*The view across Malham Tarn towards Malham Tarn House.*

a few cars pass by in summer. The first footpath signposted on the left goes past Cawden Flats to join the Pennine Way above Shorkley Hill. This is the way to go if you decide to avoid Gordale Scar. The Gordale Scar footpath is a little further along the road, passing left through a gate just before the house on the corner where the road bends right. The track up towards the Scar follows the right side of the valley ahead, and is rocky underfoot but otherwise easily walked. As you approach closer the full magnificence of Gordale Scar is revealed—a monstrous fissure in the rock with a waterfall splattering its way down one side.

Climb up the scar—after rain it can be slippery and sensible footwear is advisable. I last went up it with my family; my wife, who was in the later stages of pregnancy, led the way, and I carried our two-year-old on my back. Our dog—a Border Collie used to the rough, outdoor life—was not so keen to make his way up, no doubt sensing that he couldn't make it unassisted. With a little persuasion and a grab and a lift he came up too!

After the short climb there is a scramble up the rest of the Scar, with steps near the top to help you on your way. The top is a fine place to stop; a grassy hillside, with fine views looking east over a ravine onto a memorable landscape. From here walk on in the same general direction, following a wide, grassy track with boulders on either side. You will come to a cairn, and will then start to walk along

one of the extraordinary limestone 'pavements' that can be found in the area, passing another cairn. Footpath posts show the way, and by following these the footpath bears left away from the pavement towards steps in a long boundary wall by the roadside.

The road here comes up from Malham, and you turn right along it, ignoring the footpath sign which points along the wall. Where the road bends left, go straight ahead by an NT sign onto a track that runs across flat ground towards Malham Tarn. Pass a copse of trees on the right, and then walk down to Lings Plantation at the south-east corner of the Tarn. From here you can follow the Pennine Way round the lakeside to Malham Tarn House where Kingsley stayed. The house, which was originally built as a shooting lodge, is now a field studies centre and is not open to the public. A good view of the house can be obtained from the south side of the tarn without the extra walk round the north side which is not greatly inspiring.

To continue, turn left and head across the grass past the woods to join a footpath that leads down to the bottom of Malham Tarn at Tarn Foot. Here the footpath bears left towards the road by the side of the stream which feeds the tarn. Turn right along the road, crossing the stream and walking between walls on either side before turning left through a gate onto a signposted bridleway about 50 yards further on. The bridleway goes straight up and over a hill. The footpath which you

want bears left off it, keeping round the base of the hill with a stone wall on the left. Bearing round to the right this leads you into a strange, dry valley from where you follow the track along the side of the next valley by Comb Hill, bearing right round the ledge until you see steps that turn sharp left and drop steeply down into Ing Scar.

Head down these steps, crossing a couple of stiles at the top. Ing Scar, a huge fissure in the earth, is a remarkable sight. A good track runs along the bottom of it following the right hand side, and you keep on it until you reach a low wall with little swing gates by an NT sign. Go through these gates and walk straight on with Raven Scar to your right, until after a hundred yards or so you come to a footpath sign pointing to the right. This takes you up over an even more extraordinary expanse of limestone pavement—bear right along it, and at the far end join the steps which turn left down the hill.

As you descend you get a splendid view of Malham Cove with its sooty streaks ahead of you (have a thought for poor Tom, climbing down the cliffs here). At the bottom follow Malham Beck on a gradual incline towards the road, pausing for more fine views of Malham Cove behind you. Turn left downhill along the road into Malham, and there you'll find a good choice of cafés, tea houses, and shops—it's a pleasant place to stop in, though likely to be crowded in summer.

# Walk 13: With Richard Doddridge Blackmore on Exmoor

*Published in 1869,* Lorna Doone—A Romance of Exmoor *is a tale of excitement and romance still widely read today. Its author, Richard Doddridge Blackmore (1825–1900), has been described as 'the last Victorian', and Blackmore's 'Dooneland' (Exmoor) is now a place of pilgrimage for many thousands of Doone enthusiasts.*

R.D. Blackmore is now only remembered for *Lorna Doone* but he also wrote thirteen other novels including *Alice Lorraine, Clara Vaughan, Mary Annerley, Cripps The Carrier* and a fair amount of poetry. Nor was Lorna Doone an instant success. It was published in 1869 by Sampson Low, Son & Marston of 188, Fleet Street in three volumes, having first been rejected by some 20 other publishers. Initially sales were very slow, and only 500 copies of the first edition were sold.

The book took off on account of a completely unconnected event. In 1871 Princess Louise, Queen Victoria's daughter, married the Marquess of Lorne who was outside the royal family, an event which caused quite a sensation. A journalist commented on the connection with Lorna Doone's 'House of Lorne' ancestry, and interest was immediately aroused in the book. The tide turned when the book was published as a single volume in 1897, priced 6d, and since then it has been published in editions all over the world. It has proved particularly popular in the United States and for years it was a 'set text book' in some American colleges.

R.D. Blackmore was born in Longworth, Berkshire. His mother died of typhus soon after his birth, and when his father re-married he was brought up by his aunt who married the Reverend Richard Gordon of Elsfield in Oxfordshire. He was sent to Blundell's School in Tiverton—as indeed was John Ridd, the hero of *Lorna Doone*—where he made his first acquaintance with Exmoor. He went on to read classics and law at Exeter College, Oxford and was then called to the bar in the Middle Temple for a short time, before giving up to become a classics teacher—as a prelude to his fictional writing he wrote and published a

**The great author, Richard Doddridge Blackmore, as remembered from an early edition of Lorna Doone.**

translation of the first and second books of Virgil's *Georgics*.

The receipt of an inheritance enabled him to build Gomer House at Teddington where he settled down to become a writer and a market gardener, both equally successful occupations. His first novel *Clara Vaughan* was published in 1864, followed by *Cradock Nowell: A Tale of the New Forest* and then *Lorna Doone* three years later.

*Lorna Doone* has an excellent narrative and if you enjoyed *Wuthering Heights* I would strongly recommend it, for once you're past the first

couple of chapters and have mastered Blackmore's occasional lapses into broad Exmoor dialect it has the same highly charged romantic tension typical of the best nineteenth-century novels. (If you do intend to read it please do so before you continue with this chapter as I will be revealing some important aspects of the plot!)

Blackmore obtained much of the background material for Lorna Doone from the records of his grandfather, the Reverend John Blackmore, who had been Rector of Oare and Combe Martin. This has led to much enthusiastic research and learned speculation as to whether *Lorna Doone* is a true story or not. It does seem as if Blackmore based many of his characters on real life people—for example, a John Ridd of Exmoor was the All-England Wrestling Champion, and the Scottish Doone family led by Iain Ciar Doune ('Ensor Doone' when you say it quickly) had indeed settled in Exmoor in the early seventeenth century, occasionally terrorising the neighbourhood. Blackmore's background information about the Scottish origins of the Doones and of Lorna Doone herself was largely provided by the Reverend Richard Gordon's family.

Nevertheless, it is clear that Blackmore mixed fact with fiction when dealing with his characters and their deeds, as he did with the places where they occurred. Exmoor, with its 265 square miles, is the smallest of our National Parks, and all the doings of the Doones were within its boundaries. The Church of St Mary the Virgin in Oare is over 800 years old and excluding the eastern chancel and western tower which were later additions, it is as Lorna Doone and John Ridd would have known it. A memorial tablet placed

*Above:* **The view over Exmoor from County Gate, start point of this walk.**

*Right:* **Walking along towards the Doone Valley past the Blackmore Memorial.**

*Badgworthy Water close to the 'water slide'.*

there in 1923 commemorates R.D. Blackmore, and it is said that church records can be found mentioning the Ridd, Snow and Fry families.

Directly over the valley from the church can be seen Oare House, built on the site of John Ridd's Plover's Barrows Farm—the original farmhouse was unfortunately demolished in 1883, just too early for the book's fame to save it, although the original courtyard and outbuildings still exist. Upstream along Oare Water the hamlet of Malmsmead sports the Lorna Doone Farm, in parts over 1000 years old and reckoned to be the model for the home of Nicholas Snow, the Ridd's rival in farming matters.

Badgworthy Water (pronounced 'Badgery') leads to the land of the Doone's. On its bank south of Cloud Farm you can see the R.D. Blackmore Memorial Stone which was placed there on the one hundredth anniversary of publication in 1969, while further down the valley is the 'water slide' at the top of which John Ridd first met Lorna on St Valentine's-Day in 1675. It doesn't in the least match the description of the incredibly dangerous torrent in the book, but this is true of virtually all Blackmore's treatments of the Doone landscape. The area around Badgworthy is indeed wonderfully, wild countryside, but it does not compare with the romantic vision of lofty, scowling leaks which Blackmore describes.

The location of the Doone Valley has led to endless discussion between Doone enthusiasts. A slight majority believe that it was up Lank Combe, the rest favouring the neighbouring Hoccombe Combe. The reader is free to choose, but perhaps the most reasonable answer is to assume that the Doone Valley was the product of Blackmore's imagination, combining in one the best aspects of Badgworthy, Lank Combe, and Hoccombe Combe.

## Bibliography

There are any number of editions of *Lorna Doone—A Romance of Exmoor* available. The one to aspire to is the original 1869 first printing; failing that I acquired a late nineteenth-century 43rd edition 'Very handsomely bound in vellum at 35 shillings', published by the same Sampson Low, Marston & Co, with a preface by the author which starts: 'Few things have surprised me more and nothing has more pleased me, than the great success of this simple tale'.

An extraordinary number of books and pamphlets have been written about Lorna Doone. Quite a few of them have emanated from America where scholars have the benefit of the Anglo-American Lorna Doone Society, a privately funded research organisation which was founded in New Hampshire in 1923. Among those currently available *Who was Lorna Doone?* by Barry Gardner (Brendon Arts) makes the most of the myth and the reality, and has obviously been carefully researched. *The Lorna Doone Trail* compiled by S.H. Burton (Microstudy) takes a steadier view of the book, tracking down all the main Exmoor locations in chronological order, and comparing Blackmore's descriptions, with how they look today.

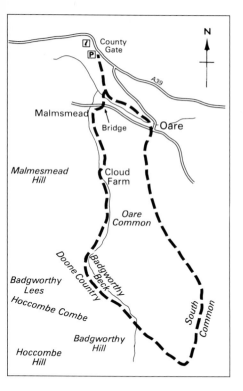

## A Walk with R.D. Blackmore

**Map:** OS Landranger 180/181.
**Start:** County Gate on the A39 coast road between Lynton and Porlock on the North Devon/Somerset border—OS Grid Ref. 793486. Free car park next to Information Centre which is open Easter to October, 10–5 pm.
**Nearest BR station:** Minehead.
**Distance:** 8½ miles.
**Time:** Allow 4–5 hours.
**Facilities:** Information Centre at County Gate sells some food; Cloud Farm sells soft drinks, ploughmans' lunches, and cream teas. Both open Easter to late October.
**Summary:** A fine walk into the heart of 'Doone Country', returning by way of Oare Church where Lorna Doone was shot.

For those new to the area this walk is an excellent introduction to Exmoor. Not too long, it takes in all kinds of Exmoor landscape and is easy walking most of the way. In summer many walkers ply along the Badgworthy Water part of this walk which is extremely picturesque. Further on the route enters wilder country, and some care is needed to find the correct way back to Oare Church on the return journey.

Start from the free car park at County Gate which is in a magnificent position on the coast road between Lynton and Porlock. From here you get an unbeatable view looking southwards over the moor, with the 'Doone Country' valley stretching off to the left. The Information Centre sells local OS maps as well as other publications dealing with Exmoor, and is of course well stocked with copies of *Lorna Doone* and various pamphlets on the legend.

From the car park walk back towards the road, as if heading towards Porlock. Just before the road, go right through a gate and follow the bridleway sign to Malmsmead down in the valley, heading along the side of a wire fence. This grass track leads steeply downhill, getting increasingly steeper all the time with a fine view laid out ahead. Walking down is not difficult, but as you have to walk back up to finish this walk, you might think it better to start and finish at Malmsmead where there is also a car park. This is quite possible and it will make the walk slightly shorter, but I would recommend the County Gate start for its magnificent views which prepare you for the walk ahead, for its useful Information Centre, and not least because it's much easier to get to by car from the main road.

At the bottom of the hill bear right before a stile to cross the East Lyn River at a bridge, heading straight ahead and then bearing left up by the side of a farmhouse which brings you to a minor road. Here you turn right past a large house with a Doone-inspired name and friendly peacocks, before taking the first left over a cattle grid signposted to Cloud Farm. The track up to the farm is mostly tarmac and provides easy walking on a fairly level surface. At the farm you can stop for something to eat or drink (unlicenced) in the pleasant garden which is just above Badgworthy Water, or use it as a base to stay the night (B&B). There is also a horseriding centre here for those who would like to ride over the moor.

To continue, go down to the river on the track which runs beside Cloud Farm, crossing by the bridge and then turning left on the track which runs along the west side. Keep along this track, and you soon come to a large rock, the R.D. Blackmore Memorial placed here to commemorate the great man. From here the track continues to follow the side of Badgworthy Water, going through a gate and into oak woods. On the far side of the woods walk on past a track going off into trees up to the right, and some way on you come to a narrow, wooden bridge. This crosses over what is generally reckoned to be the famous 'water slide' up to the right, some experts believing that the Doone settlement was in Lank Combe

at the top of it.

Crossing over the bridge you come to a much narrower track winding its way between rhododendron bushes. This brings you to more open country, heading into the wild moorland of 'Doone Country' as the track follows the right side of the valley. Ahead you will see a clump of trees downhill to the left. This area is supposed to be the site of the Old Badgworthy Settlement where other experts reckon that the Doone houses were situated, and with more trees one can imagine it being more hospitable in former times.

Where the track bears right up Hoccombe Combe, turn left downhill to the three-way footpath sign by the clump of trees and follow the direction for Exford, crossing a narrow bridge over a stream which feeds Badgworthy Water. Bear round to the right to continue alongside the river in the same southerly direction, walking along the track until it once again bears right, this time turning west along Hoccombe Water. Here you go left through a gate and walk over the fairly large bridge which crosses Badgworthy Water at the end of 'Doone Country'.

On the other side go up a short, steep hill following the signposted direction to Exbridge. When you reach the top and start to head down, look out for an unmarked, grass track going up to the left at an acute angle well before you reach the next dip where the track heads on uphill into even wilder country, approaching a long stone wall. This acute turn takes you back up northwards; from here on the route follows tracks and bridleways up to and across South Common before heading down to Oare, but is mostly unmarked and not that obvious.

A short way uphill fork right where the track forks right and left, and follow the moorland path as it appears and disappears through the heather towards the top of the ridge, heading more or less east-north-east most of the way. At the top it becomes much better defined, bearing to the left which is more towards the north. The corner of a huge green field cut into the moor comes into view, and the track carries on down to a gate leading into it. Head across this field, bearing over to the left to follow its boundary wall on the moorland side—from here you should be able to see your start point at County Gate in the distance way ahead of you.

Where the field heads down into a rough gulley, turn left through a single gate in the wall, bearing right downhill to pick up a track that runs through the heather in much the same direction. This narrow track continues on up the other side of the gulley to cross an

*In the heart of Dooneland—coming close to the supposed site of the Doone village.*

expanse of heather before coming to a gate set in a wall. Go through and walk along the right side of the field ahead which will probably be full of sheep, slowly losing height as you approach the gate to the next field. Here you continue to walk along the top of the ridge in the same northerly direction, following the right hand boundary of the field and going slightly more downhill with views of the valley ahead slowly opening out before you.

When you come to a gate on the right, turn into the next field and head downhill towards the hamlet of Oare which until this stage of the walk has been hidden from view. As you walk down the hillside, look for a clump of trees in a gulley ahead with a large house on the other side of the valley in the distance which is Oare House, built on the former site of Plover's Barrow Farm. At the top of the gulley you will find a signpost pointing the way down to Oare Church, taking you further downhill across a couple of fields and coming out at a minor road alongside the church. The turning down to Oare is quite easy to miss—if you overshoot while walking along the ridge, the clump of trees and the house will eventually come into view on the right. You then go through the left hand of two gates at the end of the field ahead and turn right downhill along a track that doubles back down to the trees.

Oare Church is a fine and interesting place—you can see the window from which Lorna Doone was shot; there's a memorial to R.D. Blackmore; and the congregation are shepherded into unusual pens! To continue from the church turn right downhill on the road, crossing the bridge over Gare Water and bearing left up the other side. After about 75 yards turn left through a double green painted gate, following the footpath sign to Malmsmead one mile distant, with a fine riverside walk ahead of you. The path eventually takes you past the back of a large farm, and then on to the stile at the foot of the hill which leads back up to your starting point at County Gate—a long climb to complete a really fine walk which will surely inspire you to reach for your copy of *Lorna Doone.*

# Walk 14: With Thomas Hardy in 'Casterbridge'

*Thomas Hardy (1840–1928) is without doubt Dorset's most famous son, blessing its principal town, Dorchester, with the fictional name, Casterbridge, and capturing the essence of rural life in his series of Wessex Novels. He was born near Dorchester and spent most of his long life near there, although his good earnings from his writing also enabled him to travel widely. His birthplace at Higher Bockhampton is now preserved by the National Trust, and the surrounding area is full of Hardy legacies.*

**Thomas Hardy.** *Photo by NPG.*

**Hardy's Cottage, now cared for by the National Trust.**

Hardy was born the son of a stonemason in a small cottage at Higher Bockhampton (Upper Mellstock) a short way east of Dorchester. His mother encouraged his interest in books although his first novel did not appear until 1871. He attended school in Dorchester, walking there and back each day, and on leaving was articled to an architect, a training which in later life enabled him to design and built the house he was to live in called Max Gate.

In his twenties he worked for a London firm of architects for a few years—this was the only period he lived away from Dorchester for any length of time, and he returned in 1867 to work as an architect and to try his hand at writing. *Desperate Remedies*, his first published work, appeared some four years later.

*Under the Greenwood Tree, A Pair Of Blue Eyes* and *Far From the Madding Crowd* appeared at yearly intervals from 1872, and the latter

proved so successful that Hardy was able to take up writing full time. Over the next 20 years he wrote 12 more novels which were all based on his beloved Wessex, but after the hostile reception of *Tess of the d'Urbervilles* and *Jude the Obscure*—a reaction which is hard to understand when reading these novels today—he gave up the novel and concentrated on short stories and poetry.

Hardy always regarded poetry as the

highest form of writing, and over the years he produced eight collected volumes, starting with the *Wessex Poems* published in 1898, but compared to his novels his poems are little read today. Among his more unusual works was *The Dynasts*, a huge, rambling collection of prose and verse which tells the story of the Napoleonic wars as seen through the eyes of ordinary Wessex men and women. In 1989 this was resurrected and presented in a highly edited form called *Victory* at the Chichester Festival Theatre.

Hardy's 'Wessex' is the south-west of England, and Wessex was also the name given to his terrier which was later remembered in the poem *Dead Wessex*. His famous Wessex Novels revolve principally around Dorset and neighbouring Devon, although the action sometimes stretches as far as Hampshire, Wiltshire and Somerset, with occasional references to parts of 'Lower Wessex' which Hardy would have known as Cornwall. He gave all the towns and villages delightful, fictional names—Chaseborough (Cranborne), Emminster (Beaminster), Kingsbere-sub-Greenhill (Bere Regis), Melchester (Salisbury), Sandbourne (Bournemouth)—which remain the same throughout his novels; and he also gave his characters a delightful local dialect, with many words and phrases requiring the assistance of a glossary if we are to fully understand them. For example, 'crumby' means appetising, 'lammicken' means clumsy, and 'dolorifuge' means solace.

One of the most popular and probably the most accessible of Hardy's novels is *Tess of the d'Urbervilles*, which tells the story of Tess, doomed by her beauty and her ancient, noble lineage. Sent by her parents on a vain mission to meet her relatives, Tess is seduced by the young son, and in an attempt to escape from what she regards as her disastrous life, she goes to work as a dairymaid in the Vale Of The Great Dairies which lies between Casterbridge and Wellbridge. Here she is pursued by Angel Clare, a man obsessed by his own goodness and the notion of purity who is unable to cope with Tess's confession immediately after their wedding ceremony, causing both of them to suffer.

Tess travels widely, crossing Egdon Heath and the Vale Of The Great Dairies, later moving to Sandbourne, and finally ending her time at far off Wintoncester (Winchester). She travels mainly on foot, and through her eyes Hardy describes a much-loved landscape of pastoral simplicity. Sadly, the surrounding countryside has changed greatly since Hardy's day, having fallen prey to a plague of new roads, new buildings, and too many cars.

Hardy and Tess would no doubt be mortified to see the majority of Wessex today, but quiet corners still remain which would be familiar to them and can be enjoyed on the walk which follows.

Hardy was married twice, firstly to Emma Gifford who he met in 1868 when he was sent as an architect to St Juliot in Cornwall. She died in 1912, and in 1914 he married Florence Dugdale and spent the last years of his life with her at Max Gate. This large and somewhat forbidding house on the Dorchester to Wareham road, designed by Hardy and built by his brother Henry in 1885, derived its name from a nearby turnpike gate kept by a man called Mac, briefly mentioned in *The Dynasts*. Hardy was quite happy here, but as he was increasingly lionised by the public he was often forced to escape his admirers by disappearing through the little green gate which led out onto the Frome meadows. Florence outlived Hardy, and on her death the house was put up for sale. Hardy's sister, Kate, bought it at an auction, and fearing it could be turned into something unsuitable to the memory of her brother, she presented it to the National Trust to be let as a family home and not shown to the public. That is how it remains today, although Hardy's study is reconstructed in the Dorset County Museum.

Hardy's coffin bearers at his funeral in Westminster Abbey included some of the prominent literary figures of the day who had visited Max Gate—Sir James Barrie, John Galsworthy, A.E. Housman, Rudyard Kipling, Bernard Shaw and Sir Edmund Gosse. His ashes were interred at Poets' Corner, but his heart was removed before the cremation and taken back for burial at the small churchyard at Mellstock (Stinsford) where Hardy's headstone remains in the graveyard today, in the countryside where you will find his true spirit.

## Bibliography

Hardy's Wessex Novels are divided into those of 'Character and Environment', 'Romance and Fantasy', and 'Ingenuity'. They are widely available in a number of editions, with *Far from the Madding Crowd* and *Tess of the d'Urbervilles* probably remaining the most popular. There are a number of Hardy biographies which have been published over the years, but for those interested in the geographical background to his novels, *The Hardy Guides* by Herman Lea (Penguin) are amongst the most interesting.

Lea was a photographer and a close friend of Hardy's. He planned to produce a photographically illustrated edition of Hardy's novels, but the project never came off. Nevertheless he assembled Hardy's work into the 1913 edition of *Thomas Hardy's Wessex* (from which *The Hardy Guides* are taken), writing on each novel at length and illustrating his work with sepia photographs showing landscapes or buildings mentioned in the novels, some of which have changed little today.

*Kingston Maurward, known by Hardy as 'Knapwater House'.*

# A Walk with Thomas Hardy

**Map:** OS Landranger 194.
**Start:** Dorset County Museum,
Dorchester—OS Grid Ref. 693908. Parking
in nearby long stay car park.
**Nearest BR Station:** Dorchester.
**Distance:** 8 miles.
**Time:** Allow 5 hours.
**Facilities:** Pubs, cafés, shops, etc. in Dorchester.
**Summary:** An easy walk visiting the place
where Hardy was born, and where his
heart is buried, and covering some beautiful
*Tess of the d'Urbervilles* country. Waymarking can be obscure across Puddletown
Heath.

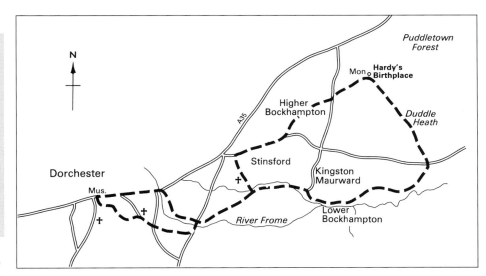

*The Hardy family tombstones in the graveyard at Stinsford.*

This walk starts at the Dorset County Museum, sometimes known as the 'Hardy Museum', in High West Street, Dorchester. Allow an hour or two to look around, for it's well laid out in a light, airy building which first opened on New Year's Day 1884, having been designed by Hardy's former employers Crickmay & Sons. It claims to have the finest Hardy collection in the world with plenty of old photos of the great man and a reconstruction of his study, as well as sections devoted to archaeology and various relics of Dorset lore.

Leave the museum and turn down the High Street, crossing into South Street and turning left down Durngate Street. At the bottom, where there's a dead-end sign, turn right up Salisbury Walk, passing some handsome houses and then going left diagonally across the green which is Salisbury Field. Cut through the houses on the far side and turn down Fordington Street past St George's Church which was well known to Hardy and is mentioned in both his novels and poems. (The grass triangle opposite was Hardy's Durnover Green.) Walk on down to the bottom of the hill, crossing the main road opposite a grocery shop and following the A352 to Wareham road sign, but almost immediately turning left down St George's Street.

This takes you away from Dorchester (Casterbridge) towards the new flyover which Hardy could never have imagined. Just before the flyover, bear left onto a track which is a footpath. It crosses the River Frome and goes under the flyover, heading off across fields towards Stinsford (Mellstock) where Hardy's heart is buried.

Cross the stile and stick to the well-worn path past the interesting remains of old irrigation control gates which dot the landscape. Stinsford comes into view with a thatched cottage prominent in the foreground and substantial buildings behind it. The path bears round to the left and enters trees as it comes to a man-made tributary of the Frome with a bridge leading to Stinsford on the left. Bear right here along the side of the waterway on a very pretty track which takes you east towards Lower Bockhampton (Lower Mellstock). Pass in front of two splendid buildings which can be glimpsed through the trees; they now form part of Dorset College of Agriculture, but the one at Kingston Maurward was once known by Hardy as Knapwater House.

Cross a track, and then come out onto a minor road at Lower Bockhampton. Turn left over the bridge and then almost immediately right onto a track after the first thatched house. This takes you through a farmyard, with yellow footpath blobs directing you on through a gate. Cross the field ahead with the Frome meandering on your right, bearing round to the left of the first house and through another farmyard. From here the footpath divides bearing left and continuing straight on; take the latter route which follows a track at the base of a hill before bearing right through a gate and across another field, heading east towards more farm buildings.

When you reach the buildings, cross the track and go straight ahead over the next field, bearing to the left of a copse. Climb over the stile here and bear left up another field, heading for the right hand side of a gorse-covered tumuli which is indicated on the OS map. Here you will find a gate and a track which you join, heading down north-east through a farmstead and eventually reaching the road by the side of a large solitary house which advertises Bed & Breakfast.

*The tributary of the River Frome close by Stinsford—a pleasant waterside walk for both you and the cow.*

Ahead lies Puddletown Heath and Forest (Egdon Heath). Cross over the road and keep straight ahead on another footpath which takes you into the trees. After crossing the stile the most obvious track goes to the right and heads up a steep hill with a glorious view behind, before plunging into the main forest. After a circuitous route you come to a 5-way cross-roads and should take the first left for Hardy's birthplace.

This main forestry track is not, however, the proper footpath, nor is it very interesting. If you don't mind the risk of getting a little lost, the more appealing alternative is to follow the footpath marked on the OS map (it is not, unfortunately, marked so clearly on the ground!) If you opt for this route, bear left, after the stile, on an indistinct track which heads off into the bushes and through woods, skirting the edge of a large, cleared area of

forest to your right. Keep your bearing to a more or less constant north-north-west, and after a while, green, rolling countryside opens out on your left. From here walk straight on, bearing left when you have the option. The track takes you through a gate and skirts the side of a pond, eventually bringing you down the hill to Hardy's birthplace. These woods are well frequented with dog walkers who can put you on the right track, so if you lose the way don't panic!

Hardy's birthplace at Higher Bockhampton (Upper Mellstock) is a thatched cottage with a pretty garden now administered by the National Trust. It was built by Hardy's great-grandfather, John Hardy, in 1800 and we are told that it has been little altered since that time. Hardy presumably had fond memories of it, for he wrote:

'It faces west, and round the back and sides
High beeches, bending, hang a veil of boughs,
And sweep against the roof. Wild honey-sucks
Climb on the walls, and seem to sprout a wish
(If we may fancy wish of trees and plants)
To overtop the apple-trees hard by.'

Hardy lived in the cottage until he was 34; he then left to marry Emma Gifford. He wrote both *Under The Greenwood Tree* and *Far From The Madding Crowd* there, as well as several other part-works and poems. The garden is open daily from Good Friday to the end of October, but you can only see the interior by appointment with the Custodian (Tel: 0305 62366). The main parlour with its Portland flagstones

*The bridge near Lower Bockhampton—you turn left to carry on towards Hardy's cottage from here.*

mirrors the room used for the Christmas dance in Tranter Dewy's cottage in *Under The Greenwood Tree*, though one marvels at its tiny size.

Upstairs is the main bedroom where Hardy was born and at first thought to be dead; he went on to live for another 88 years. We are told he did his writing at the window seat of the adjoining room; looking at this cramped, uncomfortable space, one wonders how much more prolific he might have been with a modern day word processor! Beyond the third bedroom a steep ladder leads back down to the ground floor and the old kitchen where the NT have a number of Hardy related publications and a good selection of his novels on sale.

To return to Dorchester the route to Stinsford is possibly much the same as the one Hardy would have taken as a child on his regular six-mile round walk to the grammar school in Dorchester. Head on down the track past

the few houses of Upper Bockhampton to the road. Turn left here, and after about 50 yards bear right on a track past farm buildings. Just before you reach a modern barn, bear left through a gate with a yellow footpath sign. Walk down the right hand side of the field to another gate. Ignore the stile to the left which would take you on a footpath to Kingston Maurward, and instead veer diagonally right across the field, aiming to join the conspicuous bridleway track coming down from the right where it joins the road.

To avoid walking along the road, follow a footpath sign along the north side of the road which takes you as far as the gateway of Birkin House, after which you've a short walk of a couple of hundred yards on the road past the gatehouse entrance to the Dorset College of Agriculture before turning left on the road into Stinsford. Walk past the college's dairy farm with its large herd of very noisy goats and the

church of Stinsford—St Martin's—comes into view. Walk into the churchyard by the first gate and the Hardy tombstones are immediately to your left, in the shade of a yew tree, containing the remains of most of the family, and the great man's heart. A little further on stands a more modern gravestone for the poet Cecil Day Lewis.

The graveyard is a peaceful and pleasant place. When you're ready to move on, head on down towards the Frome tributary with a thatched cottage (on closer inspection this is quite a large house) on your right. When you reach the water turn right, heading directly towards Dorchester. The track brings you out on the A35 a short distance from Gray's Bridge which is mentioned in *Under the Greenwood Tree*, *Far from the Madding Crowd*, and *The Mayor of Casterbridge*. You then come to the bottom of High Street East from where it's a short walk back to your starting point.

# Walk 15: With Henry James in Rye

*Henry James (1843-1916) was born in Washington Place, New York. After travelling in Europe and settling in Paris and London for a while, he moved to Sussex in 1898 and lived at Lamb House in Rye. His skill as a writer of novels and short stories largely went unrecognised in his own lifetime; today he is widely regarded as having made a unique contribution to English literature.*

Henry James' grandfather was an Irishman who emigrated to America and became rich, indeed so rich that at his death he was found to be the second wealthiest man in New York State. The three million dollars that he left enabled his son, Henry James the elder, to travel extensively, to study religious philosophy and other works, and to bring up his children in a cultured atmosphere that included many trips back and forth across the Atlantic.

The house where Henry James the younger was born—Number 21 Washington Place—has long since been demolished, and of course New York has been transformed out of all recognition since his day. He went with his family to live in London, Paris, Geneva and other European towns and cities, picking up languages and schooling on the way before making a first solitary trip to Europe in 1869. By this time he had already written numerous short stories and articles which were published in American journals, and on a tour around southern England he was able to make the acquaintance of leading literary figures such as George Eliot, William Morris, Dante Gabriel Rossetti and John Ruskin.

After several intermittent trips to Europe over the next few years, James made the 'Great Decision' in 1875 to settle in Paris. It did not take him long, however, to conclude that he would be an 'eternal outsider' in Paris, and so, in December 1876, he moved to London from where a steady stream of novels and short stories flowed and were received by a limited but enthusiastic audience of admirers on both sides of the Atlantic. James also attempted to write for the theatre, but without much success. His stage version of *The American* lasted 70 nights in London, and at the premier of *Guy Domville* he was booed off the

**Henry James as painted by J.S. Sargent in 1913.** *Photo by NPG.*

stage having failed to compete with Oscar Wilde's *An Ideal Husband*, a play which James abhorred but which was then the hit of the town.

By 1896 James had decided to move out of London for his summers. Having become familiar with Sussex, he chose Rye on the edge of Romney Marsh, taking the lease on Lamb House in 1897 and buying it outright for £2,000 three years later. Built by Thomas Lamb in 1721, it had housed the Lamb family until 1864 and they had effectively ruled Rye

by providing the town mayor for much of that period. It had also accommodated royalty, for having beached his ship on nearby Camber Sands, King George I had stayed three nights in the house in 1726. When the last of the Lambs had died it was bought by a local banker, and from him it passed to Henry James who later described some of his first impressions of the house in a letter, using the verbose and flowery style that characterised his writing:

'I marked it for my own two years ago at Rye—so perfectly did it, the first instant I beheld it, offer the solution of my long-unassuaged desire for a calm retreat between May and November. It is the very calmest and yet cheerfullest that I could have dreamed—in the little old, cobble-stoned, grass-grown, re-roofed town, on the summit of its mildly pyramidal hill and close to its noble old church—the chimes of which sound sweet in my goodly old red-walled garden.'

Today you can see Lamb House much as it was in the time of the Lamb family. Henry James made few changes, and apart from the invasion of motor car traffic the only major difference to it and its surroundings is that the 'most delightful little old architectural garden-house, perched alongside of it on its high brick garden-wall' is no more. It was flattened by a German bomb in 1940, but photographs show that it was a beautiful structure.

James, who remained a bachelor all his life, became a familiar figure around Rye, bicycling and walking over the surrounding flat marshland accompanied by his pet dog. He

*The walk towards Winchelsea follows a maze of drainage ditches and canals.*

was visited by many of the literati of the day—H.G. Wells, Hilaire Belloc and Rudyard Kipling amongst them—and lived in style with a butler, cook, gardener, housekeeper, parlour maid and housemaid. He also continued to maintain an apartment in London where he preferred to spend the coldest months, but despite this he was not a rich man—his grandfather's fortune has been dissipated by numerous descendants, and although his writing supported him and paid the bills it never appealed to the mass public or brought him fortune during his lifetime.

By this time James had taken to dictating his work to secretaries, working in the garden-house or 'temple of the Muse' in summer, and in an indoor study if he was at the house in winter. The popular writer E.F. Benson—later famed for his novels *Dodo* and *Lucia*—visited Henry James in Rye on several occasions, and indeed took on the lease of Lamb House after the great man died,

inheriting the Lamb tradition by becoming mayor of Rye in 1934. In Benson's last autobiography *Final Edition* there are several reminiscences of life at Lamb House with Henry James, starting with a description of his morning routine:

'He disappeared next morning after a preoccupied breakfast to a room built in the time of George II, which stood in the garden . . . When Henry James had withdrawn himself here for his morning's work, none might disturb him, and as lunch time approached one sat in the garden by the steps waiting for him to emerge, and could hear his voice booming and pausing and booming again, as he moved up and down the book-lined room dictating the novel on which he was at work to the typist . . . Such at this time was his mode of composition: he made elaborate notes of the course of his story and with these in his hand he

spoke his pages . . . The effect was of a tapestry of speech being audibly designed and executed.'

In the autumn of 1914, as the First World War got under way, James left Lamb House for London, never to return. He took British citizenship the following July for a variety of reasons—not least because he disliked being considered an 'alien' in wartime and was annoyed by the United States' refusal to help fight against Germany. Three months later he suffered a stroke; a second stroke followed, and having heard the news that he had been awarded the Order of Merit by King George V (he is said to have told the housemaid to 'Turn off the light so as to spare my blushes') he died on 28th February 1916.

His funeral service was held in Chelsea Old Church where a memorial tablet celebrates him today, and according to his wishes his ashes were interred in the family

*Above:* **Nearing Winchelsea an occasional footpath signpost helps you on your way.**

*Left:* **The beautiful church in the centre of Rye, close by Lamb House.**

grave in America. His reputation virtually died with him, and it was many years before he was recognised as one of England and America's finest novelists. Ownership of Lamb House passed to his nephew, another Henry James, who never lived there but let it to E.F. Benson and several others; on his death his widow presented the house and its garden to the National Trust.

## Bibliography

Henry James's novels are concerned with the detailed mores of society and the interaction between its members, most notably the meeting of the old world of Europe and the new world of America. Among the most highly regarded are *Roderick Hudson* (1875), *The American* (1877), *The Portrait of a Lady* (1881), *The Spoils of Poynton* (1897); and *The Wings of the Dove* (1902), *The Ambassadors* (1903), and *The Golden Bowl* (1904), all completed at Lamb House. His most famous shorter work is the psychological ghost story, *Turn of the Screw*, which has been made into a film and translated into an opera with great success by Benjamin Britten.

Among numerous biographies *Henry James and His World* by Harry T. Moore (Thames & Hudson) gives useful background information and is illustrated with contemporary photos; E.F. Benson's *Final Edition* (Hogarth) is a very good read with amusing anecdotes concerning Rye, Lamb House, and Henry James.

*Looking down the quiet street towards Lamb House.*

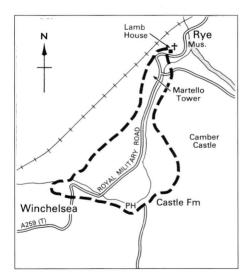

## A Walk with Henry James

**Map:** OS Landranger 189.
**Start:** Lamb House (NT) on the corner of West Street, Rye—OS Grid Ref. 920203. Park by the main BR station. Lamb House is open April to end October, Wednesday and Saturday 2–6 pm.
**Nearest BR Station:** Rye.
**Distance:** 6 miles.
**Time:** At least 3 hours.
**Facilities:** Shops, cafés, pubs, etc. in Rye; tea and coffee houses in Winchelsea; pub on A259 at bottom of Winchelsea hill.
**Summary:** An easy walk over the flat country which separates Rye from Winchelsea. The latter is well worth a visit, and the maze of drainage canals you encounter on the way hosts all kinds of wildlife.

From Lamb House turn left downhill, heading down West Street to the High Street. Turn right and then left down Market Road which will bring you to the busy Cinque Ports Street. From here go left, following the A259 road sign to Hastings. The road passes round the back of the canal basin with footpath signs pointing off to the right either side of the canal. Ignore these and walk on another 30 yards or so round to the left, where you follow the next footpath sign off to the right.

This leads you in a virtually straight line across the flatlands between Rye and Winchelsea. Keep following the footpath signs which are clearly indicated both by arrows and yellow waymarks. Most of the way you follow the route of a drainage ditch or canal, with the occasional swan paddling along amidst the

rushes. The fields inland are mostly cultivated, while to the left lies grazing land for sheep. Be warned, sheep do figure largely on this walk and you must be prepared to keep a dog under close control, particularly in the spring lambing season.

The path follows a raised, grassy bank for a time, and when the canal to your right dries out you keep on ahead across a bridge. From here the way becomes somewhat confusing with a number of footpath signs indicating tracks which don't appear on the OS map. Basically you keep straight on for Winchelsea, following the path as it bends right round the perimeter of a field, carrying straight on at a four-way footpath sign, and keeping on round the edge of the field as you make towards the right side of Winchelsea hill.

Head over towards the caravan park at the base of the hill, making for the old stone bridge where you join a minor road. Turn left to cross over the bridge, walking along the lane for 50 yards until you join the main A259 road on a hairpin bend at the base of the hill. On this bend turn right onto a track that passes a waterworks/sewage station on the left. Keep along the track which goes over a small bridge before bearing left round the bottom of Winchelsea hill, which on this northern side is well covered by trees with flat country away to the right.

Keep bearing round the side of the hill to the left, walking uphill and going over a stile. Keep on uphill through pasture land, following a sunken track that bears round to the left all the time. Eventually you come to the top of the hill by a tumulus with the remains of a recently ruined windmill on the top. There's also a trig point here, and if you climb up you get a fine view to the north-west, looking out over the plains towards Udimore.

From here follow the track on up until it levels out and passes a fine house on the left. Cross the A259 with care, and go straight ahead into Winchelsea's quiet streets. You almost immediately come to a tea house on the right and a little further there's one to the left—we tried the latter which is called the Manna Plat Coffee House and found it very pleasant. Indeed, all of Winchelsea appears quaint and attractive, and in parts gives the impression of a village without cars which is a rare luxury today. It has a museum and other points of interest, and will almost certainly reward an exploratory walk.

From Manna Plat go on down to the bottom of the street where you will find a footpath sign pointing left. This leads you down a narrow path between well trimmed hedges, and then on down a narrow flight of steps which brings you to the bottom of the hill by the infernal A259. Cross over onto the opposite pavement taking great care, and turn right past the pub on the corner, carrying straight on ahead over the bridge and onto a minor road which is signposted to West Beach. Walk on down this road which has a pavement all the way, following it for approximately half a mile. The road bends left and then abruptly right, with a sign advising drivers '10 mph Maximum'.

Here you go straight ahead onto a track which is a bridleway/footpath. Ignore a footpath signpost heading across fields to the right a little further on, and carry straight on towards Castle Farm, bearing onto the right track where it forks right and left by a gate to pass in front of the farm buildings, heading away from the canal which you have been following.

Beyond the farm buildings go through a gate just past the last animal pen—a goat lived there when we last walked by. Where the track forks left and right take the left fork for Camber Castle, following the clearly defined way across flat grassland. The castle looks at its best from a distance. Close to we found it surrounded by a high wire fence with a gaggle of municipal-style sheds and a sign saying it was closed for restoration, with no indication of when it might reopen.

A hundred yards or so before you reach the castle you come to a gate and a stile with yellow footpath arrows pointing left, right and straight on. The right hand footpath passes close to the castle, but thereafter becomes extremely difficult to follow, with a maze of drainage canals cutting off the direct route. Instead take the left hand direction, following a clear track which goes along the side of a

waterway on your right. When you come to the main canal where the houses start on the outskirts of Rye, bear left over a stile towards it—don't bear right with the track which continues to follow the other waterway in the wrong direction.

From here walk along the side of the main canal towards Rye. It's a very pretty walk with the gardens of the houses on the opposite bank all running down to the water's edge. Aim towards a solitary, white house on the right bank, and when you reach it follow the narrow track past its left hand side—here a gaggle of geese and chickens sent us on our way. Go over a stile and through a gate, and a short way on you come to the lock gates for Rye harbour. Turn left over the lock gates bridge which brings you onto the A259 once again; turn right and retrace your steps into Rye.

*The ruins of Camber Castle—less impressive when you get close by and find they've got the builders in.*

# Walk 16: With George Bernard Shaw in Ayot St Lawrence

*George Bernard Shaw (1856–1950) earns the title as the longest-surviving writer in this book, finally leaving us at the age of 94 when he was still writing furiously. A larger than life playwright, letter writer, music critic, drama critic, wit, philosopher, socialist and Nobel Prize winner, G.B.S. spent the last 44 years of his life in Ayot St Lawrence.*

G.B.S. chose Ayot St Lawrence for the strangest of reasons. If you look among the graves in the 'new' churchyard, one tombstone is to the memory of 'Mary Anne South. Born 1825. Died 1895. Her time was short . . .'. Seventy years didn't seem bad for a 'short' lifespan, and therefore the great dramatist decided to move to the New Rectory of Ayot St Lawrence in 1906, bettering Mary Anne South's lifespan by 24 years.

His longevity may, in part, be attributable to his diet—he was a committed vegetarian and never drank coffee, tea or spirits. He was also a Quaker, a Fabian and an exceptionally hard worker whose output included over 50 plays and a most voluminous and amusing correspondence. He gave over 1000 lectures airing his beliefs which included women's rights, equality of income, the abolition of private property, and the simplification of the English alphabet. He was working hard until his final illness, brought on by a fall from a ladder while pruning a greengage tree in his garden at the age of 94.

The New Rectory, built in 1902, passed into Shaw's hands in 1906 when it was put up for sale (the Rector could not afford to maintain it). Although he objected to being besieged by fans, Shaw was not above changing the name of his new home to Shaw's Corner, and advertising the fact conspicuously on the corner gate:

'Our blacksmith, master of his function,
Has on my iron gate enscrolled
SHAW'S CORNER up in letters bold.'

At first sight Shaw's Corner is a rather unexciting and bourgeois red brick house of the

**GBS as remembered in satirical form by H Furniss.** *Photo by NPG.*

type built in the home counties for the well-to-do—better suited to a bank manager than a great socialist and playwright. Once inside, however, the house is full of light and extremely pleasant, and with its fine views southwards, few would refuse the opportunity to live in such a place which is so much more homely than Rudyard Kipling's gloomy great mansion in East Sussex, Bateman's.

Shaw's study and airy drawing room are on view, as is the dining room where he died

together with its line-up of portraits of those whom one assumes were his heroes—Ibsen, Gandhi, Lenin and Stalin are among the more recognisable faces, although he might have readjusted his opinion of the latter given time. The front vestibule has an amusing collection of G.B.S.'s printed refusal cards, which he used to turn down supplications for money, requests for prefaces, invitations to open fêtes, to lecture, or to sign books and a host of other things. The kitchen has a well thumbed copy of the G.B.S. vegetarian cookery book, and a good collection of books relating to G.B.S. is on sale in the hall next to his memorably large collection of hats.

The modest gardens are also extremely pleasant and contain Shaw's writing cabin which is reminiscent of Virginia Woolf's at Monks House, but on a more austere scale. At the top of the orchard are four, white, cottage-style beehives—don't walk in front of them as they're packed with busy bees; honey is on sale in the house.

The verse above about the blacksmith and Shaw's Corner is taken from Shaw's last completed work, *The Rhyming Picture Guide to Ayot St Lawrence*, which is light hearted and makes a welcome accompaniment to an enjoyable walk around the neighbourhood. Shaw's own photographs of the village illustrate his work and show that, thankfully, the area does not appear to have changed much since his day. After commenting on a few aspects of the village, he moves on to the 'Old Church' with photographs revealing the inside (we are not allowed through the locked gate today). The story of this church's decay is a strange one. Sir Leonard Lyde who was Lord of the Manor in the 1770s objected to its presence because it blocked his view. He therefore adopted the

*Above:* **The old church at Ayot St Lawrence, partly demolished by Sir Leonard Lyle 'But not until the desecration was patent to all observation'.**

*Facing page:* **Part of the woodland walk leading from Ayot St Lawrence towards Ayot Greenway—be prepared to meet the occasional horse on this bridleway route.**

*Left:* **Shaw's Corner as seen from the front garden—an unpretentious but eminently pleasant house for the great man to live in and pen such lines as 'No dwelling place can rival Ayot; So there I labour at my job— and boil my kettle on the hob . . .'**

simplest solution and began pulling it down! The Bishop of Lincoln heard of this, and issued an injunction to prevent the demolition before it had gone too far—and that is how it remains today in a semi-ruined state.

To compensate, Sir Leonard Lyde built the 'new church' in 1778, a most impressive Palladian building (at the front at least) designed by Nicholas Revett, a Grecian enthusiast who also designed the porch of Trafalgar House in London with columns in exactly the same style. Shaw comments at length on this strange new church:

'Look west; and in amazement spy
Where partly hidden by the greenery
A Grecian temple dares defy
Our taste for medieval scenery . . .'

A few lines further on Shaw refers to the Bishops' injunction as Sir Leonard attempted to knock down the old church:

'The Bishop who alone o'ertopped him
Woke up at last and firmly stopped him;
But not until the desecration
Was patent to all observation;
And he, poor soul who meant so well,
Learnt he was on the way to hell . . .'

Finally on the new replacement:

'Christopher Wren who, untaught, yet
Designed St Paul's in the metropolis
Taught his best pupil Nick Revett
To found his art on the Acropolis;
So Nick designed this fane Palladian
To cure our ancient tastes Arcadian.'

Shaw's rhyming tour of Ayot St Lawrence also takes us to the pub, the surrounding countryside, and many buildings in the village including one which he describes as a 'Swedish pre-fab':

'Swedes: come not here to shew your sheds off.
Our builders can pre-fab your heads off . . .'

He reports in verse and photographs on the manor houses both old and new. The one you see from the new church on this walk is Ayot St Lawrence House, the 'new' red brick Georgian Mansion whose past inhabitants include a Mrs Cunliffe who lived to the age of 100—another tribute to the longevity of those who live in the village! It is now divided into flats, and the old manor house is behind it. This Tudor red brick building has in its time, played host to Henry VIII, Anne Boleyn, and Catherine Parr. Shaw reports on a walkers' right of way up the driveway past it, which has strangely disappeared today:

'Ayot Park Gate. Its owners boss it;
But we have right of way across it.'

The *Rhyming Picture Guide* dwells for a number of pages on Shaw's Corner, before concluding with this envoy:

'No dwelling place can rival Ayot;
So there I labour at my job
And boil my kettle on the hob
Deeming I have the best of reasons
For staying here through all the seasons.'

The envoy also mentions briefly Apsley Cherry-Garrard, who along with T.E. Lawrence was a close friend of Shaw's and a frequent visitor at Shaw's Corner. He had accompanied Scott on his final journey to the South Pole, and was a member of the search party which discovered their bodies. He lived at Lamer House, to the south-west of Ayot St Lawrence, from where he walked over the park to see Shaw, removing his muddy shoes before entering as required by Mrs Shaw. Unfortunately the old house was demolished and replaced by a more modern house in 1947 when Cherry-Garrard left it as he was no longer able to afford the maintenance. However, the footpaths conveniently run right past its site, and along the route Cherry-Garrard would have taken.

## Bibliography

Shaw's best known plays include *Arms and the Man, The Devil's Disciple, Mrs Warren's Profession, Man and Superman, Major Barbara, Androcles and the Lion, Pygmalion* and *St Joan*. His many other published works range from *The Perfect Wagnerite* to *The Intelligent Woman's Guide to Socialism and Capitalism*.

Shaw's wonderful *Rhyming Picture Guide to Ayot St Lawrence* was published by The Leagrave Press of Luton and is on sale at Shaw's Corner. His most recent biographer is Michael Holroyd who has written an immense work on the great man.

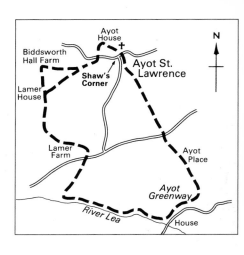

## A Walk with George Bernard Shaw

**Map:** OS Landranger 166.
**Start:** Shaw's Corner (National Trust) at Ayot St Lawrence just west of Welwyn in Hertfordshire—OS Grid Ref. 194167. Shaw's Corner is open from Easter until the end of October, Wednesday to Saturday 2-6 pm. Sunday and Bank Holiday Mondays 12-6 pm.
**Nearest BR Station:** Welwyn North.
**Distance:** 6½ miles.
**Time:** Allow 3 hours.
**Facilities:** Pub in Ayot St Lawrence.
**Summary:** A pleasant, easy walk through fine Home Counties' countryside, starting and finishing in the small hamlet where Shaw lived and where his house can be visited.

Ayot St Lawrence is only about 30 miles from the centre of London, but it is in the middle of very quiet and rather fine archetypal English countryside. It is also quite difficult to find! From Junction 6 of the A1 drive into Welwyn and turn right through the village until you come to a mini roundabout on the outskirts. Here you turn left onto a narrow road which is signposted as being unsuitable for wide vehicles.

Shaw's Corner is past the pub and the old church at the southern end of what is now a very rich hamlet. You can't miss the house because 'Shaw's Corner' is stamped in large, cast iron letters on the corner gates. There's a reasonably sized car park for visitors to the house, and with careful timing you should be able to combine this visit with a pleasant walk and a drink, or perhaps some food at The Brocket Arms which is also worth a visit.

*The new church of 1778, designed by Grecian enthusiast 'Nick Revett' on the outskirts of Ayot St Lawrence.*

From Shaw's Corner turn right down the hill. Where the road bends left with open fields beyond, you will see a bridleway sign indicating a narrow track to the left. Walk down this track which at first has high hedges on both sides. Follow it along passing woods on the right, and then go through some woods which brings you to a quiet road. Cross over here, turning left and immediately right onto the bridleway which continues in much the same direction with large woods on the left and open fields to the right broken by the occasional clump of trees.

Since it is a bridleway this track could be muddy in wet weather. Keep following it, going through woods and emerging where a big field stretches away to the left. At the end of this field you will find an old railway bridge. Turn right up onto the railway track which is marked as a local right of way despite not being shown as one on the OS map. The railway lines have long since gone on what must have been a memorably pretty train ride, and you follow it on foot up a long cutting to the next bridge at Ayot Greenway.

Here a slight scramble is required to climb up onto the bridge where you join a footpath that crosses over it. Turn left (south) from the railway, crossing a farm track with an old barn immediately on your left and a farmhouse to the right beyond it. From here the footpath goes straight down across the field ahead, although when I walked it there was no footpath sign or any indication of a footpath across the field. Walk on down past woods on the left, with the chimneys of an old house more or less ahead and the main road in sight on the other side of the valley. At the bottom of the field bear right round a fence, continuing down to the left with the 'House' marked on the OS map appearing very close. A narrow path which is at first difficult to spot heads down a short hill by the side of the fence, taking you out of the field and soon bringing you down to a track running along the side of the River Lee or 'Lea'.

Here you can turn left and visit the ford at Water End by the side of the splendidly situated Gothic 'House' where you may like to wash your feet—it's a pleasant spot, though

in fine weather likely to be crowded by cars. To resume, head back along the track which follows the river eastwards, though the water is mostly hidden and only glimpsed in a few places where you can walk down to its edge. Keep on ahead, and where the track divides go straight on and right up the side of woods. The track continues past a hillside to the right; the water meadows to the left would make a pleasant spot for a picnic, and you can get to them via a narrow track through the bushes about halfway along.

Keep on ahead, passing over a stile where a sign tells you that the herd in the field is brucellosis free. Walk along with the track coming close to the river for the last time before it bears away to the left, with a busy road coming into sight ahead. Here you turn right uphill away from the stile ahead, going under power cables and heading for a stile in the top corner of the field. Go over this stile and join a wide track where you bear left, and then come to a gate where you have to squeeze round the left side. Turn right, heading a little east of north up the wide track ahead, and keep straight on in this direction until you come to a road. You pass a crossing track with a sign saying the landowner has given permission to use it, and pass through woods before coming into the open with fields to the right and what appears to be a higgledy-piggledy tree nursery fenced in on the left. Keep on ahead, ignoring two round stepping logs by a gate to the left and walking along the side of the fence until you see large green metal gates where you join the road.

Cross straight over the road, following the footpath sign along the side of woods on the left by a tall metal fence with a cleared area which one presumes is a pheasant run. At the far end of the woods on the left, just before a clump of woods on the right, turn left through a high security gate in the corner of the fence. Walk on ahead with the woods on your left and a square clearing ringed by woods to the right, and follow the track into woods ahead. This leads you out into the open by a crossing track with the somewhat ruined buildings of Lamer Farm over to the left. Go straight ahead here along a narrow track which follows a line of trees on the right, and then bears right at a stile into more woods ahead.

Walk on through these woods, and then leave them at another high security gate ahead where you turn right on a metalled track. Continue along the track with a fine view of an avenue of well planted trees coming into sight on the right. The track bears round to the right following the edge of the woods by the well hidden buildings of Lamer House, and this is

*The riverside close by the splendid Gothick 'House'—along here there are several good spots for picnics.*

the direct route back to Ayot St Lawrence. If you want to extend the walk a little further, as I did, you can continue ahead to the far side of the clearing. The footpath runs along the side of the fence in front of the stable block that belonged to the old Lamer House—an imposing building in a fine situation, though not helped by the addition of modern sliding French windows. Keep on ahead through a gate and along the side of the woods on the left. At the far end of the clearing ignore the stile which leads to Bibbsworth Hall Farm straight ahead, and walk over to a stile on the right, following a narrow track along the side of trees which converges with the other track heading for Ayot St Lawrence.

Where you meet the main track, follow the yellow footpath sign straight ahead, ignoring the track bearing left into trees. A short way on you come to yellow footpath signs pointing left and straight on. Go left here, up over a stile, and along the edge of a field where you join a lane. From here turn right and Shaw's Corner is a short distance away. It's worth going a bit further, however, following the lane for about 50 yards and then taking the footpath sign pointing left to the 'new' church of St Lawrence. This is a strange building, made even stranger by the prosaic terrace of cottages just behind it. Walk round the back to the far side of it and you come to a cast iron gate with a path leading to the front of the church, revealing its fine Greek portico in perfect Palladian style and small, walled grave-yard.

When you've finished browsing round this splendid church, turn right, out through the kissing gate, and join a path which runs along the side of the field, passing Ayot House, an early Georgian red brick mansion which is over to the left. You soon come to the road by a white cottage, where you may like to turn left and try The Brocket Arms pub, a Tudor, black and white, half-timbered building with a wide choice of beers, good food served in large portions, and a very extensive garden. Sunday lunchtime is predictably very busy, with last orders for drink and food at 2 pm.

Just opposite the pub is the ruined old church of Ayot St Lawrence, a romantic sight—the gate is locked, presumably because it is in a dangerous condition. From here Shaw's Corner is a short distance away, at the other end of the hamlet.

# Walk 17: With Sir Henry Newbolt at Orchardleigh

*Sir Henry Newbolt (1862–1938) must rate as one of the most rousing and patriotic English poets of all time, chiefly remembered for such stirring works as* Drake's Drum, The Fighting Temeraire *and* Vitai Lampada *which brought him fame when they were published as* Admirals All and Other Verses *in 1897.*

When you're in the mood, *Drake's Drum* with its curious use of the colloquial 'et' can be quite rousing:

'Take my drum to England, hang et by the shore,
Strike et when your powder's runnin' low;
If the Dons sight Devon, I'll quit the port o'Heaven,
An' drum them up the Channel as we drummed them long ago.'

And I must also confess to liking *Vitai Lampada*, despite loathing any notion of team activities:

'There's a breathless hush in the Close to-night—
Ten to make and the match to win—
A bumping pitch and a blinding light,
An hour to play and the last man in.
And it's not for the sake of a ribboned coat,
Or the selfish hope of a season's fame,
But his Captain's hand on his shoulder smote—
"Play up! play up! and play the game!"

The sand of the desert is sodden red,—
Red with the wreck of a square that broke—
The Gatling's jammed and the Colonel dead,
And the regiment blind with dust and smoke.
The river of death has brimmed its banks,
And England's far, and Honour a name,
But the voice of a schoolboy rallies the ranks:
'Play up! play up! and play the game!'

**Young Henry Newbolt as photographed in 1889.** *Photo courtesy of the Frome Society for Local Study.*

**The church at Orchardleigh where Henry Newbolt was married in 1889, and buried in 1938.**

Henry Newbolt was born at Bilston in Staffordshire where his father was the vicar. News of the Ashanti wars was imminent during his early school life and seems to have paved the way for the rousing poetry that followed:

'We expected fighting and we prepared for it: but we felt as mighty as the heroes and heroines in a great saga and trusted ourselves to Destiny with incredible confidence.'

He won a scholarship to Clifton College in Bristol (which also schooled Sir Arthur Quiller-Couch a few years later) where 'the public school spirit' was ingrained into him forever. Newbolt approved the concepts of service, self-sacrifice, courage and justice, and held to the Christian belief in good and evil. Despite being neither keen at cricket or football, he lived to 'play the game' for the rest of his life.

A classics scholarship to Oxford followed, by which time he was writing a fair amount of poetry in the style of Tennyson's *Morte D'Arthur*. On graduating he turned first to the law for a career and became a barrister, pursuing literary interests in his spare time and

THE DOG MONUMENT

THE ADJOINING MONUMENT, FORMERLY IN THE PARK,
COMMEMORATES AZOR, A FAITHFUL DOG OF SIR THOMAS S.
CHAMPNEYS, WHICH DIED IN 1796. AZOR'S DEVOTION TO
HIS MASTER, WHOSE DEATH AND BURIAL IN THE FAMILY
VAULT HERE HE IS SAID TO HAVE SHARED, INSPIRED SIR
HENRY NEWBOLT'S BALLAD 'FIDELE'S GRASSY TOMB'
WHICH HAS BROUGHT ORCHARDLEIGH LOCAL LITERARY
RENOWN. THE MONUMENT WAS RE-ERECTED BY LULLINGTON
AND ORCHARDLEIGH P.C.C. IN 1989 FOR ITS PRESERVATION
AND IN THANKSGIVING FOR THE LIFE OF ARTHUR
DUCKWORTH OF ORCHARDLEIGH, 1901~1986, THROUGH THE
GENEROSITY OF HIS WIDOW AND DAUGHTERS.

REVD. H. BENEDICT BAKER, M.A., RECTOR

FRED CHANT
MICHAEL McGARVIE, F.S.A.        CHURCHWARDENS

**The sign for the Dog Monument at Orchardleigh, commemorating the faithful Azor.**

analysing poems and plays in laborious depth.

Newbolt first set eyes on Margaret Duckworth in the autumn of 1887, when she boarded a reserved carriage on the train taking him and his friends for a holiday in North Devon. She was the daughter of the Rev. William Duckworth, owner of the impressive Orchardleigh estate near Frome in Somerset, and for a time it seemed that young Henry had set his sights rather far above his station. Despite liking the young man, the Rev. Duckworth regarded Newbolt as a relative pauper who was 'premature in marrying before he created a business at the bar'. However, after laborious negotiations he was generous enough to settle £300 a year on his daughter, and the marriage of Henry and Margaret took place at the beautiful small church by Orchardleigh lakeside on 15th August 1889.

Henry and his best man stayed at nearby Lullington on the eve of the wedding, walking down the hill from the house to the church. We are told that 45 guests attended the luncheon which followed, with 'about 300 tenants to tea in tent'. Forty-nine years later, when Henry died, he was buried in the island churchyard of the same church and is celebrated inside with lines from *Mors Janua* engraved on a tablet in the nave:

'Death is a gate, and holds no room within:
Pass—to the road beyond.'

Newbolt's literary 'break' came in 1897 with the publication of *Admirals All*. Following on four years after the success of Kipling's *Barrack Room Ballads*, Newbolt's collection of poems which mainly concerned Britain's heroic navy were described as 'Kipling without the Brutality' and succeeded brilliantly. Twenty-one editions of 1000 copies each were sold within a year, enabling the 35-year-old barrister to leave the law and become a full time writer. William Butler Yeats praised Newbolt in glowing terms: 'You have said many wise and true and beautiful things in rhyme. Yours is patriotism of a fine sort.'

The poetry and prose which followed enhanced his reputation, but could never equal the impact of *Drake's Drum*. He edited a literary journal known as *The Literary Review* which introduced him to most of the leading writers of the time—Walter de la Mer, Thomas Hardy, H.G. Wells and Rupert Brooke among them. When he was sacked for his Liberal tendencies, Newbolt began an association with the navy that led to his work as a naval historian and consultant to the Admiralty, an involvement recorded in poems such as *Songs of the Fleet*.

Famous as a man of letters, Newbolt was offered a knighthood by Mr Asquith at a dinner party in 1913—they were more casual in those days, and it is worth noting that Henry James was also present. Sir Henry's poetic output was limited at that time and is best remembered by his short but powerful poem *A Perpetual Memory, Good Friday 1915*:

'Broken and pierced, hung on the bitter wire,
By their most precious death the Sons of Man
Redeem for us the life of our desire—
O Christ how often since the world began!'

Sir Henry and his wife spent a great deal of time at Orchardleigh. He went shooting, and swam in the lake, as recorded in August 1890: 'This morning I bathed in the lake . . . it was a bit of a Fairyland—glassy waters, kingfishers, trees full of blue mist, sunlight on everything and silence everywhere.' He also used the house and its history for the basis of his novel *The Old Country* which was a great success when it was published in 1906. The story concerns a young man who travels back through time at Orchardleigh to visit his ancestors in the Middle Ages, although the name of the house was changed as Newbolt explained to the Reverend Duckworth:

'I regret the necessity for the name "Gardenleigh" which is not nearly as beautiful as "Orchardleigh": but the public must be kept at bay, and I could not use the real name of your house without your permission.'

In one of his late letters Sir Henry wrote, 'my real ambition is to leave some poems—enough of them to make a lasting change in men's ideas of Time and Eternity'. He did not have time for poetry, however, when he was busy with writing projects that ranged from an official history of naval operations to King George V's first broadcast speech on the radio (from Bognor Regis in 1935). He also spent time promoting younger poets—of Edward Thomas he wrote 'He loved his country—he did not so much inhabit England as haunt it'. Sir Henry's last poem, *The Star In The West*, was written in 1932, six years before his death. It was one of his bleakest with none of the jauntiness of *Drake's Drum*; with the last verse he foresaw that war was again inevitable:

'Dare not to ask!—unless ye dare also to hear
The story of his cross, the first and second death—
That men have murdered Night, and made stars of their own,
And flung them down from heav'n, and peace has died by fire.'

## Bibliography

*Selected Poems of Henry Newbolt* edited by Patrick Dickinson is published by Hodder & Stoughton and includes *Admirals All*.

*Sir Henry Newbolt and Orchardleigh* by Michael McGarvie (Frome Society for Local Study) is a booklet with anecdotes from Orchardleigh, and a detailed investigation of the connection between the Dog Monument in Orchardleigh churchyard and Sir Henry's poem *Fidele's Grassy Tomb*.

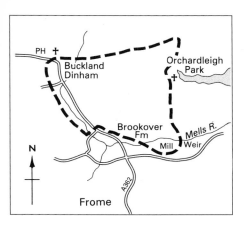

## A Walk with Sir Henry Newbolt

**Map:** OS Landranger 183.
**Start:** The church at Buckland Dinham—OS Grid Ref. 755513. Parking on roadside.
**Nearest BR Station:** Frome.
**Distance:** 5 miles.
**Time:** Allow 3 hours.
**Facilities:** Pub in Buckland Dinham.
**Summary:** A walk through Orchardleigh Park, home of Sir Henry Newbolt's father-in-law and owned by the family until 1988; the small church at Orchardleigh where Sir Henry was wedded and buried is in a most memorable setting.

Buckland Dinham is a small village on the A362 about one and a half miles north of Frome. There is plenty of room to park by the old church, and if you feel like a drink try the pleasant looking pub further on up the main road.

A narrow path runs down the side of the church, with an unusual footpath sign telling you it is the way to Lullington. Walk down the right side and over a stile, entering a field where an old faded sign informs you that all dogs off the lead will be shot. (There is no obvious reason why such drastic measures need be taken but it's possibly not worth taking the risk.) From here you get a good view of the way you will be going which is effectively more or less straight ahead—down the hill, across a field passing three isolated trees which you can't see from this point, and heading up the side of some woods into more woods beyond.

Go downhill across the field, heading for the bottom left corner where a bridge goes over a stream. From here go straight ahead towards three enormous oaks, cutting the corner of the field as shown on the OS map or walking round the side if more convenient.

The path continues ahead towards the woods running along an unploughed strip that crosses the next field. Continue on through a gate, ignoring openings to fields on the right and left, and then walk slightly uphill along the side of the next field on a path which I found undisturbed by ploughing, with woods on your left.

Go over a stile into the woods, and then follow a pleasant woodland trail straight ahead. You pass pheasant enclosures on the left, ignoring all diversions and keeping straight on until you reach a gate just past some agricultural buildings over to the right. Here you come into the main park, with a wide expanse of beautifully planted trees ahead of you and farmland over to the left. Walk ahead over the grass until you join the main tarmac drive, and continue in a very attractive setting, drawing near to the old stable block. When I last visited this it was in a state of disrepair, but by the time you try this walk it may have been converted into some ghastly executive hideaway since the whole place has recently been sold to a hotel/golf course consortium by the Duckworth family. The footpaths, however, will remain inviolate.

Just by the stable a sign points right to Orchardleigh Church. Follow the track down the side of the stables, heading downhill past the long yew hedge which encircles the main house not yet in view. Parkland and glimpses of the lake are visible to your left as you keep on downhill towards a lodge where you bear left with the track, soon coming to the tiny church which is in an incredibly beautiful position.

The church is ringed by a moat, and on the far side a lily pond stretches out before it with the simple graves of Sir Henry and his wife near the water's edge, marked by two small stone tablets laid on the ground. The 'Dog Monument' (to a poodle named Azor who died in 1796) is the large urn on a pedestal behind them, just by the church door. This is a wonderful place, and it's well worth walking round to the far side of the pond for a glimpse of the church from the far side. I met several locals who frequently walk here—their return route took them round the pond to reconnect with the outward route from Buckland Dinham. This way is not shown as a footpath on the OS map, but they were adamant that they had walked it for many years and would continue to do so—good luck to them!

The longer route which I took back heads straight up the steep hill from the church, passing the strange stone block on the left which is all that remains of the original Orchardleigh Park House which was demolished in 1860 by William Duckworth, a Lancashire lawyer who had bought the bankrupt estate and built the new house on the far side of the lake. Head

*The stables of Orchardleigh House—with plans to change the whole estate into a golf course/executive hideaway, things may have changed for the worse by the time you get there.*

*Above:* **Some of the fine broad leaf trees of Orchardleigh Park.**

*Left:* **The small island church. The Dog Monument which inspired 17 verses of 'Fidele's Grassy Tomb' is by the entrance porch.**

*Above:* **The view down to the church at Orchardleigh while walking up the hillside. The stone in the foreground is all that remains of the old manor which was demolished in 1860 to be replaced by the new house (top right behind the trees), built by the prosperous William Duckworth in 1856-58. The stable can be seen beyond the church; the large lake is hidden by the trees.**

*Right:* **The lily pond next to the church, close by where Sir Henry and his wife are buried.**

*The end of the walk—trudging up the final field a few hundred yards from the road that runs through Buckland Dinham.*

up towards a stile at the top of the hill, and as you gain height a fine view opens out behind you, from the church in the valley to the massive main house of Orchardleigh Park. Go over the stile to leave the park, and walk on along the side of the field ahead, crossing a stile and following a narrow path through trees which brings you downhill to a track following the left side of another field. Follow this well defined track ahead, passing to the left of a second belt of trees and coming to two immovable 'gates' that have to be climbed over or through before crossing the River Mells by a couple of closely spaced bridges by the old weir.

The signposting on the next part of the walk is non-existent, but be assured that the route follows the footpaths shown on the OS map. The only sign I saw said 'This Is Not A Footpath' which is remarkably unhelpful. Continue along the lane ahead, with the mill which has been turned into a modern house on your right. Carry on towards the road, and just before you reach it turn right on a sharp left hand bend by a house on the corner. There is no footpath sign to show the way here, but a wide track runs down the side of the house, crosses a cattle grid, and then bears right across a field towards a solitary, low-standing house close to the river. Where the

track bears right you leave it—again there is no sign—and continue straight ahead across the grass, looking for a bridge (with stiles at both ends) in the trees ahead which will take you across the stream. From here you go across the next field to the next more easily spotted bridge which takes you to the front of Brookover Farm, a place which is used as a horseriding centre. Turn left along the drive away from the farm, and you soon come down to the road by the south entrance lodge to Orchardleigh Park.

From the lodge turn right along the A362. You have about 200 yards of walking on what is a busy, narrow, and therefore unpleasant road. Walk towards the traffic for safety, and take care on the blind bend about halfway along.

Five minutes' walking brings you to the top of the hill where you take the first left signpost to Elliotts, heading steeply downhill on a quiet lane that leads you away from the nightmare of the road. Go past a few modern conversions of old buildings and over a stream, and a little further on just before the lane bends left there is a gate on the right with a stepping stone in the wall which signifies a footpath. Go over it and walk down towards the stream, crossing the field diagonally towards the next stile. From here on the footpath

follows close to the side of the stream most of the way to Buckland Dinham, and the church where you started soon comes into view on the hillside ahead to the right.

There are several stiles to negotiate on the way—to my way of thinking they are rather 'excuses' for stiles since their design is so appalling! Continue walking across the fields which are well protected from the noise of the road hidden on the hillside above, and after a time you will see a line of houses ahead with the footpath clearly going between them as the river bears away to the right. Walk on, crossing a lane and going straight over the stile ahead and uphill across a grassy field. Bear over to the left to cross the next stile, and carry on uphill by the side of a blackberry hedge as the ground gradually becomes level.

Cross a stepping stone in the wall ahead, and walk along a tarmacked path by modern houses on the outskirts of Buckland Dinham, heading down to the main road. This must be crossed with great caution, and one doesn't envy the residents of the village who have to do it every day. From here you can turn left to the pub, or go right on a raised pathway which bears left away from the road and brings you back to the church via some more modern houses. All in all it's a very pleasant walk, despite the horrors of the A362.

# Walk 18: With Sir Arthur Quiller-Couch in Fowey

*Sir Arthur Quiller-Couch (1863–1944), whose well-known pseudonym was a plain 'Q', is inextricably linked with Fowey, the Cornish harbour town, residing on and off at 'The Haven' from 1892 until his death. He was a prodigious writer, producing both original and edited work; a leading figure in Cornwall's public and political affairs; and a distinguished lecturer at Cambridge for some 32 years.*

Fowey, pronounced 'Foy', is situated at the bottom of a steep and very narrow road. Cars and lorries can only get down to it with difficulty, and therefore it has been spared one of the worst products of our century—traffic congestion. You can walk along its streets in relative safety, and one imagines that the buildings in this quaint town have changed little since Sir Arthur's early days.

Fowey was already an important port in the thirteenth century when Henry III granted it a charter to provide provisions for warships and their sailors. In the fourteenth century it was a trading port and the point of embarkation for religious pilgrims bound for Spain; it continued to play its part in the war games of those times with 47 ships and 770 men sent to take part in the siege of Calais in 1346. The 'Fowey Gallants' were a lawless lot who amused themselves by raiding the French coastline. When our French friends objected, a return match in 1456 resulted in half of Fowey being burnt down. Edward IV then sent instruction to the 'Gallants' not to attack their French cousins—they replied by cutting off both his messenger's ears!

In the sixteenth century Fowey continued to play a major role in naval warfare. Henry VIII forced the monks to leave and paid off two big local families; the Treffreys built St Catherine's Castle on the headland with the proceeds, and the Rashleighs were rewarded by the Menabilly Peninsula. A little later in the history of the town John Rashleigh's ship *Frances of Foye* joined the fight against the Spanish Armada, having already sailed with Frobisher to the Arctic and Drake to the West Indies, acquiring a fortune for its owner on the way.

Fowey was hit by plague in the seven-

**'Q', as sketched by Henry Lamb in 1938.** *Photo by NPG.*

teenth century, and Sir John Treffrey made the mistake of volunteering the services of the town to support the King's losing side in the Civil War. In the years that followed things settled back to normal with pilchards, smuggling and the Napoleonic Wars all contributing to Fowey's healthy economy. Only in the nineteenth century did Fowey's importance as a 'war centre' come to an end, and the town's prosperity accordingly became dependent on trading, with schooners, barquentines and brigs coming and going from the harbour. The

eclipse of sail by steam roughly coincided with the birth of Arthur Quiller-Couch, and by that time Fowey had ceased to be a major port and had simply become a very pleasant place to live, as it is today.

'Q' was born in Bodmin where his father was a doctor, on 21st November 1863. On his father's Cornish side he was descended from the Quillers and the Couches (pronounced 'Cooch', or as Q would say 'Not like a sofa'). These families came from Polperro where many can be seen laid to rest in Talland churchyard:

'By Talland Church as I did go
I passed my kindred all in a row,
Straight and silent there by the spade
Each in his narrow chamber laid.'

In deference to his mother's Devonian blood he was first educated at the Newton Abbot 'School for the Sons of Gentlemen', and later went to Clifton where he beat Henry Newbolt in the first year school poetry prize—both literary 'Sirs' to be. He went on to Oxford where he lodged in Cardinal Newman's old rooms, and established a reputation as a dapper and sometimes extravagant dresser which stayed with him for the rest of his life. Kenneth Grahame later described him as 'even more beautifully dressed than formerly . . . Man, when he chooses to give his mind to it, is incomparably the finer animal of the two and does the greater justice to his clothes'. He was galled to discover that he only achieved a second class degree—what with choosing clothes and being captain of the college boat club there were too many diversions—but he

*Looking back along the coast path towards Fowey, the town which Q loved.*

made up for it in later life at Cambridge, becoming King Edward VII Professor of English Literature and a Fellow of Jesus College.

His first recorded visit to Fowey was in 1879. He fell in love with the place immediately, and from then on was a regular visitor during his holidays:

'I stood long and gazed on the harbour, the track of the moon on its water, the riding lights of two or three small schooners at anchor in the shadow of the farther shore, and decided that this were no bad place to live. And that is all I need to say . . . of an estuary the tides of which has since woven so close into the pulse of my own life that memory cannot now separate the rhythms.'

When his father died, he found it necessary to support his mother by working as a tutor on leaving Oxford. In the meantime, he was writing his first novel, *Dead Man's Rock*, and with sound commercial instinct he sent it to Cassell's which had recently published *Treasure Island* and *King Solomon's Mines* with considerable success. Being an adventure story of the same ilk it was immediately accepted, and appeared in print in 1887, selling extremely well. The reviewers of the day loved the little mystery of the pseudonym 'Q', with some hinting that the unknown author might even be the famous Stevenson or Rider-Haggard.

Troy—'a scene of disorder or confusion . . . a maze, a labyrinth of streets'—rhymes with 'Foy' and *The Astonishing History of Troy Town* was his next book to be published in 1888. This was a romantic farce based on the town and people of Fowey, a successful recipe which he later repeated in *The Mayor of Troy*, *Shining Ferry* and *Hocken and Hunken*.

In between producing a steady flow of novels, Q worked as a prolific journalist, editor and short story writer. He was at first based in London, spending a great deal of time on the Great Western Railway travelling down to Fowey when he would write on the train, frequently completing a short story on the way. The high spots of those years included his marriage in Fowey Parish Church in 1889, and the birth of his son, Bevil, in Fowey a year later. Then he collapsed with what would probably be diagnosed today as a nervous breakdown brought on by too much work. The doctor's simple and effective advice was for him to leave London and work by the sea. With his literary reputation established this was a comparatively easy move, and he made straight for Fowey, initially renting a small house in the town before finding The Haven some six months later in 1892.

'My calling ties me to no office stool, makes me no man's slave, compels me to no action that my soul condemns. It sets me free from town life which I loathe, and allows me to breathe clean air, to exercise limbs as well as brain, to tread good turf

*This walk offers a selection of beautiful beaches en route—this is the bay at Coombe Hawne.*

and wake up every morning to the sound and smell of the sea and that wide prospect which to my eyes is the dearest on earth.'

Aside from his writing Q went on to become a major figure in Fowey and Cornish public life. From 1912 he spent the term times in Cambridge, but nevertheless found time for many other callings: Chairman of the Cornwall Education Committee, dedicated to bringing better schooling to the area; a magistrate and Chairman of Fowey Harbour Commissioners; a hard working Liberal; and Mayor of Fowey in 1937. Public honours were showered on him—he was knighted in 1910, established as a Cornish bard with the title of 'Marhak Cough', and made a Freeman of Bodmin, Fowey and Truro.

The Haven played host to some famous people. J. M. Barrie was godfather to Q's daughter Foy, and Kenneth Grahame was a

frequent visitor who was married in Fowey, staying with his fiancée at The Haven while the banns were read and spending much of his honeymoon sailing on Q's yacht *Vida*. Fowey inspired the river settings of *The Wind in the Willows*, which began as a weekly letter to his son.

Apart from writing, Q's favourite pastimes were gardening and yachting. He crossed by boat to his garden and orchard, nicknamed 'The Farm', on the far side of the harbour entrance, and as a very active yachtsman he was for many years Commodore of the Yacht Club, immaculately turned out in blazer, white trousers and yachting cap for the occasion. It was on one of his regular morning walks to the yacht club that he fell at the age of 81. Ill health followed, and although he promised to return to Cambridge for the next term he never made it, and died on 12th May 1944 while the harbour was packed with boats

preparing for D-Day. Six naval men carried his coffin into the parish church, with his boatman-gardener Joseph Welch following behind.

## Bibliography

From Q's many novels some consider the best to be *The Splendid Spur*, *Hetty Wesley* and *Sir John Constantine* which was his own favourite.

He also edited the first *Oxford Book of English Verse* (1900) which had sold half a million copies and been reprinted 20 times by 1939! Among other works this was followed by the *The Oxford Book of English Ballads* and *The Oxford Book of Victorian Verse*. *On The Art Of Writing* and *On The Art Of Reading* were compilations of his Cambridge lectures published in 1916 and 1920. His first biographer was F. Brittain, whose fond biographical study was published in 1947.

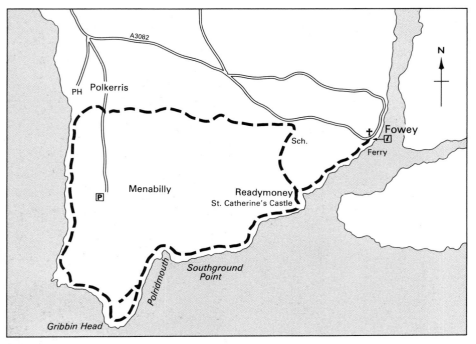

## A Walk with Sir Arthur Quiller-Couch

**Map:** OS Landranger 204.
**Start:** The square on the quay in Fowey—OS Grid Ref. 126516. Park in the main car park on the hillside above the town.
**Nearest BR Station:** Tywardreath.
**Distance:** 7½ miles.
**Time:** Allow 3 hours.
**Facilities:** Pubs, cafés, etc. in Fowey; pub at Polkerris.
**Summary:** A fine circular walk from the centre of Fowey, passing Sir Arthur Quiller-Couch's house on the Esplanade and continuing round the coastal path to Gribbin Head.

Whatever you do, don't try to take your car down into Fowey. There is a large car park clearly signposted on the outskirts, and from there it's a short walk down the lanes into the harbourside town where the main square or *piazza* is easily found on the quay.

This is a pleasant place to start from, with a fine view over the estuary and all the shops and cafés close to hand. There is a bookshop close by the church which has a large selection of books by or about 'Q', both new and secondhand. From the quay bear left up the hill away from the *King Of Prussia* and past the *Frenchman's Creek* restaurant, and then take the first left turning along the Esplanade. Head along this lane which runs parallel to the water, lined with imposing buildings to the right and with cars the exception rather than the rule.

After a hundred yards or so a steep hill goes down to the left to the Polruan foot and bike ferry. To the right is The Haven, the large house where Q lived until his death. One imagines that Fowey was a quieter place though not greatly different in those days, and Q would frequently set out across the estuary to the large garden which he kept on the Polruan side. His memorial over there is a stone obelisk at the end of Hall Walk above Penleath Point at the mouth of the estuary.

Continue along the Esplanade, passing a turning to the right and then heading downhill as the lane narrows where it passes an imposing house with fine cast iron gates on the left and approaches the small cove at Readymoney beneath St Catherine's Castle. This is a pretty place with a small beach you can bathe from. The lane passes behind the beach and then bears right uphill where it turns onto a path by the right side of a whitewashed house, with the double yellow parking lines forming a U ahead of you. Go up this way into Covington Woods, and then

*The coastal footpath looking towards Par Sands, before you turn inland for Fowey.*

*The main piazza in Fowey.*

turn sharp left towards the headland, bearing left on a track which will bring you out at the sixteenth-century St Catherine's Castle beneath the old Rashleigh mausoleum, with a fine view down the estuary and a well positioned bench if you're already in need of a rest!

From here carry on along the coast path, taking the right hand fork which leads you to a gate going into Allday's Fields above the lighthouse. The coastal path is easy to follow, and in the distance you can see the red and white striped tower which is a navigational daymark—a lighthouse without a light looking for all the world like a stick of candy—on Gribbin Head which is the point you are making for. Follow the path round the bay at Coombe Hawne—more bathing here if the weather is suitable—and on towards Southground Point. There are a number of stiles leading off to the left taking you down to small coves and beaches as you go along.

At Southground Point the magnificent bay at Polridmouth (or Pridmouth) beneath the Gribbin Head tower is revealed, as the path bears north along the edge of woods and comes down to the beach, with a cottage ahead

and a splendid lake extending along the valley. This would be a fine place to stop for a quiet picnic; on a sunny day in early September there were no more than four heads on the beach when I passed by.

Continue on past the cottage, and follow the path by the side of a wall. It then bends sharply left to resume its coastal route by a sign informing you that you are on the coastal path with Fowey leading one way and Gribbin the other. To the right is a gate, and this also leads onto a footpath, though unsignposted. It heads up towards the lane which fronts Menabilly, the Rashleigh Tudor mansion where Daphne du Maurier lived for some time, using it as the setting for *Rebecca* and *The King's General*. When her lease expired she moved to the entrance lodge where she eventually died. Unfortunately one can't see Menabilly from the path, but if you wish to cut the walk short this is an ideal opportunity as the path joins a lane which takes you directly to the church at Tregaminion.

To continue on the coastal route walk on towards Gribbin Head, heading straight up towards the tower on a broad grassy track for

a superb view at the top which would be even more superb if you could climb the nineteenth-century Trinity House tower. Unfortunately it is locked up, but this is a fine point to stop and rest awhile. Walking up to the tower cuts the corner off the coastal path which follows the headland round the left side of woods, and to rejoin it you go through a gate over to the right.

From here the path heads along high cliffs with vertical drops to clear, rocky water below. As you turn north the other side of Cornwall is revealed, with the haphazard development of Par Sands and the busy china clay port signposted by two enormous chimneys directly ahead. To the west you look straight out across St Austell Bay, while in the far distance the headland is Dodman Point, south of Mevagissey. Carry on along the coastal path making for a patch of trees ahead on the hillside. As you get closer to Par the path follows the edge of a field, and then comes to a hole in the hedge ahead with a rough piece of fence which looks confusingly like a stile. Look over here and you get a glimpse of the tiny harbour of Polkerris below, and though there seems to be a track down it is very rough and is not the way to go.

Bear right along the side of the woods and over a stile. The path continues by the trees, passing a couple more rough tracks on the left before a footpath sign indicates that the coastal path goes down to Polkerris on the far edge of the woods. Here you may turn down left if you wish to take a look at Polkerris and visit the Rashleigh Arms pub, or continue straight ahead on the footpath which takes you across a field to a gate by a lane. Turn right along this lane, and then left down a track by the side of the church at Tregaminion, a quiet place with its shady driveway dominated by hydrangeas in late summer.

Walk on down the side of the church, bearing right with the track by the farmhouse and then following it left through the farmyard as indicated by the helpful 'Footpath' daubed on the side of a barn. You come to a gate with a proper footpath sign directing you away from the farmyard, heading downhill across pasture land towards a narrow stone wall which acts as a bridge across a stream, and taking you to a stile by the side of a small ruined building. Follow the next footpath sign, going uphill and downhill to cross another stream while all the time heading east. At the top of the next hill you will see the farm buildings at Trenant ahead—the stile is set in the wall to the right, and leads to a track passing ruined barns and an old orchard in a fine setting.

Follow the path straight ahead, going uphill and towards woods. Here you step over a wall to go into the woods, bearing left down-hill by the side of an old moss covered wall. This leads you under a bridge which appears to have no obvious purpose, and you then bear right up the other side of the valley towards Lankelly Farm. Go straight ahead through the farmyard—a dilapidated stile on the right indicates that you are on course—passing a modern bungalow on the left, and then walking through a gate leading to a lane.

Turn right here, and then immediately left, continuing in an easterly direction along a quiet road. You pass pleasant houses on both sides before coming to the main road which comes in from the left on a bend. Just here there is a gate on the right leading into St Catherine's Parade running down by the side of a small lodge. Go down this pretty track which was given to the people of Fowey in the last century, and keep on until you come to the beach at Readymoney. From here it's a short walk retracing your steps back to the centre of Fowey.

*The coastal footpath not far past Gribbin head. Dodman Point is to the west.*

# Walk 19: With Rudyard Kipling at Bateman's

*Rudyard Kipling (1865–1936) was an immensely popular writer in his own lifetime, who is today best remembered for his tales from India. His success made him a very wealthy man, enabling him to live in style in the East Sussex Jacobean mansion called Bateman's which he bought at the age of 37.*

Joseph Rudyard Kipling never used his first name. He preferred his unusual second name, given to him by his parents to commemorate their meeting on a picnic at Lake Rudyard in Staffordshire—it's now the Rudyard Reservoir. He was born in Bombay where his father was a teacher of crafts at the newly opened art school, and as a child he was cared for by Indian servants as was the custom of the day. In *Something of Myself*, his unfinished autobiography, he wrote, 'Give me the first six years of a child's life and you can have the rest.' In the first six years of Kipling's life he came to know India through the servants in a way that no European adult could have done, and from these early impressions he went on to pen his most successful stories based on life in India.

His free and easy life in Bombay came to a sudden end when he was sent to England to commence his education. In *Something of Myself* he makes it clear that he hated every minute of the next five years during which time he was boarded with foster parents, dubbed 'Uncle Harry and Aunty Rosa', in a terraced house in Southsea—he called it the 'House of Desolation'. Why he should have been left with these strangers isn't clear; his mother's sisters had much more suitable families for him to stay with. Two had married famous painters—Edward Burne-Jones and Edward Poynter—while another sister's son was to be the future prime minister, Stanley Baldwin.

In 1878 Kipling went away to boarding school at the United Services College in 'Westward Ho!', Devon. At first he hated every moment of it but things gradually improved as he started to contribute to the school magazine and then became secretary of the literary society, later using some of his experiences in *Stalky & Co* (published in 1899). While many

**Rudyard Kipling as painted by P. Burne-Jones in 1899.** *Photo by NPG.*

*Bateman's from the front—imposing, but on the dark and dreary side.*

of his literary peers went to university, Kipling's parents were unable to provide the money and there were no suitable scholarships. He left the college in 1882 to return to India where his father had got him a job as an assistant editor on a daily newspaper, the *Civil & Military Gazette of Bombay*.

Despite his youth Kipling was frequently left in charge of the paper, rapidly gaining self-confidence and knowledge of writing and Indian matters. By 1886 he had started to produce a regular series of features on regional life and some occasional verse. The latter—dealing with corruption, inequality, adultery and other aspects of Anglo-Indian life—was collected into Kipling's first book of poetry (he remained anonymous) and the first edition of 350 copies rapidly sold out. It was almost immediately reprinted in Calcutta as *Departmental Ditties*.

In 1887 Kipling transferred his job to editing the weekly supplement for a newspaper called *The Allahabad Pioneer*, which involved writing extended stories about his travels around northern India. A year later his first book of

40 short stories—*Plain Tales from the Hills*—was published for the Indian market, mainly using work that had already appeared in the *Gazette*. It was a sell-out in India, but was not successful in London. Nevertheless, rumours about this aspiring young writer were creeping back to England, and in 1889, at the age of 22, Kipling resolved to leave India for good, setting off to seek his fortune as a writer in his own country.

Kipling arrived in London with little money, having stopped in Japan and several other exotic locations on the way; he remained an enthusiastic traveller all of his life. He found lodgings in Villiers Street off the Strand, and on account of his talent and extremely hard work he was famous in both England and America before the next year was out. *Plain Tales from the Hills*, *The Light that Failed*, *Soldiers Three*, *Wee Willie Winkie* and other Indian stories had secured his reputation; as had his *Barrack Room Ballads*, a collection of poems (including the immortal *Mandalay* which first appeared in the *Scots Observer*), which were recited and sung in music halls and at concerts

throughout the land.

Kipling married his American wife Carrie in 1892. By then his money troubles were over, and they decided to make their home in the United States at Brattleboro, Vermont, where Carrie's parents had an estate. They built a large, imposing house in an isolated position, naming it Naulakha (the necklace) in memory of Carrie's late brother who had co-written *The Naulahka* (spelt incorrectly despite Kipling's knowledge of Hindu!) with Kipling, the only collaboration of this kind the great writer ever undertook. Despite this fine house the couple didn't stay in it for more than three years, leaving on account of a variety of reasons—problems with Carrie's family, growing political dissension between Britain and America, and Kipling's sense of loneliness (something which later returned to him at Bateman's). Despite his American experience, most of the books written while he was in Vermont still concerned India, not least *The Jungle Book* and *The Second Jungle Book* which were wonderfully successful with children in Kipling's lifetime, but are now probably better known as Walt

Disney films. One of his few American stories from this period— *Captains Courageous*—was also later given the Hollywood treatment.

The Kiplings moved back to England in 1896 where they found a home in Rottingdean near Brighton, close to a house owned by Edward Burne-Jones. Kipling's books had made him something of a national institution but the invasion of privacy that his fame produced was a source of continual irritation to him. His poems on important matters relating to the welfare of the country which were usually published in *The Times* helped to make him the most popular patriotic poet of his day. He succeeded Tennyson as Poet Laureate in all but name; he refused to accept such titles, also turning down the offer of a Knighthood and the Order of Merit. He did, however, accept the Nobel Prize for Literature which he received in 1907.

Famous works published over the next few years included: *Stalky & Co*; the *Just So Stories: For Little Children*, illustrated by some of Kipling's excellent drawings (his father had illustrated some of his other books); and *Kim* which is considered his finest book of all, once again about India. While not working, Kipling travelled for his own pleasure, and also went to South Africa to lend his support to the British in the Boer War—this was a cause he believed in passionately, having raised a staggering £250,000 for soldiers' dependants by his poem *The Absent Minded Beggar*.

In 1902 Kipling and his family moved to Bateman's, near Burwash in Sussex. This splendidly gloomy Jacobean mansion was to be his home for the next 34 years, during which time he acquired the neighbouring water mill and farm and ran it as a small estate. His wealth from writing is reflected in this beautifully furnished house with its fine gardens. With the possible exception of Sissinghurst it dwarfs the homes of any of the other writers featured in this book, and must have consumed vast amounts of money. Carrie, who survived Kipling by three years, passed it on to the National Trust after her death.

Kipling continued to be a prolific writer, but with a few exceptions it is generally considered that his major creative years were over. *Puck of Pook's Hill* was written at Bateman's— the hill can be seen by looking south-west from the lawn and Puck's stream is by the mill pond—as was the poem *If*, and of course *Something of Myself* which he started in the year of his death. As the years rolled by he warned repeatedly about the coming war with Germany, and when war was declared in 1914 he once again took on a major patriotic role, fund raising and speech making which precluded him from writing much fiction.

His later years were less happy. Of his three children, Josephine had died from pneumonia while on a visit to New York in 1899—perhaps his sad inspiration for *They*, the story featuring the ghosts of dead children which he wrote at Bateman's; John was killed on the Western Front in 1915; and Elsie married and left home in 1924, leaving him very lonely. He became increasingly ill and, as so often happens, the critics began to turn against him, preferring the work of younger, newer writers though his popularity with the public remained largely undiminished.

Kipling also saw the coming of the Second World War, and with regret, ceased his lifelong practice of prefacing his books with the Hindu good luck symbol, a swastika, which had unfortunately been adopted by the Nazis. His last volume of short stories was *Limits and Renewals*, published in 1932 and *Something of Myself*, was published unfinished in 1937, a year after he had died from a severe internal haemorrhage while en route for a winter holiday in Cannes.

Even as early as 1906 Rudyard Kipling was occasionally labelled as a flag waving imperialist, and certainly his politics ended up being extremely right wing. However, branding him as a racist, a jingoist or whatever he is sometimes accused of today is both inaccurate and unfair, and belittles his great contribution to literature. He was a man of his age who worked for what he believed was good. He brought pleasure to millions of his readers and will continue to do so. After all, who can forget the man whose stories and poems have left so many memorable sayings: 'Oh, East is East, and West is West, and never the twain shall meet' (wrongly considered by some to be racist); 'For the female of the species is more deadly than the male'; 'You're a better man than I am, Gunga Din!'; 'If you can keep your head when all about you are losing theirs'; 'On the road to Mandalay, where the flyin' fishes play'; 'Brandy for the Parson, 'Baccy for the Clerk'; 'Let us now praise famous men'; 'He travels fastest who travels alone'; 'But that is another story'. . .

## Bibliography

*Kim (1901)* and the *Just So Stories* (1902) are probably Kipling's finest achievements for adults and children to enjoy today. He has numerous biographers: Charles Carrington's *Rudyard Kipling: His Life and Work* gives a comprehensive guide to the author; *Rudyard Kipling and his World* by Kingsley Amis is short, well illustrated, and amusingly written.

## *A Walk with Rudyard Kipling*

**Map:** OS Landranger 199.
**Start:** Bateman's near Burwash just south of the A265 in East Sussex—OS Grid Ref. 671238; car park at Bateman's (NT).
**Nearest BR Station:** Etchingham.
**Distance:** 7½ miles.
**Time**: Allow 3–4 hours.
**Facilities:** National Trust café at Bateman's; pub and tea shops in Burwash.
**Summary:** A walk through the fine countryside surrounding Bateman's; some of the footpaths and bridleways are not signposted and care needs to be taken with navigation.

Bateman's, its gardens, and water mill justify at least a couple of hours for a good look round; the National Trust café has a pleasant outside sitting area if it's fine, and don't forget to look at Kipling's splendid Rolls-Royce.

To start the walk turn right out of the Bateman's car park, and walk down the lane by the yew hedge in front of this brooding house, ignoring the turning to the left. Carry straight on and the road becomes more of a track, crossing a bridge before coming to Bateman's Mill House next to an interesting round turreted building typical of the area. Just past this building there's a footpath sign to the right. Follow this footpath which bears left round the millpond, and then carry straight on ahead on a well defined path along the side of the mill-stream (used by Kipling to provide Bateman's electricity) which is fed by the River Dudwell. In spring there is wild garlic all the way along here.

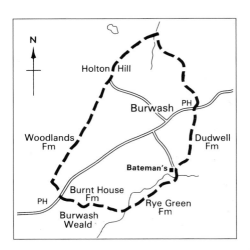

Above: "Baaaaa!" You'll meet more sheep than people on this walk, so watch out for those notices (rude and otherwise) telling you how to control your dog.

Left: A stile with yellow footpath blobs leads the way on this Kipling walk, and if you do it in spring we can promise bluebells everywhere!

*Above:* **The woods close by the River Dudwell just before you climb the hill towards Burnt House Farm.**

*Right:* **The pergola at Bateman's— Kipling was a keen gardener, and employed a suitable number of artisans to do it for him!**

Up to the left is Park Barn Farm. Carry on over a small bridge by an ancient watergate which is still working, and walk on along the grassy track. About 75 yards further on ignore the bridge to the right which leads up to Rye Green Farm, and keep straight ahead with trees on either side. Go over a stile and cross the open grassy field beyond in fine, green countryside with the River Dudwell meandering its way on your right. Keep straight across the field where the river bends away from you, following the stream running on your left with Rye Green Farm up on the hillside to the right.

The Dudwell again comes close to the path by an enormous fallen tree where you start across another rough grass field. Keep to the left alongside the stream, and go through a gate that leads into a valley with a hill and trees ahead. Follow the track through the grass, bearing right towards the river. Less than half-way along you will find a large footbridge crossing the river by a solitary oak. It has three yellow footpath signs on top which are easily missed, showing the way right, ahead and to the left which is the way you go.

A path turns left almost immediately along the riverside, but the footpath is a little higher up—they both join after about 50 yards and then come to a stile. Go over and walk through woods which are a mass of bluebells in springtime, following the path which bears right up towards a stile with a field beyond. Cross this field, heading up towards the large house ahead which is Burnt House Farm. Go through the gate in the fence at the top of this field, and walk up to the next fence where you will see footpath signs pointing left and right by a gate. Turn left here along the side of the fence until you come to another gate which you go through, following a footpath sign up to a stile and then on towards the right side of the farmhouse.

From here follow the metalled track straight ahead towards the road, bearing right through bollards. Turn right along the road, and almost immediately cross over and go left up a track—when we looked for it, the stone bridleway sign had flopped over and was easily missed. Follow this track past a rather fine converted oast house and down a hill which could become very muddy after wet weather. At the bottom turn right along a crossing track, and when you come to open ground bear right over a stile next to a gate along a narrow woodland track—do not stay on the main farm track which bears left round the outside of the trees.

Keep on along this woodland track, much of which is liable to be very muddy, heading in a north-easterly direction. Eventually you come to Woodlands Farm on the right, passing the back of a barn and coming to more open country with fine views over the countryside to the north-west. Keep straight on along a grassy track, having hopefully left the mud behind. After a time you will pass between houses with a stile and footpath sign to the left. Ignore this and keep ahead for the road at Holton Hill which you come out at opposite an orchard.

Turn left along the road here, and after about 25 yards bear right up a gravel drive past the side of a lodge. Keep on ahead with the orchard still on your right, before heading downhill towards more open country beyond the orchard. You follow an old fashioned iron fence on the right, passing the driveway to Franchise Farmhouse on the left as Franchise House comes into view. Walk on past this house which is a really magnificent looking place, keeping straight on by the iron fence across what appears to be Franchise House's gardens with a tennis court immediately to your left.

Even if it doesn't look like it, this is the footpath which runs past a small pond set in the bushes to your left. To the right you'll find a swinging gate in the fence—go through, and head across the field and on down the track which follows a hedge on its right hand side. Keep on along this track with a panoramic rural view before you. On the left you will glimpse another larger pond encircled by trees, and then you'll see the modern concrete footbridge which crosses the River Rother much further to the left.

At the bottom of the field a crossing track which is a bridleway leads left down to this bridge. There are no footpath signs showing the way here, but you go straight ahead through the opening in the hedge into the next field. Turn right along the perimeter of the field, heading away from the river and up towards a large clump of trees to the left ahead. At the top of the field you come to a stile which we found in a poor state of disrepair; cross over, and then bear left uphill across the next field towards a stile set on the edge of the trees about 75 yards distant.

Cross this stile which we found to be even more rickety, and go over a small stream by means of a convenient log bridge, following the path up through the woods which are also carpeted with bluebells in the spring. The path leads out of the woods to a grassy field going uphill ahead of you. Head up this field keeping the large barn to your left, and as you reach the brow of the hill the farmhouse at Brooksmarle which is well to the left of the footpath comes into view.

Go over the stile ahead, joining the metalled driveway at the top of the hill where you turn right, and following it all the way down to Burwash. Just before you reach the road there is a free house on the right with an attractive garden which might make a pleasant stop for refreshment. Cross the A265 that divides Burwash, and turn right for about 25 yards until you see a footpath sign pointing left down an alley by the side of a convenient café.

Turn down here between the houses, and walk downhill across the field ahead, which is likely to be muddy. Watch out for a footpath sign which had been swivelled 90 degrees in the wrong direction when we passed by, and follow the path towards Bateman's by keeping straight ahead and a touch to the right to cross the next stile. Cross stiles as you come to them, keeping on course, which is virtually straight ahead, with the help of an occasional footpath sign and a National Trust sign asking you to keep your dog on a lead in the lambing season. Soon you will come down to a lane a short way to the west of Dudwell Farm where you turn right to bring you back to Bateman's with fine views of the front façade.

# Walk 20: With Beatrix Potter in Near Sawrey

*Beatrix Potter (1866–1943) is remembered, and will continue to be remembered, for her series of children's books that started with* The Tale of Peter Rabbit *which she published herself in 1901. A further twenty-two 'Tales' followed in quick succession, all based on the same winning formula of perfect illustrations, memorable characters, and an amusing story.*

Beatrix Potter was born into a large family house in Bolton Gardens, London—the best end of Kensington—and she continued to live there for some 48 years until she finally got married, and moved to a happier life at Near Sawrey.

Throughout her childhood she was educated at home and seldom went out to meet other children, leading a solitary life on the third floor of the house, well away from her parents who were rich and by all accounts stultifyingly Victorian (she nevertheless remained more or less loyal to their whims and wishes throughout their long lives). Up in the nursery she made her own entertainment which in one year included learning half a dozen of Shakespeare's plays off by heart, and the only break in this regime came with annual three-month-long summer holidays when the family decamped—servants and all—to fairly grand houses, initially in Scotland and later in the Lake District. It was taken for granted that Beatrix would accompany her parents on these jaunts, irrespective of her age, a tradition that continued until she was well into middle age.

Beatrix's father, Rupert Potter, was an accomplished photographer, but otherwise there was no obvious root for the natural artistic talent of both Beatrix and her brother Bertram. While Beatrix sketched and painted at home, Bertram went off to become a landscape artist in Scotland and later transferred his affections to farming, an identical course to that taken by his sister many years later. Apart from some early lessons she was left to develop her own artistic style, painting miniature natural history studies. This led to her first attempt at producing a book of her watercolours of fungi which were an early and earnest interest. Despite an approach to the Director of the

**Beatrix Potter in her days as a Lakeland farmer, as painted by D. Banner.** *Photo by NPG.*

Royal Botanic Gardens the book got nowhere, not least because she was an unknown young woman. Thankfully, for posterity, she abandoned fungi and turned her attention to the *Tale of Peter Rabbit*.

Peter Rabbit existed long before the idea of the book. He was created by Beatrix to amuse Noel Moore, the son of her ex-governess who she kept in regular contact with. At the age of five he had a lengthy illness, and to keep him amused Beatrix began to send him long illustrated letters. These frequently contained news of her own pet rabbit named Peter, and on September 4th 1893 she wrote to Noel with news of the rest of the family—Flopsy, Mopsy, Cottontail and not least

Mr McGregor—with pen and ink drawings sketching out the story which was later enlarged into *The Tale of Peter Rabbit*.

Encouraged by her far sighted friend Canon Rawnsley, she submitted the story to half a dozen or so publishers, and was turned down by every one, a decision they must rue today. Undeterred she decided to print and publish the book herself, devising the small five by four inch format with a single illustration facing a few short sentences of the story on each double-page spread—the formula which is still used by her publishers today.

Beatrix had 250 copies printed and the book which had black and white illustrations, became available in 1901. She quickly sold them all to relations and friends, printing a further 200 and making another approach to F. Warne & Co who had been the most courteous of the publishers that she had originally approached. On the strength of the success of her little book they changed their minds, and offered to take over publishing *Peter Rabbit* if she would provide coloured illustrations.

With her first book successfully off her hands, Beatrix turned her attention to *The Tailor of Gloucester*, a tale of mice rather than rabbits, based on a story she had heard about a tailor. Not willing to push Warne's too hard she once again printed and published it herself in 1902, allowing Warne's to take over the following year when her own 500 copies were sold. In the meantime Warne & Co had published *The Tale of Squirrel Nutkin* (1903) which had been inspired by a visit Beatrix had made to some cousins in Suffolk. She had seen the squirrels playing in their grounds; dreamt up the idea of them sailing down the river on little rafts with their tails for sails; and tried out the initial story and pictures on various children.

*The view from the track above Far Sawrey is the landscape that Beatrix Potter loved best.*

From then on her 'Tales' followed in quick succession for the next decade with sometimes one and more often two or more new books appearing each year as she worked her way through the animal kingdom—*Benjamin Bunny* and *Two Bad Mice* appeared in 1904; *Mrs Tiggy-Winkle*, who was eventually buried in the garden at Bolton Square, and *The Pie and The Patty Pan* in 1905; *Jeremy Fisher, Miss Moppet* and *The Story of a Fierce Bad Rabbit* in 1906; and so on. Not surprisingly, she developed a close and professional working relationship with Warne's which was very much a family business. She discussed and refined her plots with them, working most closely with Norman Warne who at that time was running the company.

Norman and Beatrix became engaged in 1905 when both were in their late thirties, despite the furious opposition of her parents who would not hear of her marrying anyone

'in trade'—this attitude now seems very extreme, particularly when one considers that the previous Potter generation had made their money 'in trade'. Beatrix would probably have gone ahead with the marriage despite her parents wishes, but it was not to be. Norman suddenly fell ill and died a year later—it transpired he had been suffering from leukaemia.

Beatrix threw herself into her work, churning out books for Warne's who were now finding markets for her creations abroad. For her first French edition Peter Rabbit was transformed into Pierre Lapereau with his consorts Flopsaut, Trotsaut and Queue-de-Coton—Mr McGregor, however, remained the same. Despite pirated editions and unlicensed Beatrix Potter toys her earnings soon became considerable—50,000 copies of Peter Rabbit were sold in two years—and with her newfound wealth she turned to the Lake District.

The Potter family had first taken a house

for their regular three month summer holiday on the outskirts of the village of Near Sawrey on the west side of Windermere in 1896. They continued to be regular visitors, and in 1905 Beatrix bought her own home in the village, a farmstead named Hill Top. Beatrix described Near Sawrey in glowing terms in her secret journal, '. . . as nearly perfect a little place as I ever lived in, and such nice old fashioned people'. However, despite owning Hill Top which she updated and extended she couldn't live there, for her duty still lay to her ageing and increasingly demanding parents. With a manager in charge of the farm she stayed at Hill Top whenever she could, using the house, its garden, and the nearby village as inspiration for several more of her Tales.

Beatrix soon became intensely interested in farming, and used her earnings to buy other farms and more land in the area. The solicitor who helped her in these purchases was

*High up on the Heald, from where Windermere is hidden by the trees and acres of ferns that line the hillside.*

William Heelis, a local man with a practice based at nearby Hawkshead. In 1913 he became her husband, when Beatrix was 48, despite her parents' predictable disapproval.

From then on Beatrix Potter's life changed. She left her home in London, and lived at Near Sawrey for the next 30 years as Mrs Heelis, the formidably successful lakeland sheep farmer. After a decade of writing and illustrating she virtually abandoned her former career, with only four books published by Warne's after her marriage. She became a larger than life local character, and when her father died she moved her mother up to live in a big house on the shores of Lake Windermere so that there was no longer any need to travel to London.

Mr and Mrs Heelis decided to live at Castle Cottage on the opposite side of the road from Hill Top, a larger house which Beatrix had bought in 1909. While she disliked her privacy being invaded by English Beatrix Potter fans, she was flattered by her American admirers. This led to *The Fairy Caravan* which was published exclusively for the American market in 1928. It was much longer than any of her Tales, and pleased the residents of Sawrey by featuring the animals and surroundings that they knew. Eventually, in 1952, it was published in England, but it is considered to be much less successful than her Tales.

In her latter years Mrs Heelis devoted herself to preserving the Lake District. She continued to buy property and land whenever she was able to, and eventually left some 4000 acres and numerous farms to the National Trust when she died at the age of 77 on 22nd December 1943. Her husband followed two years later. She stipulated that none of her houses should be let for holidays, and that Hill Top should be preserved as her original Lakeland home and a resting place for the best of her memorabilia.

Today the tourists she so detested flock to Hill Top in their thousands. Despite its very ordinary outside appearance, the house is surprisingly grand inside with dark panelling, a fine staircase, and large paintings hung on the walls including a selection by her brother. Scenes from six of the Tales which used the house as their setting are easily recognisable, in particular the adventures of Tom Kitten, Jemima Puddle-Duck and Samuel Whiskers—the latter character was based on her experiences with the rats who raided Hill Top in the early days of her ownership.

The National Trust shop at the foot of the garden does a roaring trade as it cashes in on its benefactor's reputation. Beatrix Potter campaigned vigorously in the run-up to the

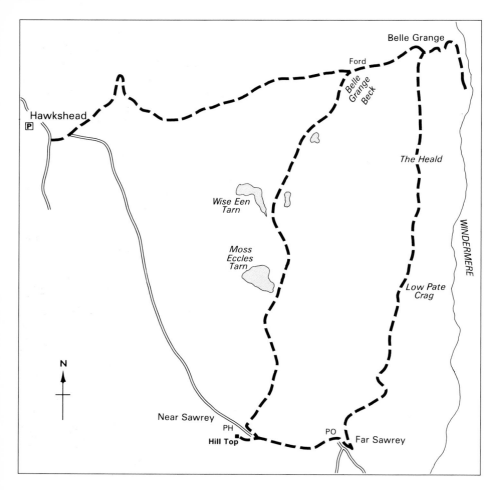

## A Walk with Beatrix Potter

**Map:** OS Outdoor Leisure 7—The English Lakes.

**Start:** Hill Top at Near Sawrey, on the west side of Windermere in the Lake District—OS Grid Ref. 371955. Car park on the north-west side of the village. Hill Top (NT) open from Easter to early November, Monday to Wednesday and Saturday/Sunday 10–5 pm. The Beatrix Potter Gallery (NT) in Hawkshead is open from Easter to early November, Wednesday to Sunday and Bank Holiday Monday 11–5 pm.

**Nearest BR Station:** Windermere.

**Distance:** Approximately 6 miles; 9 miles if you continue the walk to Hawkshead.

**Time:** Allow 3–4 hours.

**Facilities:** Pubs at Near Sawrey and Far Sawrey; coffee/tea at hotel in Near Sawrey; coffee/tea/pub in Hawkshead.

**Summary:** A walk along the heights above Windermere, returning through a beautiful landscape of tarns. The walk can be extended to the Beatrix Potter Gallery in Hawkshead.

The most direct route to Near Sawrey may be the car ferry that crosses the middle of Windermere from Bowness, but beware, in summer there are long queues, and it's probably quicker to drive round the lake. Coming into Near Sawrey from the north, you pass a large and rather splendid house on the right just opposite a telephone box by a small car park. This is 'Lakeland' (now Ees Wyke) which the Potter family rented in the summer of 1896. Further on there is a small car park on the right, from where it's a short walk along the road to Hill Top. On the way you pass The Tower Arms (NT), a pleasant pub with a small garden and reasonable food.

The walk starts from Hill Top. From the entrance turn right down the road towards Far Sawrey—in the summer you may have to contend with an endless succession of cars passing by. Follow the road downhill past a footpath sign pointing right to the church, and continue to follow it to the top of the hill where it bends right through Far Sawrey, passing a bridleway which turns off to the left and the small but well-stocked village store on the right. Keep on past the hotel where a bridleway turns up to the left and a footpath goes straight ahead.

Go left up the bridleway track past the back of the hotel. The track gradually curves round to the right, heading uphill into open country with fine views opening out behind. Keep on as the track goes up and down, and

1910 General Election on behalf of the besieged British toy industry who had been unable to make her own Peter Rabbit due to foreign competition. Our purchase of a wind-up Peter Rabbit made in Taiwan would undoubtedly have enraged her!

## Bibliography

Frederick Warne published *The Tale of Peter Rabbit* in 1902. One or more tales were published by Warne's each year until her marriage, and *The Tale of Pigling Bland* appeared in 1913. There are currently 23 in print.

Beatrix Potter's secret journal which she wrote in code for her own amusement from childhood to her mid-thirties was deciphered after many years by Leslie Linder, and was published as *The Journal of Beatrix Potter* in 1966. The definitive biography, *The Tale of Beatrix Potter* by Margaret Lane, was published by F. Warne & Co in 1946 shortly after her death.

*Hill Top at Near Sawrey, a shrine to Beatrix Potter fans, suitably (or unsuitably) commercialised by the National Trust.*

*The front of Hill Top, Beatrix Potter's first Lakeland home. Few realise that she also lived in another house in the village.*

then just before you reach the woods ahead there's a clear left hand turning between walls with a small wooden sign showing the way to Claife Head. This is typical of the footpath signs in the area which are sometimes not easily spotted. Follow this track which runs along by woods on the right, before heading downhill past a gate with a stile.

Keep on past Belt Ash Coppice, and where the track forks left and right take the second left fork uphill and head on into the woods. There follows a long woodland ramble, with occasional glimpses of Windermere to the right as you head north high above its shore-line. After a time you come to a footpath sign pointing left to Hawkshead and right to Belle Grange. Turn right here, and continue to follow the same clear track through the woods which soon resumes its northerly direction.

The track starts to head downhill, and eventually comes to a paved crossing track going downhill to the right with a National Trust sign opposite. Turning right will take you steeply downhill to the lakeside at Windermere,

and if you turn right at the bottom there's a pleasant place to sit and a wide track that continues along the lakeside. To continue, head back up the hill, carrying straight on up the track past your original turning. After a time you leave National Trust land by a notice on a wall, and cross the ford for Belle Grange Beck which is more or less dried up in summer. The track continues to head uphill, crossing a wide forestry track where you go straight ahead, following the sign for Hawkshead. The track bears left uphill, and eventually comes to another crossing track signposted right to Hawkshead and left to Sawrey and The Ferry. From here you can walk down to Hawkshead to visit the Beatrix Potter Gallery which is housed in a building that was William Heelis's office. It adds about three miles to the walk, returning the same way.

Head on for Sawrey and The Ferry, following the wide forestry track which bears round to the right uphill. On the bend ignore the narrow track going straight ahead into the woods signposted for The Ferry, and continue

to the top of the hill, bearing left and walking on past High Moss Tarn on the left to reach a gate with a blue/yellow bridleway sign showing the way ahead. This brings you to a magical landscape as the track heads on a gentle downhill slope passing between Wise Een Tarn on the right and a smaller tarn to the left—if the track is too wet and muddy, walk along the dam wall at the side of the small tarn, taking in the westerly views which are very fine.

Follow the track as it bears uphill to the left through a gate. From here it takes you past Moss Eccles Tarn which is severely beautiful, dropping gradually downhill as it passes through a gate and along the valley side. Keeping right for Near Sawrey, you'll see a fine house way over to the left by Cuckoo Brow Wood before the track passes close by a barn and then heads down through a farmyard into Near Sawrey. Here you come to a small hotel on the right which impressed us by serving a cream tea at 6.30 pm in its quiet front garden!

# Walk 21: With H.G. Wells at Uppark

*For H.G. Wells (1866–1946)—writer, scientist, philosopher, humanist, public figure and traveller—the splendid mansion called Uppark was an important influence on his early, formative years. He never lived there for any great length of time, but the experience enabled him to see how the aristocracy lived, providing the background material for Bladesover House in* Tono-Bungay.

Herbert George Wells, known to his family as 'Bertie' and later to his friends as 'HG', was born in Bromley at a time when it was still a small town some way from London, surrounded by a Kentish rural landscape. His mother, Sarah Neal, had worked as a maid at Uppark—a fine mansion near the village of South Harting on the Sussex/Hampshire border, originally built around 1690—before his birth. While she was there she met her future husband, Joseph Wells, who was the head gardener; they married in 1853 having already left Uppark.

The marriage was never a success, which was perhaps why HG never thought much of marriage as an institution—he married twice, had six long term affairs, and many brief liaisons. Sarah and Joseph settled in Bromley, where they ran a shop in the market place which allowed them to scrape together a living and bring up three sons. Self-education was Bertie's only hope of improvement, and in *Experiment in Autobiography* he described a broken leg at the age of seven which enabled him to lie in bed and read as 'One of the luckiest events of my life . . . I am alive today and writing this autobiography instead of being a worn-out, dismissed and already dead shop assistant.'

In 1880 Sarah Wells left Bromley and her family in order to return to Uppark for the next 13 years. It was then in the hands of a couple of unlikely elderly ladies. Sir Harry Fetherstonhaugh, who had inherited the house, had married his head dairy maid when over 70, educating her Pygmalion fashion, and then handing over the estate on his death some 20 years later at the age of 92. She and her unmarried sister Frances continued to run the house in his fashion, and when Lady Fetherstonhaugh died Frances took over the estate

**H. G. Wells, the visionary and social commentator as photographed by G. C. Beresford.** *Photo by NPG.*

and name of Fetherstonhaugh, living alone with her companion Miss Sutherland who was rumoured to be a natural daughter of Sir Harry. Sarah Wells had been her maid when she worked there many years before, and she was now invited to take over as housekeeper.

This was a senior position ranking with the butler as head servant, and since Sarah had had enough of both Bromley and her husband, she lost no time in going. She packed off the unfortunate Bertie to be an apprentice in the drapery trade—70 hours a week, sixpence

pocket money, and poor living conditions. He hated it and was relieved to get the sack. After a short stay with an uncle who had set himself up as a school teacher Bertie went to stay with his mother at Uppark for the first time at the age of 14. He was given a room in the attic, and it was from there and from his mother's rooms in the basement that he produced a daily news sheet of 'below stairs' gossip when the house was cut off by a Christmas snowstorm, as described in *Experiment in Autobiography*:

> 'I produced a daily newspaper of a facetious character, *The Uppark Alarmist* . . . The place had a great effect on me; it retained a vitality that altogether overshadowed the insignificant ebbing trickle of upstairs life, the two elderly ladies in the parlour following their shrunken routines.'

Bertie also discovered the Uppark library which had a fine collection of books—from among them this highly intelligent little boy delved into Tom Paine's *Common Sense*, Swift's *Gulliver's Travels* and Plato's *Republic*, reflecting the radical, agnostic and utopian themes he later used in his own books. Gaining access to this library was not, however, without its perils, as recounted in *Tono-Bungay*:

> 'The book borrowing raid was one of extraordinary dash and danger. One came down the main service stairs—that was legal. Illegality began on a little landing when, very cautiously, one went through a red baize door. A short passage led to the hall, and here one reconnoitred for Ann,

*Above:* **The South Downs way between South and East Harting. Fine walking which Wells must have known well.**

*Right:* **Looking towards the Coach & Horses, a welcome sight in South Harting, having descended the hill from the South Downs Way.**

**Uppark with the builders in. Shortly after this picture was taken the whole inside of the house was burnt out; it is now being restored by the National Trust.**

the old head-housemaid—the younger housemaids were friendly and did not count. Ann located, came a dash across the open space at the foot of the great stair-case that has never been properly descended since powder went out of fashion, and so to the saloon door . . . Oddly rat-like, is it not, this darting into enormous places in pursuit of the aban-doned crumbs of thought?'

Bertie's first winter stay at Uppark was termi-nated by his mother's decision to pack him off to become a chemist. He failed in this too, but was lucky enough to spend some time at a school in Midhurst, ostensibly learning Latin for his chemistry but in reality making up for his lack of education. Convinced that an apprenticeship would do him far more good than schooling, Sarah moved him on again and found him a place at the Southsea Drapery Emporium where he lasted for two years, with occasional excursions to Uppark which was less than an hour away by train.

This experience later proved useful for *Kipps*, but when he couldn't stand it any more he pleaded with his mother and the rest of the family to allow him to return to the school in Midhurst. She took little notice of his letters, so having considered and rejected the idea of suicide he walked the 17 miles to Uppark, lying in wait for the servants as they made their way back from the church in nearby South Hart-ing and confronting Sarah in the style of the hero of *Tono-Bungay*:

'"Coo-ee, mother!" said I, coming out against the sky, "Coo-ee!" My mother looked up, went very white, and put her hand to her bosom . . .'

Bertie got what he wanted, returning to Mid-hurst Grammar School where he was expected to teach the children in return for his own edu-cation, and visiting Uppark during the holidays. From there, exceptionally hard work and avid reading led him to win a scholarship to the Normal School of Science in South Kensing-ton in 1884, at last setting him free from family ties and introducing him to the world of the famous T.H. Huxley (grandfather of Aldous Huxley) whose lectures set him on his scien-tific, socialist and utopian way.

Holidays continued to be spent at Uppark, but Miss Fetherstonhaugh was becom-ing a difficult lady in her old age, and Bertie and his two brothers were made less and less welcome. Nevertheless he returned to Uppark to recuperate in November 1887—by that time he had scraped through his exams at the Normal School (later the Royal College of Science), and been employed at a run-down school in Monmouth where he had been diag-nosed as having tuberculosis. Whether this was the correct diagnosis isn't clear, but for many years he was prone to similar states of severe physical collapse, probably brought on the first time by a combination of overworking and an unhealthy, impoverished student life in London.

By this stage he had been writing articles for the *Science Schools Journal* for some time, with ideas that would later be expanded into such famous tales as *War of the Worlds* and *The Time Machine*. While recovering at Uppark he wrote

35,000 words of a lost romantic tale called *Lady Frankland's Companion*, no doubt based on the doddery Miss Sutherland, and worked his way through the library once again. After the excitement of London he bewailed his boring life in what he now considered to be *The House of Captivity: Valley of the Shadow of Death* (his own was not unlikely at times), describing his mother's fellow servants in a letter as 'DAMNED PHONOGRAPHS, BLOODY TALKING DOLLS'.

Finally the future began to look brighter for HG. He was given a job as a schoolmaster in Kilburn, working for John Milne, father of A.A. Milne of *Winnie the Pooh* fame who was under HG's tuition. Despite the fact that his mother's relationship with Miss Fetherston-haugh at Uppark was going rapidly downhill, he was able to make his last extended stay there in 1890, spending a month in the calm of the park when the strain of teaching, work-ing for exams, and writing had precipitated another physical breakdown.

Two years later Sarah Wells and Miss Fetherstonhaugh fell out for good. In her diary of September 1st, Sarah wrote, 'That horrid woman upset me again. Oh how hard to be obliged to stay in such a place.' She didn't have to wait long, for on 16th February the follow-ing year she was sent packing, and with nowhere else to go was reunited with her hus-band Joe. HG, who was now making a fair income, helped support both of them in a most charitable way. Apart from his success as a schoolmaster he was doing well with freelance articles. One, entitled *The Rediscovery of the Unique*, written during his last stay at Uppark, was published in the prestigious *Fortnightly Review* edited by Frank Harris. The *Pall Mall Gazette* also provided a ready market for his writing, no doubt helping to precipitate another physical breakdown which forced him to aban-don teaching and take up writing full time.

HG paid one more visit to Uppark in 1934 when he was a famous man researching his autobiography. That was the end of his for-mative affair with a great house, remembered as Bladesover House (and transported to Kent) in *Tono-Bungay*:

'I did, indeed, go back there once again, but under circumstances quite immaterial to my story. But in a sense Bladesover has never left me; it is, as I said at the outset, one of those dominant explanatory impres-sions that makes the framework of my mind. Bladesover illuminates England; it has become all that is spacious, dignified, pretentious, and truly conservative in English life. It is my social datum.'

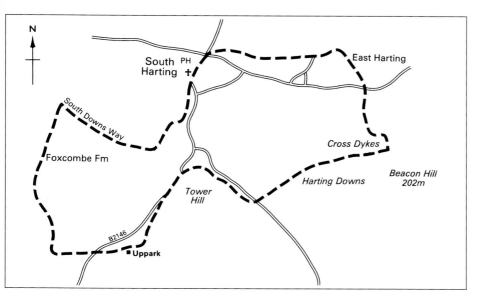

## Bibliography

Wells' scientific education paved the way for such famous science-fiction as *The Time Machine* (1895), *The Invisible Man* (1897), *The War of the Worlds* (1898), and *The First Men in the Moon* (1901). He wrote of the struggles of the lower-middle classes in *Love and Mr Lewisham* (1900), *Kipps* (1905), and *The History of Mr Polly* (1910). *Tono-Bungay* (1909) portrays the new order in England and features Uppark as Bladesover in its first two chapters; *Experiment in Autobiography* (1934) also remembers Uppark. Among many biographies *The Time Traveller* by Norman and Jeanne Mackenzie (Hogarth) is a good read.

## *A Walk with H.G. Wells*

**Map:** OS Landranger 197.
**Start:** Uppark (NT) on the B2146 just south of South Harting in West Sussex—OS Grid Ref. 779177; car park at Uppark. Optional start at South Harting—OS Grid Ref. 784195; roadside parking.
**Nearest BR Station:** Petersfield.
**Distance:** 7½ miles.
**Time:** Allow 4–5 hours.
**Facilities:** Two pubs and a tea shop in South Harting; NT café at Uppark.
**Summary:** A circular walk round the Uppark countryside including some of the South Downs Way, fine downland view and pretty downland villages at South and East Harting.

In 1989 Uppark suffered a disastrous fire which burnt out the interior of the house. An immediate decision was taken to rebuild and refurbish it in its original style, but at the time of writing there is no clear idea when it will be reopening. The grounds and café will, however, be open at least one day a week in the summer season; precise opening times can be obtained by telephoning Uppark on 0730 845317. If the house is closed you can start this walk from South Harting, walking via Uppark where you get a glimpse of the house through the main gates.

Starting from the Uppark car park, turn right and walk straight ahead down the south drive which joins the B2147 going on to Emsworth and Chichester. At the road cross over to a footpath sign, and go over the stile, walking downhill on an overgrown path with the woods on the hillside of West Harting Down visible ahead. At the bottom the path peters out; bear left on an indistinct trail and walk up the right hand side of a field, heading towards trees.

On the edge of the trees you come to another stile and a footpath sign pointing left and right. Turn right here and follow the track along the edge of the woods, ignoring the first footpath turning to the right. After a time the track drops down out of the woods and comes to Foxcombe Farm, the main house being a substantial and rather fine building in the midst of the countryside. Continue past the farm, going uphill until you come to a signposted crossing track for the South Downs Way.

Turn right along the SDW past a house on the right with a small block of stables to the left. Follow the track along and slightly uphill past a barn, ignoring a footpath turning into the trees to the right. The church of South Harting which Sarah Wells and the Uppark servants walked to on Sundays soon comes into view in the valley to your left, and a short way on there's a stile and a footpath sign pointing straight down the hill. Head down across the grass field here towards trees. Go over the stile ahead and follow the footpath right along the perimeter of the trees, bearing left downhill on a narrow track by a wire fence, and then going into the woods.

A short way on the narrow track forks left and right. Take the left fork and you almost immediately come down to a footpath sign which is in a slightly confusing position. Go down onto the sunken track which you see ahead of you, and turn left downhill along it. This brings you down past some magnificent beech trees, passing a small reservoir and on to the recreation grounds on the outskirts of South Harting. Here there is a pond with benches in a pleasant setting, as well as swings and a slide which might be welcome if children are walking with you; on a fine day it would make a good stopping place for a picnic.

From here head straight on through the gate, and join the road with the Coach and Horses Pub straight ahead. On our visit this was a welcome sight—it caters particularly well for those with dogs and children, and serves good beer and above average food. From the pub continue straight along the road past the church with its lead-clad spire. The road here is narrow with no pavement, and although it's only 50 yards or so care needs to be taken to avoid oncoming cars. Beyond the church there is pavement, and you keep straight on through South Harting, passing a turning to the left and then taking the next right turning where a road goes straight ahead.

Walk along past a few houses, with an interesting, converted chapel on the left. A little further on there's a modern estate to the right with fields to the left, and then the road starts to bear uphill. Turn left along a lane with a dead-end road sign, just by a house with white cast iron railings. Walk on past the house, and after about 75 yards turn right onto a footpath by the sign set up on a bank.

Follow the footpath across the field ahead, going down into a belt of trees and across a stile. Head straight on across the next grass field, with a fine Queen Anne farmhouse coming into view on the left and even finer views of the South Downs to the right. Go over the stile in the hedge ahead, crossing the lane and going on across the next field towards a Sussex barn which has been converted into a house. Walk up through the gate here, passing between the barn conversion and its outbuildings towards the gate ahead where you

113

come out onto a lane running through East Harting. The farmer has left an impressively polite note on this gate, requesting people with dogs to keep them under control as he is trying to reintroduce wildlife to his fields. This makes a pleasant change from the more usual signs in the 'put it on a lead or I'll shoot it' vein!

Ignore the lane to the left and head along the lane ahead, passing a number of well kept cottages and houses. The lane bears left, and just past the entrance to East Harting House you will see a footpath sign to the right by the sign for East Harting Farm. Walk into the farmyard here and bear right around the modern barns. Continue along the side of them, and then bear right across the field ahead, heading through a gate towards the road where there is another gate and stile opposite a track leading up to a modern looking house on the hillside which is where you are making for.

Cross the road and go up this track which steepens as it passes the house. It bears left on a longish uphill stretch through very pretty woodland, before turning right into more open country, emerging at the old crossroads at Cross Dykes. This is set in a beautiful valley with an old signpost that had unfortunately lost all its arms when we passed by, but still dwarfed the conventional footpath sign alongside it. To the left a chalk track goes steeply up Beacon Hill and another track goes up a more gentle hill ahead by the side of a valley with telegraph poles incongruously stretching into the distance. You turn uphill to the right, however, taking the right hand of two parallel tracks which head up Harting Downs along the South Downs Way with fine views opening out to the north. At the top of the hill the SDW levels out before heading downhill a little, and then heading up on a wide grassy track—the last climb of this walk!

On level ground again you pass a car parking area over to the left. Keep to the right here, heading into the trees ahead and out onto the road which is the B2141. Cross straight over, and follow the brown metal South Downs Way sign along a hard track which runs along the hillside through woods above the road. This gradually drops downhill, bringing you out onto the B2146 just north of Uppark. Turn left down the road, and after 150 yards or so you will come to Uppark's north driveway which leads back up to the car park.

*Looking east along the South Downs Way towards the old crossroads at Cross Dykes, and a steep hill it is too!. The South Downs Way is one of Britain's long distance footpaths running all the way from Winchester to Eastbourne.*

# Walk 22: With Hilaire Belloc in Shipley

*Most of Hilaire Belloc's long life (1870–1953) was spent at King's Land at Shipley in West Sussex. He was a prolific writer of books and journalism with over 150 published works; an energetic traveller; a bon viveur; and above all a controversialist. Today however, his larger than life personality and copious works are virtually forgotten.*

'When I am dead, I hope it may be said: "His sins were scarlet, but his books were read".'

And so they were in his lifetime, filling a yard or so of the average public library bookshelf. His output included novels, poetry, biography, travel, and many essays on religious, political and social topics, most of which have now disappeared from libraries and are more likely to be found in a secondhand bookshop.

Belloc—Joseph Hilary Pierre Belloc—was born in France, the son of a French father and English mother. His father died soon after his birth, and young Belloc was mainly brought up in London until his mother lost most of the family fortune due to unfortunate speculation, forcing her to move to a humbler life in Slindon, a few miles to the east of Chichester. Despite the lack of financial resources, Belloc was an adventurous traveller from an early age. In 1891, at the age of 21, he made his way

across the United States, supporting himself by selling sketches, and at the same time pursuing Elodie Hogan, the Californian girl who he had met in London and was to eventually marry after a protracted and sometimes frustrating nine-year courtship.

After travelling, Belloc went up to Oxford, where despite having been a brilliant undergraduate he failed to secure a Fellowship which would have provided him with a safe academic career. This rejection was occasioned by his

**The formidable figure of Hilaire Belloc, Sketched by Bernard Partridge.** *Photo by NPG.*

**King's Land, the house where Belloc lived at Shipley.**

115

'loud' and opinionated personality, and it rankled him for the rest of his life as is clearly shown in this selection of lines from his corrosive and witty *Lines To a Don*:

'Don poor at Bed and worse at Table,
Don pinched, Don starved, Don miserable;
Don stuttering, Don with roving eyes,
Don nervous, Don of crudities . . .
Don middle class, Don sycophantic,
Don dull, Don brutish, Don pedantic;
Don hypocritical, Don bad,
Don furtive, Don three-quarters mad;
Don (since a man must make an end),
Don that shall never be a friend.'

Belloc began writing in order to make a living, and he also tried his hand at the lucrative American lecture tour circuit, following in the steps of Charles Dickens and Oscar Wilde with some considerable success. His first book, published in 1896, was *Verses and Sonnets*; *The Bad Child's Book of Beasts* also appeared in the same year and sold 4000 copies within its first three months, delighting many children with such lines as:

'I shoot the Hippopotamus
With bullets made of platinum,
Because if I use leaden ones
His hide is sure to flatten 'em.'

Belloc's main interests were, however, more serious. Catholicism remained a strong influence throughout his life and whenever possible his days began with a short Mass (he maintained it was impossible to concentrate for more than 20 minutes in church). *The Path To Rome*, which furthered his reputation when it was published in 1902, was based on a month-long walk Belloc undertook from the town of Toul in the Moselle Valley to Rome, and recounts the progress of an unshaven, hard-drinking, traveller through a Catholic landscape.

Four years later Belloc, Elodie and their young children found their way to King's Land in Shipley, the house which he owned and lived in on and off for the rest of his life. Dating from the fourteenth century with many later additions, it had been the village shop and was certainly never grand—at first there was neither water, electricity or gas; and oil lamps and candles were used to light it throughout Elodie's lifetime. The combination of the ebullient Belloc, his devoted wife, and five young children all living in a state of mild chaos, attracted some visitors but appalled others— one visitor described it as a 'gypsy' encampment'.

Belloc also tried politics, standing success-

*Looking across the river towards the church at West Grinstead.*

*The Shipley Windmill, now preserved as a Belloc shrine.*

fully as Liberal MP for Salford in 1906 and 1910, but he ended his political career by despising MPs as he had once loathed Dons— 'I am relieved to be quit of the dirtiest company it has ever been my misfortune to keep'. His political creed is now very difficult to comprehend, ranging from radical left to far right—he glorified Mussolini and vilified Jews; he was always conscious of the plight of the poor and railed against the evil 'bosses' who exploited them.

Elodie died in 1914 aged only 42. Belloc wore mourning for the rest of his life, an impressive uniform consisting of a black suit, black tie, and a black overcoat or cloak, all made by Lanvin, the famous Paris couturier! He locked the door of Elodie's room at King's Land so that it stayed untouched until his own death; he did the same with his son Louis's room—he disappeared while on a bombing raid with the Royal Flying Corps in 1918.

In his later years Belloc continued to write about anything and everything, dictating some 35 books in the 1930s and frequently not bothering to read the typescripts before they went to the publishers. As age began to curtail his travels—his last lecture tour of the United States was made in 1937 and the money was used to fund a visit to the Holy Land—he spent an increasing amount of time at King's Land, sharing it with his daughter Eleanor, her husband Reginald Jebb and their

children. His daughter and son-in-law helped to run the house and farm the land which then belonged to it.

A stroke at the age of 71 left Belloc a semi-invalid for his last 10 years. He had always maintained country customs, insisting that whenever anyone close to the family died, any children in the house should 'go and tell the bees'. When his turn came at the age of 83, perhaps they went down to the bees and whispered a verse from *The South Country* in his memory:

'The great hills of the South Country
They stand along the sea;
And it's there walking in the high woods
That I could wish to be,
And the men that were boys when I was a boy
Walking along with me.'

## Bibliography

Most of Belloc's 150 or so published works are now out of print. Conspicuous amongst them were his travelogues *The Path to Rome* and *The Cruise of the Nona* (1925), and his novel *Belinda* (1928). His many biographies included *Marie Antoinette*, *Danton*, *Cromwell* and *Charles II*. A.N. Wilson has written a comprehensive biography *Hilaire Belloc* (1984) published by Hamish Hamilton.

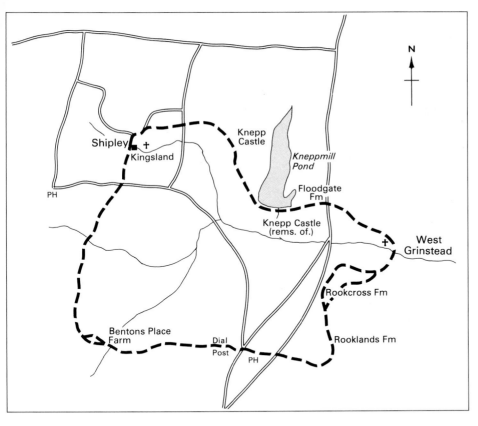

## A Walk with Hilaire Belloc

**Map:** OS Landranger 198.
**Start:** Shipley Windmill at Shipley, south-west of the intersection of the A24 and A272—OS Grid Ref. 144219. Parking on roadside. The windmill is open from 2.30 to 5.30 pm on the first Saturday and Sunday in each month from April to October; also some Bank Holiday Mondays. Tel: 040387 310 for more information.
**Nearest BR Station:** Billingshurst.
**Distance:** 9 miles.
**Time:** Allow 4 hours.
**Facilities:** Tea available in Shipley village hall on afternoons when windmill is open; pubs at Whitehall and Dial Post.
**Summary:** A walk through flat Sussex countryside to the north of the South Downs including views of Knepp Castle and its magnificent lake.

Shipley Mill is situated behind King's Land, the house where Belloc lived which is now inhabited by his grandson. There is no parking by the mill, but it's easy enough to park on the grass verge just east of the house.

A lane on the other side of King's Land leads up to the mill which is open as a monument to Belloc. When I visited in the summer of 1989 it was surrounded by scaffolding with its 'cap' removed for repair to the 'rail' so that it could revolve more freely. The English Heritage, who were overseeing the work, expected it to be completed by Summer 1990, and the collection of Belloc memorabilia was to be reinstated for visitors to browse over while the windmill ground its flour. This may well have been done by the time you visit.

The windmill is open from 2.30-5.30 pm, and during that time tea is available in the village hall, so careful timing is needed for everything to be fitted into this three and a half to four hour walk. A stop at the pub in Dial Post could also be included. From the windmill turn left out of the gate and head down the bridle-

way track that runs south. This crosses the River Adur via a couple of bridges, going along a pleasant, tree lined track with fields on either side.

When you come to a lane go straight over; or if you are already in need of refreshment, turn right for the pub at Whitehall which is not far down this lane. Continue to follow the track which is now much wider in a southerly direction. When it comes to an end, bear right through a gate into a field, passing a small, unused building named Lower Barn close by on your right, keeping to the left side of the field as you head for the next gate. Keep on along the wide track which continues in the same direction, with glimpses of Brookhouse Farm over to the right.

After a time you come to a bridle-way/footpath crossroads sign on the left. Turn left here, heading diagonally right across a field towards the corner by trees where you cross a stile and follow another footpath sign over a little bridge. The path continues along the right side of the next field into the trees where you come to a second bridleway/footpath crossroads. Turn left along the bridleway which is an overgrown track running between the fields with the large house at Bentons Place Farm ahead to the right. If this way looks too muddy, follow the footpath direction which leads to the other side of the house.

The bridleway goes through a gate where you bear right through old farm buildings, coming to the left side of Bentons Place which is an old house that appears to have been substantially rebuilt and modernised. Turn left on a track going away from the house here, and follow it along until you come to a small house on the left just on the edge of woods. Turn left by the footpath sign, turning right over a stile after about 50 yards. From there you cross a large open field, bearing a little to the left of a line of telegraph poles to reach a stile on the far side just to the right of the trees.

Head on in the same direction along the left side of the next two fields, passing a footpath turning to the left and then bearing right and slightly uphill towards a stile by a house on the right, probably passing through grazing sheep on the way. Walk straight across the next field which leads to a stile by the road going through Dial Post, conveniently opposite the pub. The main road here has been re-routed via a new by-pass which was unmarked on the 1987 OS map I was equipped with. As a result, few cars appear to pass through Dial Post which is a blessing for the village, although there's a steady hum of traffic in the background.

Turn left along the road, and just past the

*The view over towards Knepp Castle—the footpath bears away to the left across open ground, and soon brings you back to Shipley.*

B2224 forking to the left there's a footpath sign on the right. This takes you across an over-grown field on a path which seems to be seldom used. Bear right in the direction shown by the footpath sign, and you come to a new stile on the edge of the by-pass which can be crossed with care. Go over the stile on the other side of the road, and head down the right side of the field ahead, bearing right over a small bridge that crosses a stream at the bottom. This brings you to another field which goes uphill with a belt of trees to the left. The footpath sign here appeared to point to the right which is wrong—it was loose in the ground and had probably been turned round. Go uphill by the side of the trees, and at the top you'll find a fence but no stile. This is the footpath route, so cross over as best you can and walk on along the left side of the field ahead. At a gap in the hedge go through and walk down the right side of the adjacent field.

In the bottom right hand corner you will find a very decrepit footpath stile by a crossroads sign hidden in the undergrowth—this is where the footpath goes!

Take the left hand direction which follows the side of the field to the right, coming down to a tarmac crossing track at a gate. Turn left along this track, passing Rooklands Farm and a little further on coming to a group of large barns on the right just before a thatched cottage on the left which is Rookcross Farm. Turn right between the barns, and the footpath goes across the field ahead, making towards the left side of a large clump of trees about 300 yards away. There was no signpost to indicate the way here, and if you feel unsure the alternative is to stay on the tarmac lane and take the first right turn which will bring you to the crossroads track just south of Butcher's Row.

Having set out across the field and

reached the trees there is a stile ahead but this is not the one you want. Instead, go round the edge of the woods, and at the bottom corner bear diagonally left across a field, heading for a gate about 100 yards distant where you rejoin the tarmac lane at a crossroads. Go straight ahead here, following the lane as it bears right and left through the few houses of Butcher's Row, bringing you in view of West Grinstead with its church to the left and manor to the right.

Cross the river by the middle bridge leading directly up to the churchyard where you bear left round the far side of the church. Over to the right opposite the church door you will see a narrow path running up between hedges towards a metal gate. Walk up it and you will discover a footpath sign by the gate pointing along the left hand side of the garden of the adjacent house with a tennis court on the right. Carry on to a stile from where you follow the

*The bridge that leads to West Grinstead with its pretty church and lovely manor house.*

narrow track ahead as it bears right and left into a field, keeping in the same westerly direction. The footpath continues along the right side of a field towards trees ahead with the road beyond. At the trees turn right at a footpath sign by an old rickety gate in the bottom corner of the field, following the path along the trees as directed and then turning left over a stream and crossing a field taking you up to the road.

Cross the busy A24 once again with care, and go up the drive of Knepp Castle directly ahead by the side of the corner lodge. This is a private drive where there is unlikely to be much traffic, but it serves a few houses so take care. You pass the extraordinary buildings of Floodgate Farm with their waterworks on the right, and get glimpses of Knepp Castle on a hillock to the left. Keep on past some cottages in a hollow to the left, after which you come to the magnificent stretch of water which is Kneppmill Pond. A little further on you get your first glimpse of Knepp Castle as it comes into view across fields to the right—the castle is an enormous Victorian concoction. The drive bears round to the right, passing a gatehouse where you go over a cattle grid only a couple of hundred yards from the front door of the castle. Unfortunately you can't go right up to it—the footpath bears diagonally left across the park, although there is no sign showing the way. Walk across at about 45 degrees and you will come to the continuation of the drive which takes you away from the castle with fine views of the park.

After a few hundred yards a line of old oaks stretches off to the left across the park at an angle of about 30 degrees, with a few more oaks in a line to the left forming an incomplete avenue. Turn off the drive and walk along the side of the oaks to the right, continuing on the footpath which is again unsignposted. When you come to the woods ahead you will find a path—head straight through the woods along it until you reach a lane. Cross over and follow the footpath sign past the right of the house ahead, going through a gate and along the right side of a field which leads to more woods.

Carry on through these woods and you soon come to a few modern houses on the outskirts of Shipley. Turn right and left through an old iron gate, heading along the left of a field towards a lane which you reach by another old gate. Turn left here, passing the incongruous settlement of King's Reach, and the village hall is a short way on. With careful timing you'll make it there in time for tea, with King's Land and Shipley Windmill to the right.

# Walk 23: With Flora Thompson at 'Lark Rise'

*Lark Rise to Candleford is Flora Thompson's (1876–1947) autobiographical trilogy, recording through the eyes of a young girl, Laura, a world and a lifestyle that has now disappeared. The names of the people and places are fictional but were all based on reality, and that reality can still be seen when you visit 'Lark Rise' and walk across the surrounding countryside.*

In the last part of the trilogy, a gipsy visits Candleford Green and tells Laura (as Flora Thompson called herself in her autobiography), 'You are going to be loved by people you've never seen and never will see.' From this it seems clear that Flora Thompson recognised that her description of rural life in Oxfordshire in the late nineteenth century would become a classic of its kind, and it remains so today. In some ways it is a sad book, as H.J. Massingham wrote in an introduction to a 1948 edition:

> 'What Flora Thompson depicts is the utter ruin of a closely knit organic society with a richly interwoven and traditional culture that had defied every change, every aggression, except the one that established the modern world . . . we hear the thunder of an ocean of change, a change tragic indeed, since nothing has taken and nothing can take the place of what has gone.'

Flora Thompson was born as Flora Timms in 1876 at Juniper Hill. Her early years were mainly spent at the End House which is her home in 'Lark Rise', and as the oldest of 10 children (four died in infancy) her childhood can have by no means been easy—indeed the first chapter of the book is entitled 'Poor People's Houses'. Her father was a stonemason and bricklayer; her mother had been a housemaid in a nearby rectory. Between them they were ambitious for their eldest daughter, and taught her to read before she went to school. From then on she devoured books, whenever possible living in a literary world of her own which predictably distanced her from the other children in Juniper Hill.

Her short, formal education was at the

**The self-effacing and demure Flora Thompson.** *Photo courtesy of Oxfordshire County Museum.*

village school in Cottisford, where she also attended the small church. She then left Juniper Hill and her home for ever, and began work at the Fringford Post Office at the age of 14—today it's no more than 10 minutes away by car, but in those days of horse and cart it seemed a long way off. She was lucky to work and live with Mrs Whitton who we are told 'read a good deal . . . kept herself well informed of what was going on in the world,

especially in the way of inventions and scientific discovery . . . had she lived later she must have made her mark in the world'. It may-have been hard work, with daily starts at 7 am, but Flora enjoyed it and states in *Lark Rise to Candleford* that Mrs Whitton 'had more influence than anyone else in shaping my life'.

Eight years later, and beyond the timespan of her trilogy, Flora Thompson moved to Grayshott in Surrey to work in another post office. Despite the fact that the postmaster was later to murder his wife and child, Flora got on well there and records eavesdropping on the conversations of Conan Doyle and Bernard Shaw who occasionally came in to use its services, and of course took no notice of her.

In 1900 she married John Thompson, another post office clerk. They moved to work in Bournemouth, Liphook and lastly Dartmouth in 1928, producing three children on the way. Despite her husband's lack of interest, Flora continued her extensive reading, and was writing stories, essays and poems for her own pleasure until at last her talent began to bear fruit and she won a magazine competition for an essay on Jane Austen. She tried her hand—unsuccessfully—at trite, romantic stories in the hope of making some easy money, before finally writing *Lark Rise*. This began as a short story or essay based on her childhood memories of 'Old Queenie', one of Juniper Hill's characters. It was published in *The Lady* in 1937, and later expanded into the chapter entitled 'Survivals'. More of these stories followed, until Sir Humphrey Milford of the Oxford University Press encouraged her to write enough to produce *Lark Rise*. This and its successors in the trilogy were immediately successful, but for Flora in her mid-sixties this came too late:

'To be born in poverty is a terrible handicap to a writer. I often say to myself that it has taken one lifetime for me to prepare to make a start.'

At first glance the surroundings and flat countryside depicted in *Lark Rise to Candleford* are little changed, though the people certainly are. Juniper Hill ('Lark Rise') is still a small, quiet place despite the hum of the busy A43. In nearby Cottisford the village school had a new lease of life as a private house, having been closed in the 1960s, and in the church Flora's favourite brother Edwin's ('Edmund') name can be found on the First World War memorial plaque—he was killed in 1916. The old post office of Fringford ('Candleford Green') is now also a private house, and Flora's footsteps (in the chapter entitled 'Letter-Carrier') can be retraced via Willaston Farm to Shelswell Park and Home Farm:

'. . . She ran, kicking up the snow and sliding along the puddles, and managed to reach Farmer Stebbing's house only a little later than the time appointed . . . then across the park to Sir Timothy's mansion and on to his head gardener's house and the home farm . . .'.

Some of the people of these villages are descendants of Flora Thompson's contemporaries, but with a single tractor replacing 20 men most of the work has gone. Those who work now commute to Brackley, Bicester and further afield, and with many of the old cottages now refurbished and done up, rapidly increasing house prices have pushed out many locals. As with so many English countryside villages Fringford, Cottisford and Juniper Hill are merely providing dormitories for commuters; and with the loss of a local school, Sunday School and rector, they have certainly lost much of the community spirit which Flora Thompson celebrated.

## Bibliography

Flora Thompson's first published volume of verse was *Bog Myrtle and Peat*. *Lark Rise* was published in 1939, followed by *Over to Candleford* (1941) and *Candleford Green* (1943). *Still Glides The Stream* (1948) was her last, posthumously published book.

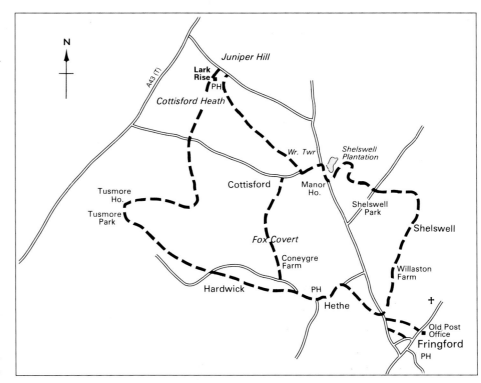

## A Walk with Flora Thompson

**Maps:** OS Landranger 152/164.
**Start:** Juniper Hill, just off A43 south of Brackley—OS Grid Ref. 579325. Roadside parking by public telephone.
**Nearest BR Station:** Bicester.
**Distance:** 10 miles (7 miles shorter walk).
**Time:** Allow 4-6 hours.
**Facilities:** Pubs at Juniper Hill, Fringford and Hethe.
**Summary:** A country walk from Juniper Hill where Flora Thompson was born, retracing her steps to school in Cottisford, and to the post office where she worked in Fringford.

Juniper Hill is a tiny place, within sight of the busy A43 but a world away from it. You can park in a lay-by by the public telephone box, though space is limited. On this walk there is quite a lot of field walking, and the going could be muddy depending on the season. Also signposting of footpaths is very poor, and at times you may find a compass a helpful aid to proving you are walking in the right direction.

Walk through Juniper Hill away from the A43, passing the pub on your right. From here Laura would usually walk along the road to school in Cottisford, though she sometimes took the more direct route across the fields which is the way we will go. About 100 yards out of the village turn right down the edge of the playing field on the unsignposted footpath, and then carry straight on ahead across the field beyond. When you reach an unploughed strip of land bearing diagonally left towards woods, head along it. This example of a farmer leaving a footpath intact deserves some applause.

When you reach the woods the main path appears to bear right, while a less distinct path goes straight ahead into the woods. Follow the latter path which leads you along the strip of woods running all the way to Cottisford. This winds its way through the trees and is in places partly blocked, demanding some ducking and diving to get by. After crossing a couple of 'tree bridges' the path brings you out to the edge of the woods, and from there on you continue to follow them round the edge of the field on the left towards the road at Cottisford. With no discernible path left by the farmer, this could be muddy and frustrating walking in winter. The OS map shows the footpath heading away from the woods before joining the road, but with no clear indication of where to go it's best to walk the most direct way.

Cottisford has a few fine buildings including the manor house sited next to the church on the edge of the woods. Having viewed these

*The view down the fine avenue of trees that lead to Tusmore Park.*

turn left along the road until you reach the old green. Opposite one of those unpleasant, modern telephone boxes stands a gleaming white house with fake lattice windows. Believe it or not this is the village school which Laura attended, but it has changed greatly since those days!

Turn right here, and follow the road downhill past an isolated house on the right and over a bridge. Just beyond this turn left over a stile and walk on ahead, passing by a large lake on the left. Near the end of the lake you will come to a gate and a fence. Don't go through, but turn right here along the edge of the field and follow its perimeter until you turn right again by the trees of the Shelswell Plantation, heading back towards the road. As the trees start to thin out look for a gate about halfway along on the left. Turn through this, and follow a good track ahead with woods on the left and a field with clumps of trees to the

right.

When you come to a tarmac lane cross over and go through the gate ahead, bearing left on a clearly defined track through parkland punctuated by trees with the occasional herd of grazing cattle. This is the start of Shelswell Park, a delightful place visited by Laura when she was working as a postgirl at Fringford. Go through a gate in the fence ahead, and at the next gate bear right where you get glimpses of the Home Farm. Follow the track round the side of a clump of woods, going through a gate by a house and over the stile ahead, with remains from Shelswell House over to your right—sadly the main house is demolished.

Walk ahead uphill across open grass, keeping alongside the edge of the park with woods on your right. This eventually brings you to a fence with a drive running down to Willaston Farm on the left, a building

recognisable by its small tower. Cross over this driveway and head straight on across the next field in much the same direction. Keep to the left and you will find a gate in the bottom left hand corner of the field, leading to an overgrown track which in turn leads through to the next field.

From here continue in the same general direction, heading to a gate that opens onto the road. Turn left down this quiet road and cross the bridge. Not far on there is a stile to the left where you turn onto another footpath. We found a sign here saying 'Put Your Dog On A Lead—Bull In Field'. Since it is illegal to keep a bull loose in a field where a public footpath passes through, I took little notice of this sign.

Follow the direction of the stile uphill across the field ahead, going across a drive and into the main street of Fringford. On the opposite side of the road a long, thatched building

122

was once the post office where Laura lived and worked. It is now identifiable by an ancient AA sign on its wall, and like most Fringford residences it appears to have been turned into a very comfortable house. There is no sign of a new post office, however, or indeed any kind of shop in this rather forlorn place—the best you can do is The Butcher's Arms, a reasonable pub on the outskirts of the village reached by turning left at the green.

To continue, walk down past the green which nowadays sadly fails to live up to the description given in *Lark Rise*. At the bottom head up a driveway which runs along the left side of a fine looking house with a large pond in front of it. Walk up close to it, and then bear left into a field and go on across a stile to cross the next field which has the same stupid bull warning. Follow the path straight ahead to a gate which takes you back to the road on the west side of the village.

Turn right to cross the bridge once again, and then bear left over a stile as indicated by a footpath sign. Head diagonally across the field ahead, walking uphill to the top where you can see over the rest of the field with the path following its left hand side. Follow this round to a gate with the houses of Hethe to the left, joining a lane which brings you out onto the road. Turn left over the bridge here and walk up through the village which is a pretty enough place, passing the pub and the cross, and then heading out of the village on the far side.

Ignore a turning on the left and carry on past a row of 1950s houses. Here you have the choice of whether to head straight back towards Juniper Hill via Cottisford, or to extend the walk via Tusmore Park, a difference of some 3 miles. To take the short route continue on past the church, and then turn down a driveway leading to Coneygre Farm. Beyond this the footpath goes ahead through the woods at Fox Covert, bearing right to cross the waterworks ahead after which it leads to the lane running through Cottisford opposite the church. From here you can retrace your steps as in the outward journey.

## Return via Tusmore Park

I was in a mood to go further on this walk, and to get a view of Tusmore Park. To go this way, follow a track off to the left just past the last houses of Hethe along the left side of a field. This leads you to a crossing track going to Tangley Farm on the left. Go straight ahead here, keeping on in much the same direction along the right side of the hedge which splits the two fields ahead. With no signposting or

*The church at Cottisford, a place which Flora Thompson knew well.*

*Above:* **The Manor House at Cottisford close by—although too poor to rub shoulders with such people in her lifetime, she has now outlived them.**

*Below:* **The lake close to the Shelswell Plantation.**

*The old post office at Fringford which is now a private home.*

obvious path, knowing which side of the hedge to be was for me a matter of guesswork, and with the fields well ploughed it was also heavy going under foot.

Keep on until you come to the few houses of the hamlet of Hardwick ahead. Here you turn right through a narrow iron gate which takes you to the road along the side of the end house. The sign here saying 'Private—No Bridleway' is directed at horses, it is a footpath. On the road turn left through Hardwick. Just past a telephone box on the right you will see a bridleway sign pointing right and left. Follow it to the right, crossing a narrow strip of grass to the gate beyond.

From here it is hard going, with no sign of a track or path. The bridleway as shown on the OS map bears left in a north-westerly direction which took me through an overgrown mass of weeds, and then across a field which was fully ploughed up. One finds it hard to imagine that the footpaths and bridleways here are put back in order, and if no path is apparent it's easiest to keep to the left side of the field. A little further on you can walk along a raised section between the fields which should be left intact due to a few trees along its length, making towards the woods ahead.

This brings you to a fine, woodland track going north-west, straight ahead through the woods. Eventually you go through a gate, and then continue along a fine avenue of beeches that mark the beginning of Tusmore Park. At the end of this avenue go through a gate and turn right along the driveway that goes past the back of the house which is sadly not open to the public. You pass huge ornamental gates with a good view of this strange looking place painted in a less than pleasant shade of yellow, and beyond the gates pass large outbuildings with a cupola and half-timber framed buildings that can be glimpsed down a driveway to the left.

Just here you turn right through a gate in the fence, walking ahead on a clear track which heads away from the house through the park which is notable for its fine trees. After a time you reach a gate with woods on your left—go through and carry on ahead with the parkland narrowing between woods both left and right. You soon reach a game reserve resembling a maximum security prison. Turn left along the high wire fence here, and at the end of the compound where the fence goes right, you go straight ahead over a small footbridge to cross a drainage ditch into the field beyond.

Walk up the side of this field—once again any semblance of a footpath had been obliterated here on my last visit—with views of the radio/radar station over on the far side of the A43 signalling that you are not far from Juniper Hill. Keep on until you join a track which leads to the road ahead, where you turn left and immediately right into the field on the other side. Keeping straight on in the same direction with the hedge on your right will take you back to Juniper Hill. As you come close to its houses you join a dusty track with an old footpath sign—one of the few to be seen on this walk—half hidden by the hedge. Turn right along this track and follow it round to the last house on the left. It has been extensively modernised, with a large extension on the back and a conservatory at the side, but it is nevertheless the house where the twin personae of Laura/Flora Thompson lived, right by the edge of the Lark Rise field.

# Walk 24: With Edward Thomas in Steep

*Edward Thomas (1878–1917) is best known for his poems, all of which were written between 1914 and 1917. Earlier in his life he earned a moderate living as a reviewer, biographer and natural history writer but his true vocation, as a poet, was cut short at the age of 39 by his death in the First World War. He was killed at 7.36 in the morning of 9th April 1917 while stationed at an artillery observation post near Arras on the Western Front. It was the first hour of the Battle of Arras in which some 150,000 British troops died. Edward's Captain wrote to his wife:*

'Your husband was very greatly loved in this battery . . . He was always the same, quietly cheerful, and ready to do any job that was going . . . I wish I could convey to you the picture of him, a picture we had all learnt to love, of the old clay pipe, gum boots, oilskin coat.'

His short time in the army appears to have been one of the most settled periods in his life. Having made the decision to volunteer, the future was entirely out of his hands. He left a diary from 1st January–8th April 1917 which is the record of a contented man, more interested in recording what remained of the countryside than the horrors of war:

'February 28th . . . Shelling town at night— moorhens in clear chalk stream by incinerator; blackbirds too, but no song except hedge-sparrow.'

Few of the men he served with could have had any idea that he was a poet, for in their company he remained secretive about his vocation. Nor did he give himself away to the public. He wrote his poems under the pseudonym 'Edward Eastaway', and at the time of his death only a small selection had been published. It was only years afterwards that they were recognised as being among the best pastoral poems in the English language.

Edward Thomas was born in London on 3rd March 1878. From his early days he hated towns and formed an idealistic love of the country. He followed closely in the footsteps of the writer Richard Jefferies who had recorded the English countryside in the late nineteenth century, and was later to write a

***Edward Thomas as painted by Ernest Henry Thomas in 1905.*** *Photo by NPG.*

definitive biography of him which appeared in 1909.

Thomas began to record his own impressions of the countryside, and at first found an immediate market for his essays which encouraged him to become a full time writer. The first of his many books was *The Woodland Life* published in 1897 when he was 19, and from then on he became a most prolific and hard working writer taking all the commissions that came his way. Among other things he wrote books about Swinburne, Maeterlinck, Keats, the Duke of Marlborough, Oxford, Windsor Castle, and walking the Icknield Way,

as well as a book of *Celtic Tales* (for children) and anthologies of folk songs. Most of this, however, was not what he wanted to do. He considered himself to be a serious pastoral writer, but because of the need for money— he had a young family to support—he felt that he had compromised himself and lapsed into hack writing.

His wife, Helen, was a liberal and progressive girl who had been dismayed when he had insisted on a conventional marriage (1899) because of her pregnancy:

'We hated the thought of a legal contract. We felt our love was all the bond there ought to be, and if that failed it was immoral to be bound together. We wanted our union to be free and spontaneous.'

Their son, Merfyn, was born early in 1900, and Edward came down from Oxford where he had read history—there was no English degree in those days—the following summer. He had resolved never to be bogged down by any kind of normal employment, and apart from a very brief period when he was taken on as an inspector of Welsh castles he did not waver from this decision. At first he found steady work as a book reviewer which built up over the years, but he was always in financial difficulties and the marriage suffered under the strain of Thomas's creative moods and depressions.

The couple did at least succeed in their great dream to always live in the country. At first they found a house near Bearsted in Kent, followed by a couple of years at a farm near Sevenoaks. They then moved in November 1906 to Berryfield Cottage at Ashford Chase

*The view from the Edward Thomas Memorial on the hillside high above Steep. The house in the valley was built next to Berryfield Cottage which passed to the new owner's gardener with the result that the Thomas family had to move out and up the hill.*

north of Petersfield, prompted by Helen who was keen for Merfyn to go to school at Bedales in nearby Steep—in those days it was a very progressive mixed school, and later, with two of their children there, Helen taught in its kindergarten.

Edward called Berryfield Cottage 'the most beautiful place we have ever lived in. We are now become people of whom passers-by stop to think: how fortunate are they within its walls . . .'. Helen commented

'At night all we could hear was the wind in the hanger, the barking of the foxes who lived there and the hooting of owls. It was a romantic and beautiful spot, and the house belonged to it and we loved it from the first.'

Three years later they moved to an even better position on the top of the hanger (a 'steep, wooded hill') at Week Green. A neighbour named Geoffrey Lupton, an idealistic old Bedales' boy with a private income, had offered to build them a house in the craftsman' spirit of John Ruskin and William Morris:

'In his workshop great oaks—which he himself years ago had chosen as they grew—and which he had seasoned and sawn and planed—were transformed into beams, doors and window frames. Everything for the house that could be made locally was so made . . .'

He also built Edward a little cottage nearby for his writing, but despite the idyllic situation and fine new home things did not go well. Edward was prone to depressions, and here he sank into what would today be termed a breakdown—he was worried about money now that he had three children to support, his serious writing was unsuccessful, his wife was

no comfort to him, and his idyllic preconception about life in the country had proved to be a myth. He spent large amounts of time away, staying with friends or visiting London to seek work, and at one stage was keen for a divorce. Finally, in August 1913 the Thomas family compromised by moving down to Yew Tree Cottage in Steep Village. It was a much simpler and cheaper house to run, and since Geoffrey Lupton allowed him to continue to use the study cottage it was a much happier arrangement all round.

By 1915 Edward's life in Steep was coming to an end. He was too old to be called-up, but in July of that year he enlisted in the Artists' Rifles, only telling Helen when it was done. Later, and one suspects after much soul searching, he volunteered to serve on the Western Front where life expectancy was anything but favourable. He lived with the army, and Helen left Steep to be nearer him. In

January 1917 he said goodbye to his wife for the last time.

Thomas's prose writing was often thinly-disguised poetry as this description of a farmer's daughter taken from *The Heart of England* so clearly reveals:

'She is at the altar of Aphrodite "full of pity"—today. She has been carried far in the goddess' dove-drawn chariot over mountains and seas, and has bathed in the same fountain as Aphrodite, nor yet seen of men—today. Delay, sun, above the sea; wait, moon, below the hills; sing, birds; rustle, new leaved beeches; for tomorrow and the day after and for ever until the end this will be but a memory and may be all she has . . .'

Nevertheless, it was another eight years before he allowed the poet within him full rein. He had worked as a poetry critic, and was encouraged to try his hand at verse by the American poet, Robert Frost, who was then living in England. Thomas's first poem *Up in the Wind* was completed in December 1914, and as with many of his poems it was a re-working of his prose. Over the next three years he completed a total of 144 poems, producing them in bursts and sometimes writing one a day. His last poem was written on 13th January 1917, two weeks before he left for France. He had hurled himself into poetry with a passion which at last enabled him to forget his worries and find contentment. The war was waiting—from the start he knew that in time he would volunteer and probably die.

His poems make fine reading today, and I have selected two here. *The Gallows* is one of many 'death poems', written before he volunteered for the Western Front. It starts like a nursery rhyme; it finishes in blackness, with the image of dead men swinging on the barbed wire of No Man's Land:

'There was a weasel lived in the sun
With all his family,
Till a keeper shot him with his gun
And hung him up on a tree,
Where he swings in the wind and the rain,
In the sun and snow,
Without pleasure, without pain,
On the dead oak tree bough.

There was a crow who was no sleeper,
But a thief and a murderer
Till a very late hour; and this keeper
Made him one of the things that were,

*A higher view looking down over the Edward Thomas Memorial, a wonderful spot from where one might see '60 miles of South Downs at one glance'.*

To hang and flap in rain and wind,
In the sun and in the snow.
There are no more sins to be sinned
On the dead oak tree bough.

There was a magpie, too,
Had a long tongue and a long tail;
He could both talk and do—
But what did that avail?
He, too, flaps in the wind and rain
Alongside weasel and crow,
Without pleasure without pain,
On the dead oak tree bough.

And many other beasts
And birds, skin, bone and feather,
Have been taken from their feasts
And hung up there together,
To swing and have endless leisure
In the sun and in the snow,
Without pain, without pleasure,
On the dead oak tree bough.'

Thomas also left poems for his wife, his three children, and his parents—one for each. To Helen he left:

'And you, Helen, what should I give you?
So many things I would give you
Had I an infinite great store
Offered me and I stood before
To choose. I would give you youth,
All kinds of loveliness and truth,
A clear eye as good as mine,
Lands, waters, flowers, wine,
As many children as your heart
Might wish for, a far better art
Than mine can be, all you have lost
Upon the travelling waters tossed,
Or given to me. If I could choose
Freely in that great treasure-house
Anything from any shelf,
I would give you back yourself,
And power to discriminate
What you want and want it not too late,
Many fair days free from care
And heart to enjoy both foul and fair,
And myself, too, if I could find
Where it lay hidden and it proved kind.'

## Bibliography

*The Collected Poems of Edward Thomas* are published by Oxford University Press in an edition that also includes his War Diary. Among a number of biographies are the memoirs of Helen Thomas, *As It Was* (1926) and *World Without End* (1931). *Edward Thomas—A Poet For His Country* by Jan Marsh (Elek) combines a biography with a critical analysis of his writing.

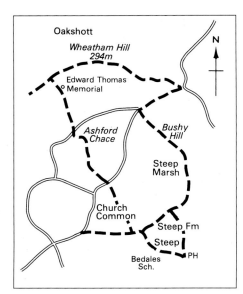

## A Walk with Edward Thomas

**Map:** OS Landranger 197.
**Start:** Steep, north of Petersfield off the A325 in Hampshire—OS Grid Ref. 745254. Park on roadside near to church.
**Nearest BR Station:** Petersfield.
**Distance:** Approximately 6 miles.
**Time:** Allow around 3 hours.
**Facilities:** Two pubs in Steep.
**Summary:** A fine walk up the hanger that towers above Steep, walking up the hillside dedicated to the memory of Edward Thomas. The route passes close by the places where he lived.

This walk passes through countryside similar to that of the Gilbert White walk at Selborne; as the crow flies the two villages are not that far distant, and both have 'hangers' dominating their landscape and affording magnificent views. The hike up to the Edward Thomas Memorial on Shoulder of Mutton Hill is severely steep, and a moderate level of fitness is required. Once up there the views are stupendous, which makes it worth reserving this walk for a fine, clear day when you can see 'sixty miles of South Downs at one glance' as Edward Thomas recorded. He was always an enthusiastic walker—in his second book of essays *Horae Solitariae* he described footpaths as 'footprints, perhaps, of the immortals'.

From the entrance to the church cross the road, and follow the footpath that goes straight ahead across the recreation field, passing a swing over to the left. The path goes into the woods ahead, where you follow a pleasant leafy

track downhill, ignoring a fork off to the right. At the bottom go over a stile and cross a stream. The most obvious footpath bears left to follow the side of the woods, but the one you want goes straight ahead across the field, following the direction of the footpath sign. Bear over to the right side of the field which is pasture land, heading towards the farmstead on the hillside. Follow the next footpath sign to a concrete track which bears left uphill between the farm buildings, bringing you out onto a lane.

Turn left along the lane for 15 yards or so, passing a sign which says that the farm sells fresh cream and organic potatoes. Then go right at the next footpath sign which takes you up another track, passing a couple of interesting modern houses hidden in the woods on the left. Keep on along this track which is very easily followed, walking along by the side of a stream on the left with the hillside sloping up to the right. A bit further on the track bears right up the hillside, and then left again on a woodland trail which was splendid when we walked along it on a sunny, late autumn day. Eventually the track breaks out into the open, coming up to a driveway which you join before walking on to the lane ahead with Shoulder of Mutton Hill towering before you.

Turn right and then almost immediately left by the signpost to get onto the footpath which will take you up the hill. Before you do this you might like to take a look at Berryfield Cottage where Thomas lived which is a short way down the lane to the left, just by the entrance to the large house of Ashford Chase. Unfortunately you can't really see much of it, and it appears to have been modernised extensively

The footpath going up the hill takes you up the side of a field. When you get into the trees ahead, take the right hand fork that heads up a very steep 'staircase'. This leads to open ground where you continue to climb steeply more or less straight up the hill, with the Thomas Memorial—a large rock with an inscription, positioned in 1937—soon coming into sight on the hillside. Just before you reach the Memorial a conveniently situated bench appears, and if the weather permits this is the most wonderful place to stop for a picnic. You are at the top of a natural amphitheatre, with the South Downs laid out before you in the distance. Over to the right you can see the radio mast on Butser Hill which marks the start of the South Downs Way, and from there you can witness '60 miles of South Downs at one glance'.

From here carry on to the top of the hill where enormous beech trees were badly decimated by the hurricane of 1987. When the ground levels off carry on ahead until you come to a clear crossing track by a footpath sign showing the 'Hanger Way'. The return route from here is to turn right along the Hanger Way, but before you do so you can turn left along the track which is Cockshott Lane to see the house built by Geoffrey Lupton a few hundred yards distant. Past the Old Litten Lane turning Cockshott Lane becomes tarmac, and when you've passed a few houses you come to Thomas's house on the left with its three high chimneys. It's mostly hidden by a hedge, but looking through the gateway you can see a plaque to the poet's memory. The small study cottage is the next house along, a little way down the hillside, and well hidden from the lane. Like all the houses on the hilltop, both command magnificent positions.

Retrace your steps back to the Hanger Way, carrying on straight ahead and passing a footpath which goes off to the left some way on. Eventually you bear right and start to head downhill through the woods on this track which can be very muddy—indeed there's a sign which says as much! Mud permitting the track takes you along another fine woodland trail, leading you down Wheatham Hill to the bottom of the hanger. When the buildings of Wheatham Farm come into view some way ahead, turn right over a stile. This leads you down a field along a pretty avenue of small trees towards a belt of bigger trees where you come out onto a lane.

Turn right along this lane, and after about 200 yards look for a footpath sign on the left just opposite another fine avenue of trees marking the boundary of the fields. Turn left along the footpath which heads across a field with a wire fence on either side, and then goes down the side of Bushy Hill past woods on the left. Cross over the stile near the bottom of the hill with a large Lutyens-style house up on the hillside to the right—one of many like this in the area—and then bear right across the meadow ahead, following large yellow footpath blobs on the telegraph poles towards a massive stile on the edge of woods ahead, also marked with yellow paint.

Climb over the stile and bear left down the side of the woods. A short way on the path appears to bear round to the right through the woods when it comes to a 'barrier' ahead. This is the only part of the route which is not well signposted; you go straight ahead over the barrier which is easily climbed, skip over the mud, and walk on down the left side of the field ahead. Head on to the bottom left hand corner of the field where you come to a narrow bridge

*Edward Thomas' last home in Steep, one of three workmen's cottages in a village which had then been 'untouched by jerrybuilders' (Helen Thomas).*

taking you across a stream to a three way footpath sign.

Walk on ahead here, passing by the western end of an enormous battery chicken house which appeared to have fallen into disuse when we passed by. Follow the clear path on over a stile with a barn on the left, and carry on uphill into more woods where the ground levels out and the path runs between a large white cottage with a steep pitched roof on the right and its white outbuilding on the left. One has the impression of walking through someone's private garden, but small white signs point out the footpath route clearly.

Walk on ahead into more woods, heading slightly downhill. Eventually you come to a footpath sign pointing left up a narrow track, and right down towards a lane. Go right here, passing through a gate and heading uphill on the lane towards Steep Farm on the hilltop. Just before you reach the entrance gates a lane leads off to the left which will take you to the Harrow pub if the time is right. From there you could retrace your steps, or walk back

along the road to the church where you started from. To continue from Steep Farm bear right round the high walls of the farmstead, following the footpath ahead and ignoring the stile on the right. Walk on past the buildings, heading over a stile and then crossing a narrow bridge to the right which takes you up a track leading back to the church at Steep.

There are a few other things to see in Steep. The church is interesting, and from there you can head west along the road for a couple of hundred yards until you come to Mill Lane on the right where the War Memorial commemorates Edward Thomas amongst others. Further on down the same road Number 2 Yew Tree Cottages, where the Thomas family lived, comes into view on the right just before you reach the Village Stores. It's set back from the road, between two similar pebble dash houses which have both been modernised. Some way on is the Cricketers pub, though you may prefer to try the Harrow which is in a much quieter position at the other end of the village.

# Walk 25: With Virginia Woolf at Monk's House

*For Virginia Woolf (1882–1941) Monk's House was the country retreat where she spent much of her time during the last 22 years of her life. It has been preserved for posterity by the National Trust, and remains much as Virginia and her husband, Leonard Woolf, would have known it, placed within sight and easy reach of fine walking country on the South Downs.*

Virginia Woolf is frequently described as 'one of the greatest writers of the twentieth century', though in truth such works as *The Voyage Out, To The Lighthouse,* or *Orlando* are not so widely read today. They are difficult in the same way that Proust is difficult, but whether she is read or not she will always remain famous as a founding member of the 'Bloomsbury Group'.

Virginia Woolf started with a literary, not to mention a financial, advantage. Her father—Sir Leslie Stephen—was a famous literary figure of his day who is now mainly remembered as the editor of the vast 63 volume *Dictionary of National Biography,* a work that kept him occupied for some 18 years. Virginia revealed her father's same literary instinct from an early age, while her sister Vanessa, who later married Clive Bell, opted to pursue the visual arts—mainly painting.

When Sir Leslie died in 1904, the sisters and their two brothers—Thoby and Adrian—left the comforts of the family home at Hyde Park Gate to move to 46 Gordon Square in Bloomsbury, and in so doing created that mythical set known as the 'Bloomsbury Group'. Bloomsbury was then considered a rather unsuitable place to live, but through Thoby's friends—made whilst an undergraduate at Cambridge—Virginia and Vanessa gathered together an impressive group of intellectuals and artists who started to pay regular visits to their house for earnest and frivolous discussions. The topics of conversation included many things that would have been considered highly unsuitable for the ears of two young, well-bred ladies; the idea that they should have aired their views on such subjects was even more outrageous. Many of those in the 'Group' are still well known today—Lytton Strachey, Clive Bell, Desmond MacCarthy, Maynard

***Virginia Woolf by G. C. Beresford in 1902.*** *Photo by NPG.*

Keynes, Saxon Sydney Turner, and of course Leonard Woolf—and most remained close to Virginia throughout her lifetime.

Virginia became engaged to Leonard Woolf in May 1912, and married him in St Pancras Registry Office some three months later—no church for them! Leonard Woolf resigned his job and his prospects with the Colonial Office in Ceylon in order to marry, and from then on he continued to make many sacrifices in order to care for Virginia. The price of her undoubted brilliance was severe bouts of mental illness and depression. She had suffered her first attack as a child, and these attacks recurred intermittently and blighted her

life—her first attempted suicide was recorded as early as 1913. The impending publication of some of her books was an incredibly stressful time for her, as she wondered how the critics would receive her work. This was frequently the catalyst that brought on her illness afresh.

In between these unhappy times were many comparatively happy years, and in his excellent biography Clive Bell, her nephew, makes it clear that she was frequently a delightfully funny aunt, and not the moody, introspective, forbidding intellectual that one might imagine. One of her greatest disappointments remained her decision—taken jointly with Leonard and her doctor—not to have children, in the belief that she would have been mentally unable to cope. While always a close and loyal friend to her sister, Vanessa's apparently happy family life with children around her would sometimes cause Virginia pangs of jealousy.

Virginia's association with Sussex and the downs began in 1910. She stayed with her brother, Adrian Stephen, at the Pelham Arms in Lewis, and thereupon resolved to acquire a country retreat away from the stresses of London which aggravated her illness. She initially rented a small villa in Firle, before taking the lease on Asheham House near Beddingham the following year. In 1916 Clive and Vanessa Bell leased the farmhouse at Charleston (open to the public in season) on the Firle Estate just east of Rodmell, providing the intellectual, artistic and literary coterie which revolved around the Stephen sisters with two bases from which to enjoy the beauty of downland Sussex.

Virginia and Leonard Woolf were forced to leave Asheham in 1919 when its owner

*Above:* **The view from the churchyard close by Monk's House—miles of forlorn downland.**

*Right:* **Monk's House, a cosy home for the Woolfs and ideal for satisfying Leonard's passion for gardening with its south facing conservatory.**

**On the top of the South Downs, walking along Front Hill towards Iford Hill.**

asked for it back. Virginia bought the Round House in the centre of Lewis on an impulse, but on taking Leonard to visit it they saw a poster advertising the sale of the Monk's House in Rodmell, a few miles to the south. They bought it at an auction a few days later for £700—would that we could buy our houses so casually these days!

Monk's House, which is only a few miles from Asheham, dates from the early eighteenth century. When the Woolfs moved in it had no water, gas or electricity and compared very unfavourably with Asheham in terms of general grandness. Virginia recognised, however, that its views of the downs were more extensive, and that the countryside around was better for walking, something she greatly enjoyed in company with her dogs. Its situation next to the church and churchyard must have seemed pleasant, and the garden had

much more potential than Asheham—this was fully exploited by Leonard who created its charming nooks and crannies; he ran three hothouses and employed a gardener to keep the house fully supplied with plants.

Inside the Woolfs made the rooms bigger, and with the help of her more artistically astute sister and Bloomsbury friends, Virginia furnished it with some of the most interesting trappings of the day. Amongst others, furniture, ceramics and paintings were provided by the artistic duo, Duncan Grant and Vanessa Bell; Vanessa's children, Quentin Bell and Angelica Garnett; and Roger Fry of post-impressionist fame. As Virginia's reputation grew, so did her earnings, and the Woolfs were able to install all the necessary equipment to make Monk's House a comfortable place in which to live.

Monk's House remained primarily a

retreat for weekends and holidays, Leonard Woolf's busy working life frequently keeping him in London. Apart from being very active politically as a Socialist, he and Virginia founded The Hogarth Press in 1917. They did this by simply buying and installing a printing press at Hogarth House, which was then their home in Richmond, and in their time they published writers as diverse as T.S. Eliot and Katherine Mansfield. Virginia was also asked to publish James Joyce's *Ulysses*, but felt that such a small press was unable to undertake such a large project.

By the Second World War the Woolfs had lost their interest in The Hogarth Press, and spent increasingly more time at Monk's House. Luckily they were in Sussex when their London flat in Tavistock Square was bombed, but as Leonard was both a Socialist and a Jew, the imminent German invasion filled them

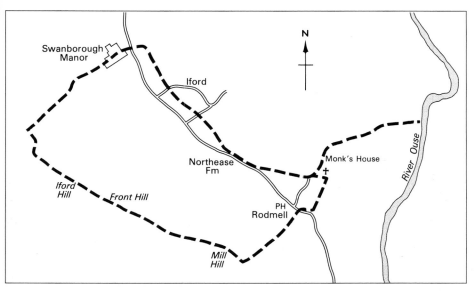

## A Walk with Virginia Woolf

**Map**: OS Landranger 198.
**Start**: Monk's House at Rodmell in East Sussex, on the Lewes to Newhaven road; OS Grid Ref. 420063; car park on the road just beyond Monk's House.
**Nearest BR Station**: Southease.
**Distance**: 6 miles.
**Time**: Allow at least 3 hours, including time to look at Monk's House.
**Facilities**: Abergavenny Arms pub in Rodmell.
**Summary**: An easy downland walk above Rodmell; the footpaths are well signposted and finding the way is straightforward.

with dread. The Woolfs were under no illusions about how they would be treated, and arranged means of committing suicide should this be necessary. By 1941 the danger of invasion seemed to have passed, but Virginia was about to enter her last illness. When depression came she was convinced that this time she would go irretrievably mad, a fate which had always terrified her. On 28th March 1941 she drowned herself in the River Ouse, despite having appeared perfectly calm when she went to see a doctor the previous day. She left a very touching note for Leonard:

'Dearest,
I feel certain I am going mad again. I feel we can't go through another of those terrible times. And I shan't recover this time. I begin to hear voices, and I can't concentrate. So I am doing what seems the best thing to do. You have given me the greatest possible happiness. You have been in every way all that anyone could be. I don't think that two people could have been happier till this terrible disease came. I can't fight any longer. I know that I am spoiling your life, that without me you could work. And you will I know. You see I can't even write this properly. I can't read. What I want to say is I owe all the happiness of my life to you. You have been entirely patient with me and incredibly good. I want to say that—everyone knows it. If anyone could have saved me it would have been you. Everything has gone from me but the

certainty of your goodness. I can't go on spoiling your life any longer.
I don't think two people could have been happier than we have been.'

Rodmell today is still comparatively untouched by modern progress, and the walk which follows is a fine one which Virginia would have known. She would nevertheless have found much to complain about in the Sussex of the 1990s. Even in the 1930s she railed against the destruction of the countryside. Asheham was bought by a cement company who gouged open the land around it, and the flat coastal plain south of Rodmell which had been wild land was overrun by the creation of unlovely Peacehaven. In a letter to Ethel Smyth in 1932 she described those responsible for such horrors as 'damnable buggers'—what would she say today?

## Bibliography

Virginia Woolf's principal works are *The Voyage Out* (1915), *Night and Day* (1919), *Jacob's Room* (1922), *Mrs Dalloway* (1924), *To the Lighthouse* (1927), *Orlando* (1928), *The Waves* (1931), and *The Years* (1937).
Virginia Woolf's nephew, Quentin Bell, has written the definitive biography of his aunt (1972, The Hogarth Press), published in two volumes covering the periods before and after her marriage. It's an immensely readable and enjoyable book, whatever your level of interest in Virginia Woolf.

From Monk's House take the small lane running down the side to the church at the back of the garden. Walk through the churchyard with fine downland views ahead, and in the far right hand corner you'll find a stepping hole cut in the wall with a footpath sign on the other side. Step through and walk straight ahead through a farmyard and along a track with views of the downs to your left. You soon come out onto the Rodmell Road—turn right here along the pavement for about 50 yards until you come to a blue bridleway sign for the South Downs Way.

Follow this sign, crossing over the road and going up a short, grassy track by the side of a house with a conservatory, and then up a long, metalled track past a few houses. This will eventually take you up to the top of the downs where you come to a gate with a footpath sign ahead, with views over towards Fore Hill and Breaky Bottom. (Those with OS maps can easily extend this walk to the south-west.) On the right there's a narrow track with a bridleway sign which is easy to miss. This is the way you go, passing a small house on the right and a large and imposing pink and white house with extensive gardens in a fine position on the left.

Walk along the bridleway which soon comes out into open country with fine downland views both right and left. The track goes down along Front Hill, heading up Iford Hill and passing crossing tracks on the way. The going is good, and eventually the bridleway becomes a concrete track as shown on the OS map—no chance of mud and smooth enough to push a pram on, but somewhat tedious.

*Another view from the churchyard at Rodmell with some oil seed rape brightening the scene.*

Keep straight on with views over to Iford and The Brooks on your right, and Woodingdean over to the left. Eventually you come to a fence with bridleway signs indicating that you leave the concrete and turn right and left along its perimeter. You'll see another concrete track heading down into the valley towards Swanborough Manor—follow it down if you like a hard surface under your feet, or go on a little further and take the next track downhill which is likely to be more muddy and rutted. Both these tracks bring you down towards houses, passing a modern barn conversion on the right. Carry on down the track, and you soon come to the road by the side of Swanborough Manor.

Cross straight over the road here, following the footpath sign into a field. When we walked this way the path had been completely ploughed up and sewn over, so follow the general direction as shown by the sign, heading diagonally across the field close to the left corner of a house and aiming at a gate about 50 yards beyond it. Go through this gate and then straight across the next field, heading more or less parallel to the road. Cross a stile and continue across another field in the same direction, which brings you to a stile just outside Iford by a large house with a walled garden over to the right and trees to your left.

Keep on through Iford, passing an imposing white house with large gardens, and a classic Georgian house painted pink on your left. Follow the footpath signs through kissing gates, keeping straight ahead until a footpath sign indicates that you bear diagonally right across a field, heading for Northease Farm where you turn right and join the road. Walk along the left side of the road, first on the pavement and then on the grassy verge which is fairly safe from passing traffic. Beyond the school playing fields a footpath is indicated going straight ahead where the road bends right just past a large house with an enormous picture window. Head across the field for Rodmell with its church to your left. Go over a stile, straight past the tennis court of a fine old house, and ahead over a step in the wall. This leads you to a track which joins the road near the church, a short distance above Monks House.

To finish the day you could walk down from Monk's House past the car park, and go along the track ahead which is a bridleway, leading to the River Ouse where Virginia Woolf perished so tragically. The landscape here is flat, featureless and somewhat depressing—no help at all in her hour of need.

# Walk 26: With D.H. Lawrence at Zennor

*David Herbert Lawrence (1885–1930), one of Britain's finest twentieth-century writers, spent two years of his nomadic life at Zennor on the wild north coast of Cornwall. The harsh environment reflected his passionate struggle with life and his fellow men, ending in ignominious rejection.*

Lawrence was born into a poor Nottinghamshire mining community. With the support of his mother, and despite illness which dogged him all his life, Lawrence won a scholarship to study as a teacher at Nottingham University College. His mother had also been a teacher, and their relationship was celebrated in *Sons and Lovers*, one of his many semi-autobiographical novels.

After two years he abandoned teaching as a career, and from then on lived as best he could as a full time writer. At the age of 27 he met Frieda, a relation of the German 'Red Baron' (von Richthofen), who was married, had three children, and was six years his senior. To mark the start of what was to be a lifelong and stormy relationship, Lawrence and Frieda eloped to Germany where the unfortunate Lawrence was briefly arrested as a spy. (In the light of this, his later experience

at Zennor seems even more bizarre.)

Lawrence and Frieda were soon back in England. In 1915 his most recent novel, *The Rainbow*, caused a stir when a magistrate declared it obscene and ordered all existing copies to be destroyed. Today the 'obscenity' is impossible to discern, and the ban was no doubt partly due to Lawrence's veiled criticism of the First World War; his heroine ridicules her lover in uniform. Jingoism was the order

**D. H. Lawrence in his Mexican Phase, painted by Dorothy Brett in 1925 when he had long given up on England.**

**The farmhouse at Tremedda close by Higher Tregerthen where Lawrence lived.**

of the day and Lawrence was sickened and horrified by the war, and by his country. He was twice called up and rejected as unfit by the army—once while at Zennor— a humiliating experience which is graphically described in *Kangaroo*.

Depressed by the war and by *The Rainbow*, Lawrence moved with Frieda to what he hoped would be a new life in Zennor at the end of 1915:

'We shall stay in Cornwall till our money is gone—which will take three or four months—then I think we may as well all go and drown ourselves. For I see no prospect of the war ever ending, and not the ghost of a hope that people will ever want sincere work from any artist.'

First they stayed in the Tinner's Arms in the village before moving to the group of cottages at Higher Tregerthen the following March—'What we have found is a two roomed cottage, one room up, one down . . . It is just under the moors, on the edge of the few rough stony fields that go to the sea. It is quite alone . . .'.

At Zennor, as at other places, he had hopes of founding a community of 'Rananim'—based on the Hebrew name for 'green, fresh or flourishing'—with like-minded people disassociating themselves from the evils of the world. This utopian dream never materialised, but as a first step he persuaded the literary couple—John Middleton Murry and Katherine Mansfield—to move into one of the adjoining cottages. The arrangement didn't last long, not least because of his tempestuous behaviour with Frieda. Katherine wrote:

'He simply raves, roars, beats the table, abuses everybody . . . What makes these attacks insupportable is the feeling one has at the back of one's mind that he is completely out of control. Swallowed up in acute insane irritation . . . They are both too tough for me to enjoy playing with . . . And I shall never see sex in trees, sex in running brooks, sex in stones and sex in everything.'

Despite, or perhaps on account of the storms, he wrote his passionate novel *Women in Love* at Zennor, and later he used his experiences there for the extraordinary chapter entitled *'The Nightmare'* in his novel *Kangaroo*, written five years later in Australia. Kangaroo is the nickname of one of the main protagonists; Lawrence is the hero or anti-hero in the guise of 'Richard Somers', and Frieda is

*The coastal footpath looking west towards Zennor Head.*

'Harriet'. In a flashback to his life at Zennor, 'Somers' recounts how the Lawrences were persecuted.

The trouble started on Christmas Eve 1916, when Lawrence and Frieda were visiting an American journalist, Robert Mountsier ('Mosell'), at a nearby cottage. The police sergeant called and asked all kinds of questions, and from then on it became obvious that they were under suspicion. In *Kangaroo* that was not the end of it:

'When Mosell got back to London he was arrested, and conveyed to Scotland Yard: there examined stripped naked, his clothes taken away. Then he was kept for a night in a cell—next evening liberated and advised to return to America.'

Later the Lawrences visited Cecil Gray ('James Sharpe'), a dilettante musician, at nearby Bosigran Castle to the south-west of Zennor. Knowing there were informers outside, 'They talked in occasional snatches, in mockery of the enemy that surrounded them. Then Somers sang to himself, in an irritating way, one German folksong after another, not in a songful, but in a defiant way . . . And in the silence, the tense and irritable silence that followed came a loud bang. All got up in alarm, and followed Sharpe through the

dining-room to the small entrance-room, where a dim light was burning. A lieutenant and three sordid men in the dark behind him, one with a lantern.'

In the novel they are accused of flashing a light out to sea—in real life one of Gray's curtains had come undone—and an unpleasant scene ensues. After the men left, 'the three went back to their room, fuming with rage and mockery. They mocked the appearance and voice of the lieutenant, the appearance of the weeds, and Harriet rejoiced over the one who had fallen into a ditch. This regardless of the fact that they knew that *some* of the watchers were lying listening in the gorse bushes under the windows.'

The Lawrence's cottage was searched in their absence, a violent intrusion later recaptured by 'Harriet' in *Kangaroo*:

'She looked in the drawers—everything turned upside down. The whole house ransacked, searched. A terrible fear came over her. She knew she was antagonistic to the government people: in her soul she hated the fixed society with its barrenness and its barren laws.'

Finally, on 11th October 1917 Lawrence and Frieda were ordered to leave Cornwall—'The police-sergeant, in rather stumbling fashion, began to read an order from the military authorities that Richard Lovat Somers and Harriet Emma Marianna Johanna Somers, of Trevetham Cottage, etc., should leave the county of Cornwall within the space of three days.'

Lawrence wrote in a letter, 'I cannot even conceive how I have incurred suspicion. We are as innocent even of pacifist activities, let alone spying of any sort, as the rabbits in the field outside. And we must report to the police. It is very vile. We have practically no money at all—I don't know what we shall do.' Yet one does have some understanding for the suspicion of the authorities: ships had been sunk by German submarines within sight of Higher Tregerthen ('Trevetham'); Lawrence was thought to be a subversive anti-war writer; the couple had a number of strange visitors, and Frieda was related to the infamous Red Baron!

Not all Lawrence's time at Zennor was so bleak. He proved to be a most successful gardener—'My gardens are so lovely, everything growing in rows, and so fast . . . It looks like a triumph of life in itself'—and he spent

a great deal of time helping at the neighbouring farm, chatting to the owners, the Hockings (the 'Thomas' family in *Kangaroo*):

'He was very thick with John Thomas and almost always at the farm . . . And he seemed to be drifting away, drifting back to the common people, becoming a working man, of the lower classes . . . "I declare!" said John Thomas, as Somers appeared in the cornfield, "you look more like one of us every day".'

After Zennor the Lawrences continued their life of wandering, visiting and living in Italy, Ceylon, Australia, Mexico and America. In 1925 Lawrence became seriously ill with tuberculosis, moving for the last time to the south of France in 1929—the same year that his first exhibition of paintings was raided by the police in London. He died on 2nd March 1930 at a sanatorium in Venice, but even after his death controversy continued. His last completed novel *Lady Chatterley's Lover* was prosecuted for obscenity in both the United

States and England when it was first published complete in 1959—thankfully both sense and the power of Lawrence's writing prevailed.

## Bibliography

In addition to those mentioned above, Lawrence's other novels include *Aaron's Rod*, *The Lost Girl*, *The Trespasser*, *The White Peacock*, *The Plumed Serpent*. He also wrote several travel books, numerous poems, and at the end of his life became an accomplished painter. Among many biographies *The Life of D.H. Lawrence* by Keith Sagar (Eyre Methuen) brings Lawrence to life in an impressive way, quoting extensively from his 5000 or so letters.

## *A Walk with D.H. Lawrence*

**Map:** OS Landranger 203/Pathfinder SW33/43.
**Start:** The Wayside Museum at Zennor, on the B3306 north of Penzance in Cornwall— OS Grid Ref. 453383. Free car park nearby. The Wayside Museum is open daily, Easter to end of October, at 10 am.
**Nearest BR Station:** Penzance.
**Distance:** Approximately 5 miles.
**Time:** Allow 2–3 hours.
**Facilities:** Pub in Zennor; tea or coffee available at Wayside Museum; cream teas at farmhouse on Trewey Hill.
**Summary:** A fine circular walk, passing the cottages where Lawrence lived outside Zennor, and returning along the dramatic coastal footpath.

Zennor is reached by the narrow coast road running north from Penzance and west from St Ives. You can park at the bottom of the hill by the old chapel which has now been turned into a hand-made furniture factory—such is progress. Next to it is the Wayside Museum which gives an interesting insight into life as it used to be in Zennor, but with no records of the Lawrences' unfortunate sojourn there. For such a small museum it has a good shop with a wide selection of books and pamphlets on the area, including the local OS maps.

The first part of this walk is an easy stroll across fields but the return leg along the coastal path is a real up and downer on what is sometimes a quite slippery trail. It can be hard going, and would not be appealing on a wet and windy day—so plan this walk with care! From the car park turn left up the hill towards the church. On your left you pass the pub where Lawrence lodged—it would still be recognisable to him, and for us today it has a garden and serves food.

Turn left up between the pub and the church, and then turn right onto a track which

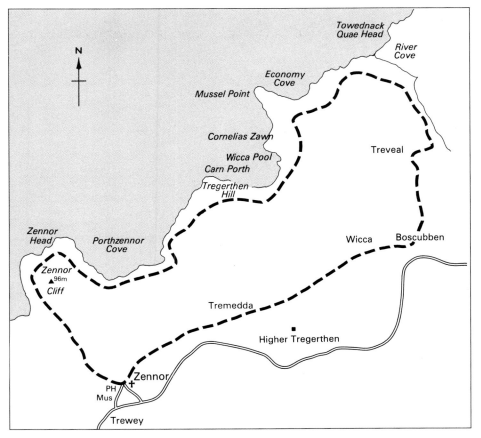

*The view of Zennor—a small community which rejected Lawrence and his friends at a time of national stress.*

runs between the church and farm buildings, heading off across fields in a direction more or less parallel with the road. Finding the way is fairly easy, even though there are no signposts. Sometimes tracks lead off in the wrong direction across grass fields, but keep following the strange old stepping stones through all the walls which appear as slabs of stone laid like prehistoric cattle grids. These mark the route of the public footpath, as opposed to the modern farm gates which are for the farm tracks.

Follow the path along a gentle, flat landscape, with strange boulders in the grass looking for all the world like fossilised sleeping seals. Cross over a lane behind the first set of farm buildings you come to at Tremedda, and a little further on the path passes equally close to the next set of farm buildings at Tregerthen. When I walked by, a heavy rebuilding programme was in progress, possibly develop-

ing the buildings into holiday homes. To the right there is a cluster of three cottages on the hillside which is Higher Tregerthen where Lawrence lived in splendid isolation. The cottages are now somewhat disfigured by modern additions—a tale of woe for all of Cornwall—and should not be confused with the two larger houses on the hilltop above the road.

Carry on along the path which goes close behind Tregerthen, heading into bushes and trees where you bear left and ignore a possible right hand fork. The path goes round the left side of an overgrown, ruined building, and then resumes its course across the fields. A solitary black and white post indicates the way towards the farmstead at Wicca where the path goes through the farmyard between the buildings to join a tarmac track—there's a map on a board on the wall here showing where you are and where you can go.

Continue walking along the lane ahead

to the next farmhouse at Boscubben. The lane bears round the back of this house, and you then take the left fork downhill past a couple of signs telling you that the track is a footpath and banned to motors. Follow this track downhill towards the farmstead at Treveal where it bears left round the first house and then sharp right downhill away from the farm buildings, passing a quaint, whitewashed cottage on the left.

Having left the tarmac the track now narrows as it heads down into the gully ahead. About halfway down you come to footpath signs, pointing ahead and to the left. Take the left hand turning signposted to Cove which takes you along the side of the gully above the River Cove on a narrow track, passing enormous fuschia bushes which are laden with flowers in late summer. This path soon comes to the headland facing Towednack Quae Head where you join the coastal path with a fine view over the mass of rocks called the Carracks.

From here you turn left to head west along the coastal path, and the far headland which soon comes into sight is Zennor Head. This is the one you are making for, and although it doesn't look far, you can reckon that on foot it will take you at least an hour of walking up and down helter-skelter fashion, following the contours of the various coves. Some of the going is rocky and can be quite a scramble, but despite these drawbacks it is a magnificent walk along a wonderful stretch of wild, majestic coastline.

Keep following the narrow path which is always plain to see. Zennor Head is not always in view, but you know you are getting close to it when after a short climb uphill to the left the path bears right downhill over a rushing stream at Tremedda Cliff. From here you can see the mass of Zennor Head with its distinctive pile of rocks to the right, and a footpath sign sends you on the track that runs round its side. Below you can see sandy Porthzennor Cove, and once past the pile of rocks on Zennor Head you bear round the headland, with a fine view of the lean spit called Gurnard's Head opening out in the distance, with beautiful beaches below in the coves of Pendour and Veor.

The path heads inland from here and Zennor soon comes into view. Walk past the continuation of the coastal footpath which goes off to the right, and keep on ahead, joining a tarmac lane and walking on up towards Zennor where you emerge just behind the pub. If five miles is not enough for you, this fine walk can easily be extended with the aid of an OS map. You could carry on eastwards from Treveal, cutting across on the footpath to return along the coastal path via Trevega Cliff or Hellesveor Cliff some three miles further on. Alternatively, at the other end of the walk you could continue along the coastal path from Zennor Head to the next headland at Carnelloe, returning inland via Ponjou on a path which takes you directly to the museum; or go further west to Gurnard's Head and return via Treen and Ponjou.

Although not served by a footpath, I can also recommend the excellent teas served in season at the farmhouse a short way up Trewey Hill above Zennor, half a mile or so from the car park. Head uphill out of Zennor in a westerly direction (it's a one-way village, so you have to follow the one-way system by car), and then go along the coast road for a short distance, taking the first left hand turning uphill to a sign saying that teas are served at the first old farmhouse on the right.

*Magnificent scenery but slow walking—the section of the coastal path which this walk follows weaves up and down, in and out, and is not for foul weather.*

# Walk 27: With T.S. Eliot in East Coker

*Thomas Stearns Eliot (1888–1965)—poet, playwright, philosopher and Nobel Prize Winner—came to England, stayed, and became totally anglicised. Today he is probably best remembered for* The Waste Land, *the long poem of despair which earned him his reputation in the 1920s.* East Coker *was one of the equally famous* Four Quartets.

T. S. Eliot was a very formal man which accounts for the public 'T.S. 'rather than 'Tom Eliot'. He invariably dressed in sober suits, and completely suppressed any sign of his American upbringing or accent. He never lived at the small Somerset village of East Coker, and we don't know when he first visited it, but he was attracted to the place by his ancestors who had lived there some 300 years before.

Stephen and Katherine Elliott are recorded in the parish register of 1563. Over the next century various 'Elliotts' regularly appeared, gradually losing an 'l' and a 't' to become Eliot. They survived the plague of 1645, but then disappeared after 1664 to reappear in America. An Andrew Eliot had emigrated to Salem and become a jury member of the infamous Witch Trials. Andrew's direct descendants were Henry and Charlotte Eliot of St Louis, Missouri, and Tom Eliot was born to them in 1888.

The Eliot family were comfortably off, with two large homes in the area, and Tom appears to have had an agreeable childhood. His brilliance led him to Harvard at the age of 18 where, while studying philosophy and metaphysics, he discovered Dante and the culture of Europe. This prompted his first trip across the Atlantic for a year's sabbatical at the Sorbonne, despite his parent's puritanical disapproval—they feared for their son's welfare in such a sin-soaked city. After three further years of metaphysics, Eliot travelled to Oxford in 1914 for a year's study on a Sheldon Travelling Fellowship, a prelude to the illustrious academic career that appeared to await him.

Despite working hard and preparing *Knowledge and Experience in the Philosophy of F. H. Bradley* for his doctorate, there were diversions.

**T. S. Eliot, photographed in relaxed mood by Kay Bell Reynall in 1955.** Photo by NPG.

(Bradley was a late nineteenth-century Oxford philosopher, and in the last year of his life, Eliot confessed that he could no longer make head nor tail of what he had written about him.) Within a year of arriving in England Eliot had met and married Vivien Haigh-Wood. There was no official engagement, and the marriage took place in secrecy at a registry office in Hampstead. Vivien's more liberal parents took the news well, but when Eliot travelled alone to face his parents on the other side of the Atlantic they proved less forgiving. Henry Eliot refused to continue giving financial support to his son, and the two parted on bad terms never to meet again—his parents never met Vivien.

Nor did the marriage work out well. Vivien proved to be mentally unstable, and after years of strain Eliot abruptly separated from her in 1933.

After nine years of careful preparation Tom Eliot was on the verge of completing his doctorate and commencing a career as a lecturer in comparative religion at Harvard. He turned his back on America, however, returning to London to support himself and his wife, first as a school teacher, and then by working in the Colonial and Foreign Department at Lloyds bank from 1917 to 1925. Despite this somewhat prosaic employment he soon built up a circle of friends that included most of the leading literary lights of the day—not least the American modernist poet Ezra Pound; the philosopher Betrand Russell (who it seems had a brief affair with Vivien); and Leonard and Virginia Woolf who published Eliot's early poetry at The Hogarth Press.

Eliot also worked on a couple of literary journals in his spare time, and it was in the *Criterion*, which he was then editing, that *The Waste Land* first appeared in 1922. Most of it had been composed at a sanatorium in Lausanne where he had been recovering from a nervous breakdown, and in its original form it was a thousand or so lines long; it was cut to less than half by the help of Ezra Pound. This brought its own problems, for when *The Waste Land* was published in book form by The Hogarth Press it was too short to fill the allotted number of pages. Leonard Woolf asked Eliot to fill the space, and hence his famous *Notes on the Waste Land* which in reality shed little light on this virtually incomprehensible poem.

*The Waste Land* is a cry from the heart by the common man. The fact that it has no clearly defined meaning has contributed to its timeless success—academics and would-be intellectuals still love to puzzle over its verses and come up with their own explanations. The *Oxford Companion to English Literature* claims that *The Waste Land* established Eliot 'as the voice of a disillusioned generation' in the years following the First World War. Its success also brought about a change in his employment, for he left the bank to become a director of Faber & Gwyer (later Faber & Faber) in 1925, building up their poetry list and gradually setting himself up as a daunting figure of cultural authority.

Two years later Eliot became a British subject. He was also baptised and confirmed as an Anglican, having previously been an agnostic, whereupon religious life and church matters became deeply important for the rest of his life. In the 1930s he turned to the stage achieving a notable success with his Thomas à Becket play *Murder in the Cathedral*; and much later great acclaim with his black comedy—*The Cocktail Party* (1950). One wonders what he would have made of Andrew Lloyd Webber's money-spinning interpretation of *Old Possum's Book of Practical Cats* which he wrote for children in 1939.

Eliot's last great poems were the *Four Quartets* which were first published together in 1943. *Burnt Norton*, *East Coker*, *The Dry Salvages*, and *Little Gidding* are places which were important to him, and also represent the four seasons and four elements of life. The first verse of *East Coker* starts with the famous saying attributed to Mary Queen of Scots, awaiting her death at Fotheringay:

'In my beginning is my end. In succession
Houses rise and fall, crumble, are extended,
Are removed, destroyed, restored, or in their place
Is an open field, or a factory, or a by-pass
Old stone to new building, old timber to new fires,
Old fires to ashes, and ashes to the earth
Which is already flesh, fur and faeces,
Bone of man and beast, cornstalk and leaf.
Houses live and die: there is a time for building
And a time for living and for generation
And a time for wind to break the loosened pane
And to shake the wainscot where the field mouse trots
And to shake the tattered arras woven with a silent motto.'

Eliot was awarded the Nobel Prize for Literature and the Order of Merit in 1947. Ten years later he married for the second time. At the age of 68 his wife was his 30-year-old secretary, and once again Eliot insisted that the wedding should be completely secret; no one was told, and by his request it was conducted at an out of the way church at 6.30 am on a cold, January morning when it was still pitch dark outside. Despite this strange beginning and the age discrepancy, the marriage was by all accounts very happy, although Eliot's last years were marred by his growing infirmity due to emphysema, a disease of the lungs. He died in London on 4th January 1965; after a cremation at Golders Green his ashes were interred in the church of St Michael at East Coker in accordance with his wishes. As you enter the door a memorial can be found on the right hand side with the opening and closing words of *East Coker*—'In my beginning is my end. . . In my end is my beginning'.

## Bibliography

Poetry selections include *Collected Poems 1909-1962*, *Four Quartets*, *Selected Poems*, *The Waste Land and Other Poems*, and *Old Possum's Book of Practical Cats*—all published by Faber & Faber.

Plays, include *Murder in the Cathedral*, *The Family Reunion*, *The Cocktail Party*, *The Confidential Clerk*, *The Elder Statesman*—all published by Faber & Faber.

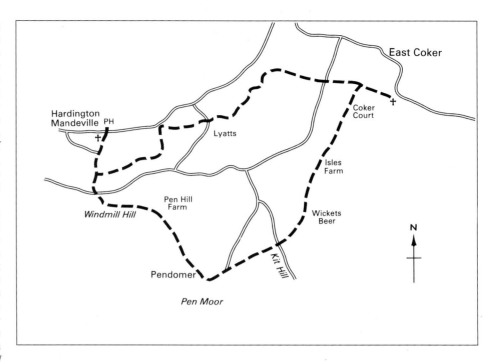

## A Walk with T.S. Eliot

**Map:** OS Landranger 194.
**Start:** From St Michael's Church at East Coker, south of Yeovil in Somerset—OS Grid Ref. 539123. Park by church or on roadside in village.
**Nearest BR Station:** Yeovil Junction.
**Distance:** Approximately 6 miles.
**Time:** Allow 3 hours.
**Facilities:** Pubs at East Coker and Hardington Mandeville.
**Summary:** A circular walk in country close to the Somerset/Dorset border, starting from the village where T. S. Eliot's ancestors lived, and where his ashes are interred.

East Coker is a small village just south of Yeovil between the A30 and A37 main roads. Coming from the east, St Michael's Church is up a lane off a bend just past the pub, with the driveway splitting left for the church and right for Coker Court. This is an enjoyable walk, but be warned, the footpath signposting is dire, and there's a distinct lack of proper stiles. The whole route is on public footpaths, and if you get a little lost have the courage of your convictions and forge on ahead!

To start this walk head downhill from the church, and then turn left up a narrow lane by the almshouses. Follow this lane uphill past a crossing track, and then on to a pair of semi-detached cottages by the corner of a field where the lane comes to an end at a gateway.

Ignore the tarmac track doubling back to the left which leads to Coker Court, and go ahead through the gate and then immediately left over a stile. From here head straight up the hill through the Coker Court parkland, and continue ahead over the hilltop, heading down towards a belt of trees on the other side with a house some way over to the right. When you reach the trees cross over an excuse for a stile, and head down a narrow woodland track which soon leads to a crossing track which you ignore and instead go straight ahead on an indistinct track that continues downhill through the woods. This brings you out of the woods at a bend in the lane just above Isles Farm. Cross straight over the lane, going over a stile into the next field. Walk on across this field in much the same direction which eventually brings you downhill to a gate in the far corner.

Cross over another lane here and carry straight on into the next field, heading uphill for a gap in the hedge on the hilltop. Start to bear more to the right across the next field when the farmhouse at Wickets Beer comes into view over to the left, heading towards another gate and another lane at Kit Hill. Cross straight over, going through the right hand of two gates as indicated by a yellow footpath arrow—the first seen so far on this walk. Keep on with the hedge on your left, veering left and downhill, with a good view westwards opening out ahead. Pass a copse on the left as you cross into the next field, and continue on down the left side which brings you down to a lane just north-east of Pendomer.

Turn left along this lane, passing a couple of houses on the left and one on the right— look for the strange little effigy set in the wall. The footpath turns right down the far side of this house, but it's worth going on to see the quaint little church which is reached by going through a gate and walking through part of the garden on the right of the fine old rectory/farmhouse which has a similar effigy set in its wall. The church is in a fine position, and tranquil, apart from the occasional noise of a high speed train passing by. A bench beneath the tower at its western end is conveniently placed for a short rest.

To continue head back down from the church and turn left onto the unsignposted footpath which runs along the south-west side of the house with the effigy. Pass through the gate and walk along the track which follows the side of a field, and then go through the next gate and across the field ahead towards Pen Hill Farm which is distinctive on the hillside. Bear over to the left to get through the hedge ahead which brings you to a wide track running up the hillside on the left of the field.

*A lonely line of wind-blown trees signify open country close by the small church at Pendomer.*

*Above:* **East Coker has many handsome, well to do houses such as the one shown here.**

*Right:* **The lonely farmhouse at Isles Farm which you pass close by, having climbed over the parkland of Coker Court.**

Follow this track up for a hundred yards or so, and then when it bears right towards the farm, you turn left over a stile on the edge of a small patch of woods. Cross another stile almost immediately, and then walk on up the right hand side of a large field. At the next hedge cross a stile into a meadow, and turn right to walk up to the top of Windmill Hill, the highest point of this walk, with more good views westwards.

At the top bear over to the left to find the gate which brings you out onto the road above Hardington Mandeville, where amazingly enough there's a footpath sign showing that you have indeed come the right way. Cross straight over the road here and walk down the hill ahead with houses on both sides. (If you want to find the pub, walk on down the hill and turn right at the bottom—the pub is about 150 yards further on, on the left.) The next footpath turning is a tricky one to spot. About 150 yards down the hill, just before you reach a short lane off to the left, there's a 'step' with a couple of pipes across it set into the front wall of a small house. This is about 75 yards before you come to a large, modern bungalow perched up on the right, which is distinctive because it has electronic gates, a meadow behind it, and a converted chapel next door.

The footpath doesn't look like a footpath! It goes up the side of the small front garden that goes with the small house, passes along the side of the house by an oil storage tank, and then goes over a stile into the field beyond. From here on the level of signposting is very poor, there are few stiles and most of the field boundaries are thick hawthorn hedges next to deep ditches—finding the way demands some skill! Walk on ahead, passing a house up by the roadside to the right, and cross over into the next field as best you can. Walk on across this field and then turn right through a gap to continue in the same direction towards the small farmhouse ahead.

Bear round the right side of this house—no footpath signs here!—crossing a drive and hopping over electric sheep fences that may bar your way. Once past this house bear left, heading downhill towards a patch of trees over to the right. This brings you down to the next field, and on down by the side of a small house to a lane where you will find another footpath telling you that you have been walking in the right direction.

Turn right down this lane, and then almost immediately turn right again, following a footpath sign for 'Lyatts' up by the other side of the house. Head uphill on a grassy track, and when the big farmstead at Lyatts comes

*Looking along the main street of East Coker close by the pub. The church is up to the left.*

into view ahead, bear left downhill to find a well hidden stile in the hedge which will take you into the next field. From here head straight downhill, crossing a couple of closely spaced stiles at the bottom to reach a 5-bar gate by the road, near to a couple of cottages and a short way downhill from Lyatts.

Turn right along the lane here. Just past the houses where the lane starts to bear uphill turn left onto a signposted footpath—this is the last signpost you will see! A local warned us that the way was not obvious. Basically you are heading for a large, modern house on the hillside by the side of a belt of trees, hopefully not encountering impassable hedges on the way. Cross over the small bridge ahead, and then bear right along the base of the next field in an easterly direction. Where convenient, take a sharp left to turn north up towards the house, making for the track which runs up the

left side of its large garden—we found some searching was necessary to find the right way here!

Once safely on the track walk on uphill, passing a pond on the right, dug in 1989, and a collection of newly planted trees. Eventually this leads up to a lane where you turn right, passing the front drive of the house, and heading on towards the driveway of another house ahead. Just before you reach this, turn left onto an unsignposted track which bears round the perimeter of a large clump of woods. Follow it round the side of the woods—the going could be muddy—bearing round to the right. The track improves as it passes Westfield Farm on the left. Cross straight over the lane ahead, and walk on up a fine avenue of trees which signals your re-entry into Coker Court's parkland, continuing straight on to get back to your starting point.

# Walk 28: With Vita Sackville-West at Sissinghurst

*The Honourable Victoria Mary Sackville-West (1892–1962) was, in her day, a highly esteemed writer of fiction, poetry, history, travel and gardening, as indeed was her husband, Harold Nicholson. Today their many books are largely forgotten, and they are remembered instead for their strange lifestyle, and the wonderful home they created at Sissinghurst Castle.*

Victoria, who was known as Vita all her life, came from an illustrious English family. She was the only child of Lionel—the third Lord Sackville—and Victoria Sackville-West, who by circuitous means had inherited Knole, near Sevenoaks, which at that time was one of the largest and most splendid English houses in private hands. Vita's mother, Victoria, was the illegitimate daughter of the second Lord Sackville, who begot her and a number of other children by a Spanish dancer named Pepita who he had met in Paris—this story is extraordinary in itself, and Vita's book *Pepita* which describes her grandmother is well worth reading.

Both mother and daughter were a strange mixture of English, aristocratic reserve and fiery Latin exuberance. Despite the staff of 60 servants at Knole, life was not always easy; the family's financial situation was precarious and indeed Vita's mother fought and won two famous court cases which highlighted the Knole inheritance and the large sums of money needed to run it. In later years these sums became so great that like many other fine houses Knole passed into the hands of the National Trust. (Knole is just over 20 miles from Sissinghurst—open Wednesday to Sunday, from Easter until the end of October—and both could be visited in the same day.)

In October 1913 Vita married the young, ambitious diplomat, Harold Nicholson, at the chapel in Knole with a grand society wedding. Helped by Sir Edwin Lutyens, one of her mother's many admirers, they converted Long Barn—south of Knole on the west side of the A21 near Sevenoaks Weald where Edward Thomas had lived from 1904–6—which they described as 'a cottage', into a fairly grand

**Vita Sackville-West photographed in usual arty form by Howard Coster in 1934.** *Photo by NPG.*

seven bedroomed home with separate cottages for the gardener and the children that were to come. With money from her mother Vita was also able to buy a house in Ebury Street in London.

At first their marriage was a great success. Vita produced two boys—Ben and Nigel who were both in time successful writers—but then broke up the marriage by abruptly falling in love with Violet Keppel, a similarly upper-class girl who later also became a well known novelist. Vita and Violet ran off together on numerous occasions, with Vita frequently dressing up as Violet's boyfriend 'Julian'. Despite periods of wild living in London, Paris or Monte Carlo, Vita was never recognised as a woman, although like her mother she was extremely good looking. In mid-affair Violet got married to a man named Denys Trefusis—apart from being pushed by her parents her reasons for marrying him are incomprehensible, particularly as she had promised Vita that Trefusis would never be allowed the pleasure of proving his manhood.

Over a three year period this intensely passionate affair created a scandal. Harold had at first been unaware of what his wife was up to, being abroad most of the time, but as the affair became more and more like a farce, he and Denys Trefusis began to chase their errant wives around Europe in the hope of bringing them back. In time Vita's enthusiasm for Violet faded, and she returned to Harold and from then on restricted herself to less passionate affairs. These were usually with women—most notably Virginia Woolf whose *Orlando* is a celebration of Vita, and of Knole where the original manuscript may be seen today—while Harold quietly contented himself with men which it seems had always been his inclination. In this way they cemented their marriage, and remained dedicated to each other for the rest of their lives.

In 1930 a move from Long Barn was prompted by a rumour that the adjoining land was to be sold to a farmer whose proposed chicken huts would spoil the view. Vita was by then a best selling author, and had the wherewithal to buy the ruined remains of an Elizabethan manor house named Sissinghurst Castle south of Maidstone. Little was left of the original building and the garden and surrounding land was in a terrible state, having been used as a dumping ground by generations of farmers. Despite these drawbacks Vita was set on the place, not least because she was a direct descendant of Sir John Baker who had lived there in the sixteenth century.

*A corner of the garden at Sissinghurst which Vita and Harold made famous, close by the South Cottage.*

'The place caught instantly at my heart and imagination. I fell in love; love at first sight. I saw what might be made of it. It was Sleeping Beauty's Garden; but a castle running away into sordidness and squalor; a garden crying out for rescue. It was easy to foresee, even then, what a struggle we should have to redeem it.'

In true aristocratic style, Vita, Harold and the two boys at first slept in camp beds in the tower, reserving Sissinghurst for weekends. Then, as the surviving buildings were renovated they set up a system whereby they could live separately and meet occasionally. When Vita was not gardening in the day, she worked on her books in the tower—usually by night—where she was not to be disturbed. Among her better known books written at Sissinghurst are the novel *The Dark Island* (1934), the biographical study *St Joan of Arc* (1936), and *Pepita* (1937). Today the Woolf's archaic press which printed the first edition of T.S. Eliot's *The Waste Land* can also be seen on the floor above her sitting room. Vita and Harold had their bedrooms in the solitary South Cottage where he also wrote books such as *The English Sense of Humour* (1947) and the biography *King George V* (1953) in his sitting room. The boys meanwhile lived separately at the Priest's

*Above:* **Oast Houses let you know you are in Kent, though most are now converted into private houses. This is the view while en route towards Buckhurst Farm.**

*Right:* **The twin towers of Sissinghurst—derelict when the Sackville-Wests took it over, it must have made an extraordinary home.**

House at the other end of the garden where there was a dining room and kitchen. They all met for more formal occasions in the 50-foot-long library in the main entrance building where over 4000 books were stored. Despite the size of the place there were no guest bedrooms, and by all accounts it was never particularly comfortable.

Over the next 30 years Harold designed and Vita planted what was to become one of the most famous gardens in Britain. In praise of Harold, Vita wrote:

'I could never have done it myself. Fortunately I had acquired, through marriage, the ideal collaborator. Harold Nicholson should have been a garden-architect in another life. He has a natural taste for symmetry, and an ingenuity for forcing focal points or long distance views where everything seemed against him, a capacity I totally lacked.'

The gardens were first opened to the public in the 1940s, since when they have attracted many thousands of visitors. Vita died from cancer at Sissinghurst in 1962, followed by Harold six years later. A year before his death, ownership and administration of Sissinghurst was passed over to the National Trust.

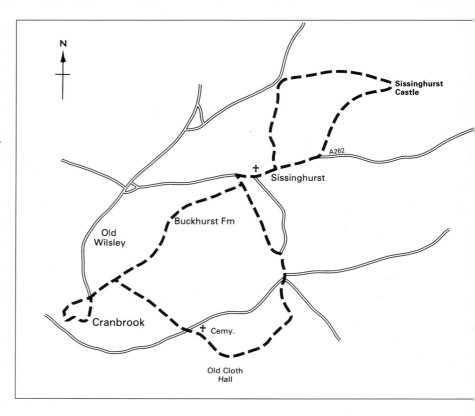

## Bibliography

Vita was already a compulsive writer in her teens. Nigel Nicholson's *Portrait of a Marriage* tells us that between 1906 and 1910 she wrote eight full length novels (one in French) and five plays (unpublished), all based on the history of Knole. They were unpublished, but among her successes in later life were *Knole and the Sackvilles* (1923) and *The Edwardians*, also based on Knole, under the pen-name Chevron. Her best selling novels which helped finance Sissinghurst included *All Passion Spent* and *Family History*. Travel books based on her journeys to visit Harold while he was working as a diplomat in Persia include *Passenger to Teheran* and *Twelve Days*. She also produced a fair amount of poetry, of which her finest work is considered to be *The Land*.

Harold Nicholson's diaries, edited by his son Nigel, were published in three volumes in 1969.

Nigel Nicholson's highly entertaining *Portrait of a Marriage* also includes long, autobiographical sections by Vita, and is primarily concerned with her affair with Violet Keppel. Both were published by Weidenfeld & Nicholson which Nigel Nicholson co-founded.

## A Walk with Vita Sackville-West

**Map:** OS Landranger 188.
**Start:** Sissinghurst Castle (NT), off the A262 east of Royal Tunbridge Wells, Kent—OS Grid Ref. 808383. Sissinghurst is open from Easter to mid-October, Tuesday to Friday, 1–6.30 pm; Saturday and Sunday 10–6.30 pm.
**Nearest BR Station:** Staplehurst.
**Distance:** 6 miles.
**Time:** Allow 3 hours
**Facilities:** Café at Sissinghurst Castle; pub and tea house at Sissinghurst village; pubs, etc. at Cranbrook.
**Summary:** A circular walk round the country south of Sissinghurst Castle, revealing the changing face of Kent with its hops, orchards and oast houses.

Sissinghurst Castle and its gardens are now a major National Trust attraction, so in the main summer season it's wise to arrive as early as possible. One can't imagine that Vita Sackville-West would have done the walk that follows—she would have been much too busy writing, gardening or travelling, but for us visitors it makes a pleasant Kentish ramble.

From the car park at Sissinghurst walk through to the farm shop, and turn left onto a track that heads away from the castle, running alongside the car park. A little further on it passes a house with stables over on the right and from here it appears well used by horse and can consequently be very muddy—walking boots or gumboots are a must. On the left there are open fields, and on the right the pretty woods are packed with bluebells in the spring.

The track passes an isolated, small building with the strange name of 'Horse Race House' on the right, and a little further on there's an orchard on the left as the track joins the road on a bend. Here you turn immediately left over a stile, and walk on down the track ahead, keeping to the right with apple orchards on both sides divided by a high hedge. Spring is the best time of year here with apple blossom all around you!

Keep on down between the orchards until you come to woods on the left. Bear round to the right along the edge of the woods, and when you come to a field of hops bear left down a narrow track away from the apple trees, heading towards the sound of the road. Walk up past a surprisingly innocuous sewage treatment plant, joining a metalled track which

148

akes you up to the busy A262.

Turn right and walk along the verge of this road in comparative safety, coming to pavement and walking on through the village of Sissinghurst, passing the church and The Bull public house. Go past the left turning to Golford, then cross the road, and a short way past an antiques shop-cum-tea house turn left down a gravel track before you get as far as the right turning signposted to Staplehurst.

Keep left through a gate and go on past a large Georgian house. Here the path narrows and splits, going straight on or turning right, which is the way you go, along a narrow path which at first runs parallel to the road past tennis courts and playing fields, with views over fields and woods to your left. Keep on along this pleasant track, going down steps to a lane and up some steps and over a stile on the other side. From here head downhill to the left over a grassy field, making for a stile set to the right of a clump of conifers. Buckhurst Farm is over to your left, with a rather fine converted oast house behind you.

After the stile keep on uphill along a track with woods on your left—the going can be muddy here. At the top of the rise you eventually come to another stile where you follow the footpath sign along a hard concrete track going straight ahead. To your right is Wilsley House, a somewhat ostentatious looking place perched on high ground, surrounded by a forbidding wire fence which appears to be there to protect its adjoining golf course. To your left there are fine views over the fields, with occasional trees and woods and a splendid white windmill in the distance.

Where the concrete track runs out, keep on ahead along a narrow path which follows the side of the field. Ignore the stile on the left unless you wish to cut out visiting Cranbrook which is not the most exciting place, but does offer shops, pubs, and a notable church. Walk on along the path, and then cross over a stile by the side of a modern house festooned with classical, architectural trimmings. This brings you to the road where you turn downhill to the left, walking some 200 yards into Cranbrook.

When you come to a duckpond on the right, turn up towards Cranbrook Church which despite Cranbrook's urban nature is a splendid place. The patron saint here is Saint Dunstan, the Archbishop of Canterbury who died in 988, and though of Saxon origin the church owes most of its present form to the Dutch weavers who flooded into Cranbrook in the Middle Ages and demanded a bigger and better place to pray in. It mainly dates from 1350–1550, with the blocked-up door at

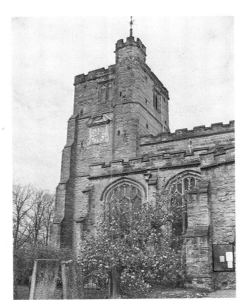

*The entrance to the church at Cranbrook, where the new front door cost 17 shillings and 7 pence.*

the foot of the west tower being the only trace of the Norman church which superseded the Saxon one. It has fine, double, stained glass windows on the north side which date from around 1450, and a beautiful magnolia tree by the south porch; the parish records tell us that the new door which was installed here in 1569 cost seventeen shillings and seven pence.

Walk on into Cranbrook for a look around if you wish. To continue with the walk, bear clockwise round the outside of the church, following the churchyard wall until you come out by the playing fields. Keep to the right across the fields, which bring you back to the road by the modern house with its incongruous classical portico adorning the front door. Cross the road and retrace your steps along the footpath towards Wilsley House. Just before you reach the concrete track, turn right over the stile which is not signposted, walking down between two fields which have a line of pollarded trees on a slightly raised mound marking the boundary, heading more or less south-east.

When you come to the bottom of these two fields with woods and a fence ahead, turn right along the perimeter of the woods, walking round the side of them before bearing left downhill. In the dip cross the left hand of two bridges to go over a small stream, and then head uphill towards a conspicuous timber-framed house; the stile you are making for is immediately in front of it. This brings you out

on the road where you turn left for a short way on the grassy verge, and then turn immediately right up a metalled lane beside the churchyard.

Follow this lane past the entrance to Old Cloth Hall, and keep along it as it bears left past a sign for Dulwich Prep School with a duckpond on the right. Walk on past a black, corrugated iron barn, opposite Coursehorn Barn, passing a stile with a footpath sign to the left, and walk on until the track bears right round the side of a field past a modern barn conversion. The footpath is unsignposted here, but bears diagonally left across the field from this bend in the track, bringing you to a gate in its bottom left hand corner. You can't see this as it's in a hollow, but it's by the far end of a line of trees which divide the fields.

If there is no sign of a path here you may prefer to walk round the perimeter of the field to reach this gate, which on our visit was in an advanced state of disrepair and neglect, as was the footpath which continues from it. Turn left through the gate which is just by a house, and find your way along the track which runs by the side of the fields up towards Golford. Badly overgrown and partly blocked by fallen trees, this track demanded our full concentration, but it does eventually join a better track by a house on the left before coming out on the road at Golford. Hopefully this footpath will be cleared and properly signposted by the time you visit.

Turn right along the road, then left past the telephone box, going downhill and passing a solitary warehouse on the left. Where the road bends right, turn left through a gate by a telephone pole along a footpath which we also found unsignposted. Go ahead to the next gate, and just before you reach it turn right down a line of trees by a fence. A stream joins the side of your path, and you then go over a stile into woods which were smothered with wild garlic on our visit. Walk over a bridge, and then keep right over the second bridge. This footpath through the woods was badly overgrown and the way was not that easy to follow when we walked it, but if you keep to the right of the stream you will come out on the far side, to the right of a large raised pond.

From here the track goes straight across an open field, heading up towards a white house with the village of Sissinghurst beyond. Walk up into the village, and then either return to Sissinghurst Castle along the outward footpath, or follow the busy A262 to the main entrance. Be warned that beyond the village the A262 has no pavement, and on fine afternoons the castle drive has a continuous flow of cars which makes walking less than pleasant.

# Walk 29: With T.E. Lawrence at Clouds Hill

*The quiet part of Dorset just to the west of Wareham is the resting place for T.E. Lawrence (1888–1935), the celebrated and controversial hero known as 'Lawrence of Arabia' who wrote* Seven Pillars of Wisdom, *based on his experiences in the Arab war which Winston Churchill described as one of 'the greatest books ever written in the English Language'.*

Lawrence was born in Tremadoc in Caernarvon, North Wales, the illegitimate son of a wealthy Anglo-Irish landowner and a Scottish governess. In the moral climate of the times both father and mother suffered from a sense of guilt which was to some extent passed on to Lawrence and his four brothers, playing its part in the remarkable life that lay ahead of him.

He was naturally brilliant, and having travelled extensively through Syria to study the old crusader castles he gained a first-class degree in Modern History at Oxford in 1910. He learnt Arabic and then plunged into a life of archaeology, spending most of the next four years in Syria working on an excavation site at Carchemish on the banks of the Euphrates. During that time he made frequent forays into the surrounding area, including a six week survey of the Sinai desert, and when war was declared in 1914 Lawrence's knowledge of the terrain secured him a place in the army at Cairo.

Lawrence had built up a strong affinity with the Arabs, approving of their hard lives based on a strong element of self-denial. He had gained a healthy dislike for the Turks who kept the region under their oppressive control and became Germany's allies in the war, and he worked tirelessly to ferment the Arab revolt which broke out in 1916. He was appointed liaison officer to the Emir Feisal who was one of the principal Arab leaders, living in his camp and with his army, and dressing in Arab clothing on the grounds that it made him less conspicuous and was more comfortable.

Lawrence assumed an important position in Feisal's entourage, and took an active part in guiding Arab policy against the Turks. He developed the idea of commando-style attacks with small forces, and began to destroy Turkish bridges, railways, and locomotives by the dozen, riding with his personal bodyguard of 'hired assassins' and being greeted by cries of 'Aurans! Aurans!'. He fought alongside the Arabs with single-minded determination, but all the time he feared that the various promises made to them by the British would never be honoured. He also suffered heavily, both physically and mentally. He described his first killing—the execution of an Arab who had killed another tribesman—with disgust, and the remorseless killings and massacres by and against the Turks left their mark on him, accounting in part for his strange behaviour after the war.

**T. E. Lawrence sketched by Augustus John.** *Photo by NPG.*

**. . . and the tombstone in the graveyard where he is buried in the hamlet of Moreton.**

*The woodland path on the other side of the river from Moreton, passing the ruined 'spyway'.*

He came near to death on several occasions, most notably when he inadvertently shot his own camel through the head during a charge of 400 camel-mounted warriors against the Turks, and was only saved by lying in front of its body. Many of his long desert crossings were undertaken in extreme discomfort, and he suffered numerous bouts of dysentery and fever, but the incident which appears to have injured him most happened when he was captured in Deraa, a Turkish stronghold and a vital railway junction. He had entered the town wearing his customary Arab clothing, intending to reconnoitre the area, and was stopped by some Turks who dragged him off to their Bey who was a homosexual. When Lawrence failed to fulfil the Bey's desires, he was beaten and whipped, finally escaping the next day.

At the end of the war Lawrence continued to work on the Arabs' behalf, pressing their claims on the War Cabinet in the hope that some of the many promises they had been made would be honoured. However the British and the French were more interested in carving up the Turkish territories for their own benefit, and Lawrence soon became severely depressed at what he saw as his own failure. He decided to write his own account of the desert war, *Seven Pillars of Wisdom*, using the title which he had given to an earlier travel book which he unfortunately destroyed in manuscript form before the war. The name refers to the seven cities of Cairo, Smyrna, Constantinople, Beirut, Aleppo, Damascus and Medina, coupled with a quotation from the Book of Proverbs: 'Wisdom hath builded her houses, she hath hewn it out of seven pillars.'

He began work on the book during the Peace Conference in Paris, sometimes writing as many as 30,000 words in 24 hours. The first draft was finished by the end of August 1919, and Lawrence revived plans which he'd had as an undergraduate for setting up his own printing press. At the end of the year, however,

he lost the whole manuscript while changing trains at Reading, and despite advertisements offering a reward it was never recovered, a blow which would have sorely tried any writer.

To escape the public attention that he attracted after the war, Lawrence moved to Oxford where he had been elected a Fellow of All Souls College in November 1919. He sought out the companionship of other writers, becoming close friends with Robert Graves and Thomas Hardy and his wife who he often visited later in Dorset. Rewriting *Seven Pillars* plunged Lawrence into a deeper state of melancholy and introspection; having been a national celebrity he craved for obscurity and finally succeeded in enlisting in the R.A.F. as an aircraft mechanic under the assumed name of John Hume Ross. He was mentally battered, and sought to subject himself to a monastic lifestyle, 'leading painlessly to the oblivion of activity'. He also planned to write a book on the R.A.F., later to appear as *The Mint*, but his

*Lawrence's cottage in the woods—a quiet, dignified, ascetic kind of retreat for this strange man.*

life as 'Ross' didn't last long for the press discovered his true identity, and he was formally discharged from the R.A.F. on 23rd January 1923.

He transferred to an equally humble position, becoming a Private of the Tank Corps at Bovington in Dorset under the new alias T.E. Shaw, a name he eventually adopted by deed poll. He hated army life with a masochistic relish, and his only relief was to ride his Brough motor bike at speed and retreat to the nearby cottage named Clouds Hill which he began to rent in 1924. He repaired it from an almost derelict state with the help of a Pioneer Sergeant Knowles, and used it as a regular resting place, either alone or with friends:

'I don't sleep here but come out at 4.30 pm to 9 pm nearly every night and dream, or write or read by the fire, or play Beethoven and Mozart to myself on the box.'

Lawrence later used his connections to transfer back to the R.A.F. after a hint at suicide in 1925. He continued working on *Seven Pillars of Wisdom*, having enlisted the critical help of E.M. Forster, George Bernard Shaw and his wife, Charlotte. He was also preparing a shortened, popular version called *Revolt in the Desert*, and as Lowell Thomas's book, *With Lawrence in Arabia* was about to be published at the same time, he applied for a posting to India to

escape the publicity—not the sort of author publishers would welcome today!

A limited number of a subscribers' edition of *Seven Pillars of Wisdom* was published in 1926, while *Revolt in the Desert* went on sale to the public in 1927, selling over 40,000 copies in the first three weeks and guaranteeing Lawrence some much needed income. He had also finished writing *The Mint* which was largely his own recollections of the unpleasant side of life in the services, but the book was effectively suppressed and was not published until 1955 in Britain, and then in an edited form.

In his spare time Lawrence also translated Homer's *Odyssey* for a fee of £800. Greatly recovered mentally he was making plans to retire to a refurbished Clouds Hill which he had now bought. Here he intended to write a book called *Confessions of Faith*, which would embody some of *The Mint* and be about 'that reserved element, the air'.

He left the R.A.F. on 26th February 1935, moving to Clouds Hill where he was for a time pestered by the press. There were rumours that Churchill was about to ask him to help the government reorganise the Defence Forces, and there is little doubt that his future could have been as exciting as his past if he had been willing to co-operate. On the morning of 13th May 1935, fate intervened. Lawrence crashed his motorbike on the narrow road near Clouds Hill, having been to Bovington to send a telegram. He had swerved to avoid two boys on bicycles, and while they were uninjured Lawrence had fractured his skull and never regained consciousness. He died six days later at the army hospital in Bovington, and was buried in the nearby churchyard at Moreton where this walk begins.

## Bibliography

After the limited edition of 1926, *Seven Pillars of Wisdom* was published by Jonathan Cape in 1935. *The Mint* by '352087 A/C Ross' was published by Jonathan Cape in 1955.

There are numerous biographies of Lawrence, some of which verge on the salacious. Robert Graves wrote the first authorised life in 1927; more recently his nephew Richard Perceval Graves' *Lawrence of Arabia and His World* (Thames & Hudson, 1976) is an accessible introduction to Lawrence, profusely illustrated with his own photos.

## A Walk with T.E. Lawrence

**Map**: OS Outdoor Leisure 15.
**Start**: Moreton— Grid Ref. 805894; park on roadside by post office.
**Nearest BR Station**: Wool.
**Distance**: 6 miles.
**Time**: Allow 3 hours.
**Facilities**: Teas sometimes available at post office.
**Summary**: An easy walk with straight-forward navigation which takes you from Lawrence's grave, to his cottage, Clouds Hill, and to the place where he crashed his motor bike.

Whether Lawrence would have walked on this route himself is open to question, since he usually preferred racing around on his motor bike! Moreton is a hamlet of a few houses, just off the B3390 Tolpuddle to Warmwell road.

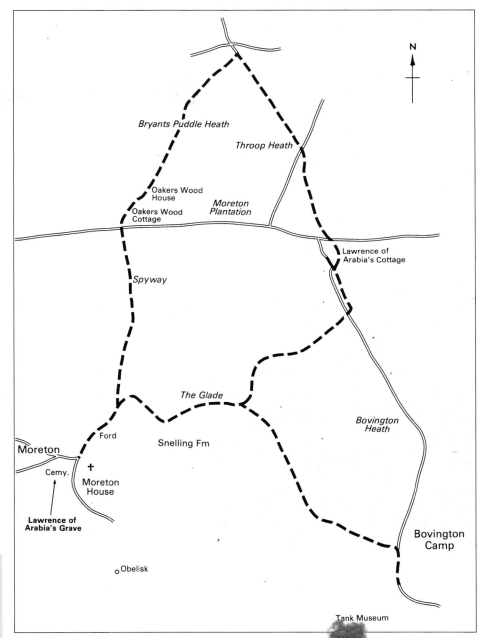

Park on the roadside by the post office-cum-village stores on the corner, and walk back up the road past the entrance to the church. A little further on there is a small graveyard on the right where Lawrence's grave may be found at the far end in a peaceful setting.

From here head back down the road to the River Frome, crossing the bridge and going straight on along the track ahead. Bear left over a small bridge past pretty woods, and a little further ▓▓▓▓ the track bends right you will see a ▓▓▓▓ of yellow footpath arrows to the left. Follow the one which points diagonally right across a field, skirting a copse of trees and passing over stiles and on into the rhododendron-filled woods ahead.

The path through these woods is well marked with yellow blobs, eventually leading between tall pine trees with a soft bed of needles under foot. It comes out by a crossing track where you turn left past a ruined building at Spyway, and then head on down to the road. Cross straight over and follow the bridleway sign for Culpepper's Dish, heading into woods along the hard track which bears left past Oakers Wood Cottage. Keep on ahead following the blue bridleway blobs on the track which eventually bears right into Forestry Commission land with pines planted in uniform rows like soldiers.

Head down the hill across Bryants Puddle Heath, passing under overhead power lines and carrying on up a short hill with Rimsmoor Pond over to the right. Beyond a crossing track, the track dips down to the right where you follow the yellow footpath sign on a muddy track forking right, ignoring the left hand bridleway sign. Keep straight on ahead, through a gate and along a driveway past the left side of Culpepper Cottage, which brings you out on the road just east of the strangely named Culpepper's Dish.

Turn right along this dead straight, very quiet road for about half a mile with forestry plantations on both sides. When you come to a road crossing at Throop Heath, follow the bridleway blob straight ahead onto heathland amongst gorse, heather and pines. The track soon joins a tank track coming from the left, with numerous MOD signs on the right—they don't, however tell you what to do if you meet a tank coming straight at you! Keep along the tank track for a short while, bearing right where you see bridleway blobs on a bend where the tank track bears off to the left. Head up into trees and up a short hill where you join the road a short distance from Clouds Hill.

Cross the road, turn right for a short distance, and then almost immediately left up a narrow path by a footpath blob next to an MOD sign telling you to beware of pyrotechnics. Follow the footpath blobs on a pretty track through the woods, with what appears to be a tank Grand Prix racing track on your left! Turn right where the blobs indicate you should do so, and you will come out on the road about 100 yards south of Lawrence's cottage.

Clouds Hill (NT) is well hidden from the road by bushes. It is open from Good Friday until the end of September on Wednesdays, Thursdays, Fridays, Sundays and Bank Holiday Mondays, 2-5 pm. It is also open on Sundays, 1-4 pm, from October until the end of March. It was a ruin when Lawrence took it over, and its simplicity clearly illustrates the ascetic nature of this great man who described it—on quiet days—as 'an earthly paradise'. Over the entrance is a Greek phrase inscribed by Lawrence which freely translated reads

*The view upstream towards Moreton House. The church close by is well worth a visit.*

*The track which passes Rimsmoor Pond on its way across Bryants Puddle Heath.*

'Why worry?'. Upstairs the 'music room' is the most comfortable room in the house, where Lawrence and his army friends escaped from their barracks to listen to music and to consume snacks consisting of olives, salted cashew nuts, baked beans and Lawrence's own mixture of China tea. Downstairs the 'book room' is mainly filled by Lawrence's enormous couch-cum-bed, the walls lined with books and mementos of his early travels. Apart from the kitchen the only other room is the tiny 'bunk room' which, with its narrow ship's bunk, was reserved for single guests. The inside walls are covered in aluminium sheeting which Lawrence believed made a good insulating material—cool in summer and warm in winter.

Having soaked up the strange atmosphere of Clouds Hill, turn left back down the road and left again back onto the same footpath. After about 10 yards turn right along a very indistinct footpath which runs parallel to the road—finding your way along it is not that easy, but if in doubt stick close to the road. After a while you come to a cleared area with a huge tank training ground to your left, and a sign warning you not to take photos. On the right by the roadside is a tree planted in memory of Lawrence, near to the place where he crashed.

Cross over the road here, and walk between the big concrete tank bollards, following the footpath which is indicated straight ahead to the right of the tank track. After about 300 yards the tank track bends left, and at a footpath sign the path turns right down through trees next to another warning about pyrotechnics. Go down this path, keeping to the left. There is one, short, muddy section, and then the path joins a wide track which brings you down to a T-junction crossing track with a bar to stop any vehicles. The left hand turn here goes to Bovington if you wish to divert to the Tank Museum which is just over a mile away; or turn right for home, following the level track through open country with old irrigation canals on either side.

Go past a house on the right on the edge of The Glade, and then turn right by the entrance to Snelling Farm. When you come to a T-junction bear left as shown by the footpath blobs, and this brings you back to the River Frome with fine glimpses of Moreton House as you cross the bridge.

Before leaving Moreton, a visit to the Church of St Nicholas is recommended. This is a most attractive church, mainly dating from the eighteenth and nineteenth century. In 1940 it was largely destroyed by a German bomb, and was only rebuilt and re-dedicated 10 years later. It now boasts 12 very unusual engraved glass windows, the work of Laurence Whistler undertaken over 30 years between 1955 and 1984.

# Walk 30: With Dylan Thomas in Laugharne

*Dylan Thomas spent the last four years of his short life (1914–1953) at the Boat House in Laugharne, the small Welsh coastal town where he had lived on and off since first discovering it in 1934. They were not his happiest years, but the Boat House remains a splendid monument to this troubled genius.*

Towards the end of his life Dylan Thomas wrote a piece about Laugharne for broadcast on the BBC:

'Off and on, up and down, high and dry, man and boy, I've been living now for fifteen years, or centuries, in this timeless, beautiful, barmy (both spellings) town, in this far forgetful, important place of herons, cormorants (known here as billy duckers), castle, churchyard, gulls, ghosts, geese, feuds, scares, scandals, cherry trees, mysteries, jackdaws in the chimneys, bats in the belfry, skeletons in the cupboards, pubs, mud, cockles, flatfish, curlews, rain, and human, often all too human, beings; and, though still very much a foreigner, I am hardly ever stoned in the streets any more, and can claim to be able to call several of the inhabitants, and a few of the herons, by their Christian names . . .'

Dylan Thomas's reputation lives on—'the madcap drunkard who scandalised America, wrote *Under Milk Wood* and numerous poems, and died after downing 18 whiskies'. The truth is more prosaic. Dylan Thomas was incapable of looking after himself or his family. He was born with a healthy disregard for possessions and money which, in the early days didn't trouble him, but later, when he had children to support and overdue tax bills to pay, it drove him to distraction with worry.

He could have been rich and famous—indeed Hollywood was beckoning when he died—but instead he remained poor and tragically miscast. On what was to be his deathbed he boasted 'I've had eighteen straight whiskies. I think that's the record', but his bravado and gross exaggeration was only a mask to hide

**Dyland Thomas sketched by Michael Ayrton in 1945.** *Photo by NPG.*

his true character; he was killed by worry, stress, and general illness as much as by alcoholic poisoning. His lungs were weak from childhood and he had predicted that he would be dead by 40—for no self-respecting, great poet could live longer, and Keats, who he always hoped to surpass was dead by 25.

Dylan Thomas was born and bred in Swansea where his father, D.J. Thomas, was a teacher of English with a fine reputation. Though Welsh, Dylan Thomas never bothered to work with the Welsh language; indeed he never worked at any academic pursuit which deflected from his singleminded ambition to

become a great poet. He began to write serious verse as a teenager, and these poems filled his first published book, *Eighteen Poems*, of 1934; *Twenty-Five Poems* followed in 1935.

Thomas first discovered Laugharne in 1934, when he was still living at home in Swansea but spending considerable amounts of time in the company of bohemian young artists in London. He crossed to Laugharne with Glyn Jones, a lifelong friend from Swansea, travelling on the ferry from Llanstephan which in those days plied across the estuary. Although only there briefly, he wrote at length about his visit to Pamela Hansford Johnson, a young poetess who qualified as his first girlfriend:

'I am spending Whitsun in the strangest town in Wales. Laugharne, with a population of four hundred, has a town hall, a castle, and a portreeve (mayor). The people speak with a broad English accent, although on all sides they are surrounded by hundreds of miles of Welsh country. The neutral sea lies at the foot of the town, and Richard Hughes writes his cosmopolitan stories in the castle . . .'

He went on to describe some of the local sights and sounds:

'I can never do justice to the miles and miles and miles of mud and grey sand, to the un-nerving silence of the fisherwomen, and the mean souled cries of the gulls and herons, to the shapes of the fisherwomen's breasts that drop, big as barrels, over the stained tops of their overalls as they bend over the sand, to the cows in the fields that lie north of the sea, and to the near breaking of the heart as the sun comes out for a minute from its cloud and lights up the ragged sails of a fisherman's boat. These things look ordinary enough on paper. One sees them as shapeless, literary things, and the sea is a sea of words, and the little fishing boat lies still on a tenth rate canvas . . .'

Dylan Thomas married an Irish/French girl called Caitlin (pronounced like 'cat') on July 11th 1937.

'I was married three days ago; to Caitlin Macnamara; in Penzance registry office; with no money, no prospect of money, no attendant friends or relatives, and in complete happiness.'

Their first home was a studio above a fish market in Newlyn where they stayed throughout the summer, before moving back to Swansea to live with Thomas's parents when their money ran out completely. After alternating between Swansea and Caitlin's mother's home in Hampshire, they at last found a home of their own in Laugharne. This was accomplished in April 1938 with the help of Richard Hughes, the celebrated author of *A High Wind In Jamaica* who had rented the fine house adjoining the castle and befriended Dylan Thomas. He found the young couple a terraced fisherman's cottage in Gosport Street. In those days it had neither running water nor any kind of modern convenience.

Dylan Thomas described his new house in graphic terms:

'Green rot sprouts through the florid scarlet forests of the wallpaper, sneeze and the chairs crack, the double bed is a swing-band with coffin, oompah, slush-pump, gob stick, and almost wakes the deaf, syphilitic neighbours . . .'.

Nevertheless he and Caitlin liked it there, and they were probably never as happy again.

Thomas worked hard at his poetry but the pub continued to play a dominant role in his life—work in the morning; the pub, usually Brown's where he loved the gossip, at mid-day; lunch at home; more work in the afternoon; and then Brown's or the Cross Hands in the evening. In a letter to a forthcoming visitor he commented, 'I hope you like drinking, because I do very much and when I have money I don't stop. There are three good pubs here, the best bottled mild in England, and no prohibitive drinking hours.'

He made regular visits to Richard

*The start of the walk from the castle at Laugharne, heading towards the Boat House.*

Hughes' house at Laugharne Castle, and it was there, in the kitchen, in 1939 that he said 'What the people of Laugharne need is a play about themselves.' This prompted *Under Milk Wood*, the famous verse play about a village that is declared mad, while in truth, it is the world outside which is insane. Laugharne and its inhabitants, and to some extent New Quay in Cardiganshire where he had also spent some time, were the role models for the play, and though never quite finished and only given its first performance in 1953 during his penultimate visit to the USA, it remains his most famous work.

In August 1938 Dylan Thomas and Caitlin moved to Sea View behind the castle—'a tall and dignified house at the posh end of this small town'. However, financial problems intervened, and in October 1938 they were driven out of Laugharne by their debts. They returned in May the following year in better financial health, and had their first son, Llewelyn, christened in the Anglican church. Augustus John, a regular visit to Laugharne Castle and a close neighbour of Caitlin's mother's in Hampshire, was an attendant godfather, as was Richard Hughes.

Then war broke out. Thomas was passionately against becoming involved, believing that thousands were being led to their deaths by the whims and wishes of misguided rulers and politicians. He wrote from Laugharne:

'It is terrible to have built, out of nothing, a complete happiness . . . and then to see the immediate possibility of its being exploded and ruined through no fault of one's own... the brutal activities of war appal me—as they do every decent-thinking person. Even here the war atmosphere is thick and smelling: the kids dance in the streets, the mobilised soldiers sing 'Tipperaray' in the pubs, and wives and mothers weep around the stinted memorial . . .'.

Dylan Thomas later volunteered to be a member of a bizarre, anti-aircraft battery that was privately funded and almost entirely staffed by painters and writers, but he was rejected due to his weak lungs, a decision that depressed him.

The Thomas family left Laugharne during the war, when Dylan worked mainly on screenplays for government-financed documentary films, dividing his time between London and a number of other homes which he found in England. By 1948 he was homesick for Wales again, a feeling he summed up in these memorable lines:

'I did not want to be in England, now that they were there.
I did not want to be in England, whether they were there or not.
I wanted to be in Wales.'

Despite having worked steadily and hard, Dylan Thomas still had no money and no home of his own. Margaret Taylor, the ex-wife of the historian A.J.P. Taylor came to his rescue as she had before. She had housed Dylan Thomas and his family—by then the first son, Llewelyn, had gained a sister, Aeronwy, named after the River Aeron on whose

*The Boat House itself is in a wonderful position, but was not enough to save poor Dylan from himself.*

bank she was conceived—in Oxford and at South Leigh nearby, and now bought the Boat House at Laugharne for their use. With them, in 1949, went Dylan Thomas's parents who were elderly and unable to fend for themselves. A cottage called the Pelican House, opposite Brown's Hotel in Laugharne's main street, was rented for them, and despite his travels, Dylan Thomas never let a day pass by without calling in to see his father (who was by then virtually blind), either to chat, to talk over the crossword, or, while he was able, to go over to Brown's for a beer.

The Boat House with its writing shack where *Under Milk Wood* was effectively finished amidst piles of discarded paper, is in a glorious, unrivalled position, but the last four years of Dylan Thomas's life spent in this house, were not happy. His third child—a boy named Colm—was born here, raising his spirits for the first few months, but his marriage was degenerting steadily, with money worries providing a continual source of friction. Thomas was driven to undertake four lecture and poetry reading tours of the United States which, with his magnificent voice, brought him fame, and should have brought him fortune. However, he squandered most of the money he earned, and hearing tales of his outrageous behaviour and infidelity in America, Caitlin became increasingly embittered.

In December 1952 Dylan Thomas's father died after a protracted illness, ending an important, lifelong relationship between father and son. Almost a year later Dylan left Laugharne for the last time. Stress at home, a punishing schedule on his tours, and his own lifestyle had left him a very sick man. Nevertheless, hounded by the need to earn more money, he flew to New York in the autumn of 1953 for his fourth and last tour which was to have ended with a collaboration with the composer, Stravinsky, and the writing of a libretto for an opera about the world after a nuclear Armageddon. He died three weeks after arriving in the States.

## Bibliography

Constantine Fitzgibbon's *The Life of Dylan Thomas* (Plantin 1965) is an excellent biography by one who knew him and sympathised with him throughout his turbulent life. J.M. Dent's publication of *The Collected Poems* in 1952 made Dylan Thomas famous. Dent also published some of his short stories under the title *Quite Early One Morning* and the verse play *Under Milk Wood* posthumously. Among his best known poems are *A Refusal to Mourn the Death, by Fire, of a Child in London*; *If my head hurt a hair's foot*; *Do not go gentle into that good night*; *The hand that signed the paper*. He left recordings of these and other works which are magnificent.

*Laugharne's castle—an extraordinarily fine place for such a small, out of the way town.*

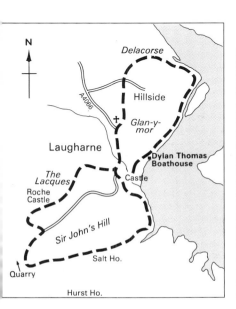

## A Walk with Dylan Thomas

**Map:** OS Landranger 158/159.

**Start:** The castle at Laugharne on the A4066 south of St Clears in Dyfed, South Wales—OS Grid Ref. 302107. Free car park next to the castle. The Dylan Thomas Boat House is open April to mid-November, 10–6 pm daily.

**Nearest BR Station:** Whitland.

**Distance:** Walk via Boat House 2½ miles; walk via St John's Hill 3 miles.

**Time:** Allow 1½ hours for each walk.

**Facilities:** Pubs, cafés and tea houses in Laugharne, including small café at the Boat House.

**Summary:** Two views of Dylan Thomas's Laugharne. First a walk past his Boat House, up the estuary, to the church where he lies buried; second a walk along St John's Hill on the other side of Laugharne, with magnificent views over the coastal sands.

Laugharne, pronounced 'Larne', is well worth a visit, and these two walks give you a good introduction to it. Either walk can be done first, depending on your timetable and when you plan to visit the Boat House. In between them you'll have plenty of time for a good look round, and perhaps lunch or tea; if time is pressing, or the weather is unfavourable, I suggest you do the Boat House walk only.

For the Boat House walk start from the large car park by the side of the fine old castle which was founded in the twelfth century by Rhys ap Gruffyd. Cross the stream that emerges from under its walls, and walk beside it along the foreshore below the gazebo where the novelist Richard Hughes allowed Dylan Thomas to work while he was at Sea View.

159

*Dylan's grave—easily identified by its plain, wooden, white cross.*

Keep along the foreshore by a sea wall, and then where you see a footpath sign take the track going uphill. This leads you to a hillside path that goes to the Boat House, passing Dylan Thomas's writing shack which has been left as if the artist had just vacated it—maybe for a quick drink or two up at Brown's Hotel. The view from here is splendid, and one wonders how he could have worked at all! It is similarly spectacular from the Boat House itself, and you should allow an hour for this part of the visit. Although the house is small, you will be shown an excellent film on the life of Dylan Thomas; there are all sorts of things of interest on sale; and there is a pleasant tea room downstairs.

From the Boat House continue along the hillside path which soon goes into woods ahead. There follows a very pleasant walk through these woods, following the track which bends round to the left past a couple of old, ruined buildings. At the end of the woods cross a stile, and then walk straight ahead along the side of a field, following the path which skirts its perimeter at the foot of a hill. Follow this round to the left, and then cross a ditch and a stile by a tremendous gnarled oak tree before walking ahead to the farmhouse at Delacorse which you can see in front of you.

The footpath goes left and then goes right to join a track by the left hand side of the house which now caters for bed and breakfast. Walk on up this track which takes you steadily uphill for some distance, leading you to the heights above Laugharne. Here take the first left turning following the sign to Hillside, and after about 50 yards take the right turning downhill. Follow this on down past a large house on the left, and a little further on you will come to a kissing gate leading into the splendid old graveyard of St Martin's Church. Apart from an extraordinary collection of gravestones and tombs, this also has some fine old yew trees—one was known as the 'Fox Tree', since the heads of foxes and similarly 'undesirable' creatures had to be nailed to it for three church services before the reward for destroying such creatures could be paid.

The church itself is handsome, and was visited by the well travelled Samuel Taylor Coleridge on 17th November 1802. A replica of the memorial commemorating Dylan Thomas in Westminster Abbey is at the west end of the north wall, on the left as you go into the church. The great man's grave is easy to find—it's virtually in the middle of the new churchyard over the bridge, and is made conspicuous by a white painted wooden cross.

From here walk on down to the road, and then turn left along the pavement into Laugharne. You pass Brown's Hotel on the left where Dylan Thomas was well known for his consumption of alcohol, and opposite there's a good secondhand bookshop with a selection of his works on sale. From here keep on down the high street past the Town Hall clock tower of *Under Milk Wood*, and you soon come back to the car park where you started from.

The second walk around St John's Hill takes you in the other direction, south-west from Laugharne. From the car park follow the track round the shoreline towards the well wooded headland, passing under the shop with the large 'Antiques' sign. Where the track bears left go past a path going directly uphill, bearing right a little further on onto a track which goes uphill through woods, about 75 yards before you come to the low lying walls which hide the sewage works.

Follow this woodland track up until it levels out and follows the hillside with really magnificent views out across the mudflats of the Afon Taf, bearing round the headland well above the low, flat grasslands that stretch out to Laugharne Sands with Pendine Sands some way on to the west. Keep along this track which follows the contours with a few ups and downs, passing a few ruined dwellings on the way.

Where the track forks right and left, take the left fork which heads downhill, bringing you down by the side of Salt House at sea level. The enthusiastic yappings and yelpings which one can hear from some way off inform you that this is a kennels, and on my visit the dogs were mainly locked up; those that weren't were small and well used to strangers.

From Salt House turn right onto a track, walking along by the base of St John's Hill towards a far off quarry works with a few farmsteads on the marshes over to the left. At the quarry turn right uphill on a road, and then fork right onto a lane with a dead-end road sign. This leads you up to the main A4066, but despite being an 'A' road it's fairly quiet and not too unpleasant to walk along for the half a mile or so that's required.

Keep going until you come to a lane forking off to the left which leads up to Llandawke. Turn up here, passing a decrepit footpath sign on the right, and carry on for a couple of hundred yards until the road bends left by a white cottage. Although this lane appears quiet beware of the quarry lorries which appear to use it as a short cut. Turn right at the footpath sign behind the cottage, crossing a small stream to go through a gate, and then heading uphill on a track through the grassland. From here follow the contours along the hillside before heading down towards a group of modern houses further along the side of the A4044.

You will find a grassy track running behind these houses. Head along it, passing an isolated, small building by the side of a stream and then following the track alongside this stream for some way until you reach the road above Laugharne, walking past a few cottages on the way. This is a pleasant walk, and the stream continues to follow by the side of the road, passing an old water pump and then coming to the cross which brings you out opposite Laugharne's fine castle.